A HISTORICAL GUIDE TO
Henry David Thoreau

HISTORICAL GUIDES
TO AMERICAN AUTHORS

The Historical Guides to American Authors is an interdisciplinary, historically sensitive series that combines close attention to the United States' most widely read and studied authors with a strong sense of time, place, and history. Placing each writer in the context of the vibrant relationship between literature and society, volumes in this series contain historical essays written on subjects of contemporary social, political, and cultural relevance. Each volume also includes a capsule biography and illustrated chronology detailing important cultural events as they coincided with the author's life and works, while photographs and illustrations dating from the period capture the flavor of the author's time and social milieu. Equally accessible to students of literature and of life, the volumes offer a complete and rounded picture of each author in his or her America.

A Historical Guide to Ernest Hemingway
Edited by Linda Wagner-Martin

A Historical Guide to Walt Whitman
Edited by David S. Reynolds

A Historical Guide to Ralph Waldo Emerson
Edited by Joel Myerson

A Historical Guide to Henry David Thoreau
Edited by William E. Cain

A
Historical Guide
to Henry David Thoreau

EDITED BY

WILLIAM E. CAIN

OXFORD
UNIVERSITY PRESS

2000

OXFORD

UNIVERSITY PRESS

Oxford   New York
Athens   Auckland   Bangkok   Bogotá   Buenos Aires   Calcutta
Cape Town   Chennai   Dar es Salaam   Delhi   Florence   Hong Kong   Istanbul
Karachi   Kuala Lumpur   Madrid   Melbourne   Mexico City   Mumbai
Nairobi   Paris   São Paulo   Shanghai   Singapore   Taipei   Tokyo   Toronto   Warsaw

and associated companies in
Berlin   Ibadan

Copyright © 2000 by Oxford University Press, Inc.

Published by Oxford University Press, Inc.
198 Madison Avenue, New York, New York 10016

Oxford is a registered trademark of Oxford University Press.

Library of Congress Cataloging-in-Publication Data
A histroical guide to Henry David Thoreau /
edited by William E. Cain.
p. cm.—(Historical guides to American authors)
Includes bibliographical references and index.
ISBN 0-19-513862-7;—ISBN 0-19-513863-5 (pbk.)
1. Thoreau, Henry David, 1817–1862—Criticism and interpretation.
2. Literature and history—United States—History—19th century.
3. Literature and society—United States—History—19th century.
I. Cain, William E., 1952– II. Series.
PS3054 .H57   2000
818'.309—dc21   99–055276

1 3 5 7 9 8 6 4 2

Printed in the United States of America
on acid-free paper

Acknowledgments

I am grateful, first of all, to Robert A. Gross, Dana D. Nelson, Lawrence A. Rosenwald, Cecelia Tichi, and Laura Dassow Walls for their excellent work in this volume. I want also to express my thanks to T. Susan Chang, former Humanities Editor at Oxford University Press, for inviting me to be part of the Historical Guides series. Both Elissa Morris and Jennifer Rozgonyi of Oxford University Press have also been very helpful and supportive. For their insight and cooperation, I would also like to thank Leslie Wilson, Special Collections, Concord Free Public Library; Ruth R. Rogers and Jill Triplett Bent, Special Collections, Clapp Library, Wellesley College; my colleagues in the English department of Wellesley College; and my wife Barbara and daughters Julia and Isabel.

As I have worked on my sections of this collaborative project, I have thought often of three scholar/critics of American literature: Laurence B. Holland, who taught with uncanny power and passion Thoreau and other writers of the American Renaissance; Richard Poirier, whose forthright, stimulating books and essays I have long admired and from which I have learned so much; and Eric J. Sundquist, whose literary criticism I find inspiring and whom I have known as a friend since our days together in graduate school.

Contents

A HISTORICAL GUIDE TO
Henry David Thoreau

Introduction

William E. Cain

Honored in the United States and around the world for his resolute individualism, his insight into and celebration of nature, and his piercing social criticism, Henry David Thoreau stands among the major authors in the American literary canon. But his work did not secure its renown until decades after his death in 1862. In his lifetime Thoreau (with the accent on the first syllable, as in "thorough") published only a handful of poems, a number of essays, and just two books, *A Week on the Concord and Merrimack Rivers* (1849) and *Walden; or, Life in the Woods* (1854). The first book was a failure, and the second only a modest success. His Concord neighbors were aware that Thoreau was a writer, but few had any idea of the scope and scale of his writing. Nor did they appreciate how different he was from Ralph Waldo Emerson, the sage from whose influence Thoreau was felt to be struggling to break free. Many who knew Thoreau, even his friends, found him cranky, opinionated, difficult; some went further, calling him complacent and conceited. The people in the town thought him strange—a Harvard-educated young man who sauntered in the woods and meandered from one odd job to the next.

At different junctures in his life, Thoreau was a teacher, surveyor, pencil-maker, handyman, and natural historian. But above all he was a writer. This is the most important fact to know about him—that he was always writing. He began writing regularly while he was a student at Harvard in the 1830s and soon began keeping a journal that over the next twenty-five years totaled 2 million words. He wrote poetry and prose in the 1830s, but his real start came in the early 1840s, when he produced essays, poems, and translations for the Transcendentalist journal *The Dial*. He edited, revised, and stitched together work he had already done—combining it with much new material—to construct his first book, and, perfectionist that he was, he devoted years to writing, organizing, and reorganizing his second.

Though his name is associated with the pleasures of the moment, Thoreau is one of the most deliberate and disciplined authors in American literary history. In his tireless, exorbitant need to fashion a suitable language for sensations, feelings, impulses, and intuitions, he resembles such authors as John Ruskin (*Modern Painters*, 5 vols., 1843–1860), Walter Pater (*Studies in the History of the Renaissance*, 1873), Henry James (*The Portrait of a Lady*, 1881; *The Golden Bowl*, 1904), and, in the modern period, Gertrude Stein and Ernest Hemingway. Even his journal is highly crafted and designed, most of the time based on notes and jottings that Thoreau then shaped into artful sentences. He persisted with his journal until serious illness intervened, and on his deathbed he was still writing: adding to his calendar of flowers and shrubs, compiling lists of birds, making selections from his journals, and preparing articles for publication. New work by Thoreau continues to make its way into print, including natural history manuscripts issued under the titles *The Dispersion of Seeds* (1993) and *Wild Fruits* (2000). His complete writings, published by Princeton University Press, will require twenty-five volumes.

As a writer and social critic, Thoreau is bold and fortifying, a power to be reckoned with and drawn upon for strength and inspiration. He is, observed Walt Whitman:

> one of the native forces—stands for a fact, a movement, an upheaval: Thoreau belongs to America, to the transcendental, to the protesters. . . . One thing about Thoreau keeps him very near to me: I refer to his lawlessness—his dissent—his

going his own absolute road let hell blaze all it chooses. (Traubel, *Whitman in Camden*, 3:375)

With the possible exception of Whitman himself, Thoreau has been the American author most beloved by reformers, naysayers, and dissenters. The Indian religious and political leader Mohandas K. Gandhi read and translated Thoreau's writings when he campaigned in the 1900s and 1910s for Indian civil rights in South Africa, and he returned to these texts in subsequent decades when he called for Indian independence from the British: "My first introduction to Thoreau's writings was, I think, in 1907, or later, when I was in the thick of the passive resistance struggle. A friend sent me the essay on 'Civil Disobedience.' It left a deep impression on me" (Cited in Salt, "Gandhi," 728). "Civil Disobedience" also was a "rallying tract," among "resisters of the Nazi occupations in Europe" (Miller, "Afterword," 255). Martin Luther King, Jr., read the essay in college in the 1940s and remembered it in 1955 in the midst of the Montgomery bus boycott: "I became convinced that what we were preparing to do in Montgomery was related to what Thoreau had expressed. We were simply saying to the white community, 'We can no longer lend our cooperation to an evil system'" (*Testament*, 429).

While "Civil Disobedience" and parts of *Walden* have propelled broadly based reform and protest movements, Thoreau's main message is a personal one. He disliked groups, organizations, and institutions, which, he believed, threaten to divert persons from honestly reflecting on their own lives and revivifying them. Thoreau demands that readers face fundamental questions: What constitutes the life you lead? How can you be satisfied with it? What *is* your work and what are you working *for*?

For Thoreau, learning how to live means simplifying, casting off. In *Walden* he writes:

No method nor discipline can supercede the necessity of being forever on the alert. What is a course of history, or philosophy, or poetry, no matter how well selected, or the best society, or the most admirable routine of life, compared with the discipline of looking always at what is to be seen? Will you be a reader, a student merely, or a seer? Read your fate, see what is before you, and walk on into futurity. (III)

Thoreau's immediate, highly personal appeal ensures that he will always have many avid readers. But the limit of this response is that it can lead us to miss seeing Thoreau in historical context—as a writer embedded in the issues and controversies of mid-nineteenth-century America, a writer who cultivated his own garden yet who thought (and wrote) all the while about the intellectual movements and trends and social and political events of his era. Thoreau examined and commented acutely on education, utopian theory and practice, labor and working conditions, immigration, poverty, and inequality; he probed the relationship between individual rights and the powers of local, state, and federal government; he assailed the enslavement of African Americans and the mistreatment of Native Americans; and he inquired into and brooded on the relationship between literature and social reform, literary nationalism, and the literary marketplace.

Thoreau said more than once that people pay far too much attention to newspapers and hence lose sight of permanent truths, yet friends and neighbors recalled that he read newspapers zealously. He was more absorbed in the issues of the day than he lets on; as a writer, intellectual, and worker, he knew much about the society of which he resisted being a member. His preoccupation with finding and articulating genuine value is born from his extreme discomfort with so much under way around him, in particular the lust for getting and spending, the subordination of individuals to the state, and, for millions of enslaved African Americans, the denial of the freedom that America in theory guaranteed. Thoreau did not lead a life of quiet desperation himself, but he witnessed many who did, and he wanted to show them that they could cast off the consciousness that society had imposed on them.

In the biographical introduction that follows, I survey Thoreau's life and literary career and highlight the social and political issues and historical events to which he responded. The essays in the next section also treat Thoreau from a contextual point of view. The chronology (pp. 243–64) is similarly intended to help readers place Thoreau's writings in their biographical and historical contexts. And the photographs and illustrations within the chronology sharpen our sense of Thoreau as a man of his times and illuminate the changes and controversies in the America that he wrote about.

In the first essay in the second section, Dana D. Nelson comments on the nature of work, the marketplace, and gender in mid-nineteenth-century America, and she notes the impact of the slavery crisis on Thoreau's social and political ideas. But Nelson's primary aim is to trace the themes of labor, manhood, race, and ethnicity that he, like other authors of the period, explored. In the 1840s and 1850s, what did it mean to be "a man," to be "manly" in one's private and public lives? What was the meaning of a man's work, and the range of his social and political responsibilities? Nelson points out that when Thoreau refers in *Walden* to the enslavement of blacks he is seeking not to contrast it with the freedom enjoyed by whites but, instead, to dramatize the bondage that all men experience within an exploitative economic system. Thoreau's concern with the meanings of manhood and the competitive pressures of the marketplace economy, she argues, led him to investigate the history of the American Indians, whose culture, original to the land, the white settlers and their successors had displaced with their own.

Taking note of Thoreau's interest in homemaking and hospitality, Cecelia Tichi next describes the relationships between *Walden* and nineteenth-century domesticity. Drawing on recent work in feminist criticism and material culture studies, Tichi connects the themes of *Walden* to the ideas about gender and work that Catherine Beecher, Harriet Beecher Stowe, Lydia Maria Child, and other women writers and reformers of the period examined. She focuses on Thoreau's interest in the dwelling house, the parlor, and the activity of housekeeping, as she considers the ways in which he criticizes and seeks to reform the nation's skewed domestic life and protect it from the incursions of the market economy.

As Laura Dassow Walls shows, Thoreau also was keenly interested in natural history and science. He took his scientific work very seriously, but for him the challenge was to contribute to the objective study of nature without losing his own literary identity and highly individualized conception of himself. We can see this not only in *Walden* but even more, especially in the 1850s, in the journal that Thoreau devoutly maintained. In Thoreau's day, notes Walls, literary culture typically defined itself in opposition to science and technology, which were, it was claimed, separating persons from nature. He took issue with this distinction, redefining the meanings of "science" and "technology" and exemplifying his conception of the bonds between self and nature in the kind of focused, meticulous, yet personalized writing he practiced in his journal.

Lawrence A. Rosenwald takes for his subject the arguments and contexts of Thoreau's essay on civil disobedience. He discusses the theory and practice of "non-resistance" as exemplified in the life and work of Amos Bronson Alcott, William Lloyd Garrison, and Frederick Douglass, and he addresses Thoreau's responses to the Mexican War, the expansion of slavery, the role of government and the duties expected from citizens, and the possibility Thoreau entertains that "resistance" to the state sometimes may require violence and bloodshed.

In the final essay, Robert A. Gross analyzes the responses to Thoreau by his Concord neighbors. It was not his social or political radicalism, or his wayward walking in the woods, that disturbed them. As Gross explains, it was Thoreau's individualism that mystifed and riled the Concord townspeople. Thoreau refused to sign petitions; he would not train with the militia; with the exception of the Concord Lyceum, he was unwilling to take part in any group or institution; and he went to jail rather than pay his poll tax. Focusing on several persons who knew and commented on Thoreau, Gross describes the process through which Thoreau's individualism was portrayed, in the decades after his death, as a form of eccentricity: he became a New England "character." For the men and women of Concord, Thoreau's life and work illuminated in troubling ways the changing boundaries between the individual and the community, and thus the making of his reputation, in Gross's words, dramatizes for us the interplay of "social history and cultural memory."

Thoreau was proud of his writing and hoped that he would

reach many readers, for he had important lessons to teach them. But he both did and did not care about the world's opinion. Thoreau is witty, playful, engaging, even seductive in his prose, but time and again he will then take on a severe, upbraiding tone or flash an unpleasant edge in a phrase or sentence. Thoreau dares us to dislike him—which is another way of saying that he demands that we measure our principles against those that he embodies. Deeply interested in the events and crises of his own era, he sought to instruct Americans about the essential meaning of their society and history and, beyond that, to express truths about the art of living well that would make his books and essays permanently relevant.

REFERENCES

King, Martin Luther, Jr. *A Testament of Hope: The Essential Writings of Martin Luther King, Jr.* Edited by James M. Washington. San Francisco: Harper & Row, 1986.

Miller, Perry. Afterword to *Walden*. New York: Signet, 1946.

Salt, Henry S. "Gandhi and Thoreau." *Nation & Athenaeum* 46 (1 March 1930): 728.

Thoreau, Henry David. *Walden*. Edited by J. Lyndon Shanley. Princeton: Princeton University Press, 1971.

Traubel, Horace. *With Walt Whitman in Camden.* 3 vols. 1905–1906. Reprint, New York: Rowman & Littlefield, 1961.

Henry David Thoreau
1817–1862

A Brief Biography

William E. Cain

Thoreau was born on his maternal grandmother's farm, on Virginia Road, in Concord, Massachusetts, on July 12, 1817, the third child of John and Cynthia (Dunbar) Thoreau. On October 12 he was christened David Henry Thoreau, named after an uncle who had died in Concord in July. Not until the mid-1830s did he identify himself as Henry David Thoreau. Like much else about this private man, so candid about his principles yet guarded about himself, the reason for the change of name is unclear. Perhaps Thoreau switched his first and middle names to affirm a measure of independence from his family and to signify the new person he had become through his Harvard education and friendships with Ralph Waldo Emerson and other Transcendentalists. Some of his Concord neighbors saw his change of name as rebellious and downright foolish. But "Henry" was what Thoreau's family had called him since birth, and there is no evidence that they objected to his decision.

John Thoreau was "a small, quiet, plodding, unobtrusive man, thoroughly genuine and reliable, occupying himself for the most part in his own business, though he could be friendly and sociable when occasion invited" (Salt, *Life,* 2). He had little luck as a storekeeper and teacher, but his fortunes improved after he settled in 1823 in Concord, roughly twenty miles west of Boston, a town that had been given its name in the 1630s to attest to the peaceable relations in the area between the white settlers and the Indians from whom the site for the town was acquired. In this farming community, population about 2,000, John Thoreau enjoyed success as a manufacturer of pencils, setting up his small factory in an ell of the family home.

John's wife Cynthia was known for her firm opinions, sharp personality, and blunt tone. Ralph Waldo Emerson's son Edward Waldo Emerson remembered her as "spirited, capable, and witty, with an edge to her wit on occasion" (*Thoreau*, 13). Active in the antislavery cause well before it gained wide support, she was a member of the Concord Women's Anti-Slavery Society (formed in 1837), which was aligned with the radical Boston abolitionist William Lloyd Garrison. As her neighbor Jean Munro LeBrun recalled (1883), Cynthia Thoreau later "was unsparing in her denunciation of the fugitive slave law," which Congress passed in 1850 and which required northerners to assist in the return of escaped slaves; and she "was one of the first to give aid and comfort to fugitives" (Meltzer and Harding, *Thoreau Profile*, 3). Several aunts, also staunch foes of slavery, lived with the Thoreaus, and Cynthia Thoreau took in boarders to supplement the family's income.

Of the three other children, the oldest was Helen, born on October 22, 1812, five months after her parents were married. She taught school in towns near Concord but suffered from poor health and in 1849 died from tuberculosis—the same illness that would take her brother Henry's life in 1862. John, Jr., born on July 5, 1815, was lively and outgoing, a lover of nature who made a study of the birds nearby. Some reports indicate that he was the more promising of the Thoreau boys, yet the family chose Henry—it is not clear why—as the son who would receive an education at Harvard. Thoreau's younger sister Sophia was born on June 24, 1819. She taught school for a short time but devoted herself to the family business and household; in the 1860s she edited and prepared Henry's manuscripts for posthumous publication.

Thoreau attended public grammar school in Concord and then, with his brother, enrolled in Concord Academy, where they were taught by Phineas Allen, a Harvard graduate whose curriculum included classics, composition, debate, geography, history, and science. Thoreau entered Harvard College in 1833; he did not do well on the entrance exam, and it is said that Harvard president Josiah Quincy told him, "You barely got in." His coursework was wide-ranging and rigorous (see Cameron, *Harvard Years*)—Greek and Latin, mathematics, physics, philosophy, history, English, theology, and foreign languages (Italian, French, German, and Spanish).

Between terms in 1835–1836 Thoreau taught school in Canton, Massachusetts, and in January–February 1836 he boarded with the Unitarian minister Orestes Brownson (1803–1876) a trenchant social critic and author. Brownson was at work on his Transcendentalist manifesto *New Views of Christianity, Society, and the Church* (published later in 1836). He and Thoreau studied German, and Thoreau developed a passion for Johann Wolfgang von Goethe's *Italian Journey* (1816), an exhilarating record of the author's residence and travels in Italy from 1786 to 1788 and an account of his interests in natural history and botany.

Thoreau spoke critically of his college education; in response to a remark by Emerson that Harvard offered many branches of learning, he muttered, "All of the branches and none of the roots." But the thirty-five faculty included excellent scholars, such as Benjamin Peirce in astronomy and mathematics, Henry Wadsworth Longfellow in foreign languages (he had studied in Europe from 1826 to 1829 and returned there for further work in 1835–1836), and Edward Tyrrell Channing in composition and oratory. Thoreau did moderately well, ranking nineteenth (roughly in the middle) in the class that graduated in 1837, and he would have done better if his studies had not been interrupted by illnesses.

At commencement, August 30, Thoreau spoke on "the commercial spirit of modern times considered in its influence on the Political, Moral, and Literary character of a Nation"; he stressed that "this curious world which we inhabit is more wonderful than it is convenient, more beautiful than it is useful—it is more to be admired and enjoyed then, than used. The order of things should be somewhat reversed,—the seventh should be man's day of toil, wherein to earn his living by the sweat of his brow, and the other six his sabbath of the affections and the soul" (*Early Essays*, 117). These *Walden*-like words derive from multiple sources: Thoreau's resistance to the day-to-day work routine he beheld in his father's life; his love of nature, kindled (Thoreau recalled) as early as 1822 by his first experience of the beauties of Walden Pond; his zeal for acquiring knowledge; and, above all, his enthusiastic response to Emerson's book *Nature* (1836), which Thoreau read in the spring term of his senior year and echoed in his final college essays.

In chapter one of *Nature* there is a key passage that prophesies the shape of Thoreau's own life and work:

> The lover of nature is he whose inward and outward senses are still truly adjusted to each other; who has retained the spirit of infancy even into the era of manhood. His intercourse with heaven and earth, becomes part of his daily food. In the presence of nature, a wild delight runs through the man, in spite of real sorrows. Nature says,—he is my creature, and maugre [despite] all his impertinent griefs, he shall be glad with me. Not the sun or the summer alone, but every hour and season yields its tribute of delight; for every hour and change corresponds to and authorizes a different state of the mind, from breathless noon to grimmest midnight. . . . In the woods too, a man casts off his years, as the snake his slough, and at what period soever of life, is always a child. In the woods, is perpetual youth. Within these plantations of God, a decorum and sanctity reign, a perennial festival is dressed, and the guest sees not how he should tire of them in a thousand years. (*Essays and Lectures*, 10)

In *Nature* Emerson described the riches that an investment in nature could yield, and on August 31, 1837, in his Phi Beta Kappa Society address "The American Scholar," delivered in the First Parish Church in Cambridge to the students in Thoreau's Harvard class, he evoked the splendors and defined the duties of a new intellectual identity. The scholar, Emerson explains, is *"Man Thinking.* In the degenerate state, when the victim of society, he tends to become a mere thinker, or, still worse, the parrot of other men's thinking" (*Essays and Lectures*, 54). In Emerson's view, society victimizes persons by prescribing soul-killing tasks and imposing self-stultifying identities. Each of us gives in and goes along, as if there were no choice but to accept the pattern that others have made and that they insist we conform to.

Emerson gave a spiritualized rendering to sentiments similar in part to those that Andrew Jackson had voiced on the national scene, during his campaign for the presidency in 1824 (he lost to John Quincy Adams) and again during his successful second run for the office in 1828. Jackson made his appeal to the common man and the popular majority, attacking wealth, privilege, and the rule of elite moneyed interests. An extremely controversial, fiery figure, Jackson was praised by his supporters as a true man of the people and denounced by his political enemies for (as they saw it) his pride, ambition, and tyrannical use of the veto power, especially in the bitter battle over the charter of the Second Bank of the United States, an institution that Jackson despised as the epitome of oligarchy. On the one hand, he assailed the abolitionists for the disorder that they threatened to cause in the nation, while, on the other hand, he angrily stood against southern nationalists who upheld the primacy of states' rights and challenged Jackson's authority as president. He was a slaveholder, a Tennessee aristocrat, an Indian fighter who during his presidency enforced a brutal relocation policy on Native American tribes in the South. Yet he was also the national and Democratic Party leader who opened up the government, making it accessible as never before to "the people"—he portrayed himself as their "direct representative"—and advocating their right to make their voices heard in political debate.

When Emerson spoke to the Harvard class, the nation was reeling from the financial panic of 1837—caused in large measure by Jackson's economic policies—and the choices for a fulfilling career, even for bright, well-educated men, seemed few and grimly narrow. The panic, a severe economic downturn that lasted until the early 1840s, was triggered by rampant, risky speculation in western lands, canals, and railroad operations and by huge state debts and overextended lines of credit by banks. Its consequences included many bank failures (618 in 1837 alone) and slowdowns in public works. Unemployment was widespread, and between 1836 and 1842, for those fortunate enough to find work, wages plummeted by one-third.

It was not simply economic pressure, however, that Emerson knew faced the young men to whom he spoke; it was also self-doubt and social and familial disapproval:

> For the ease and pleasure of treading the old road, accepting the fashions, the education, the religion of society, [the scholar] takes the cross of making his own, and, of course, the self-accusation, the faint heart, the frequent uncertainty and loss of time which are the nettles and tangling vines in the way of the self-relying and self-directed; and the state of virtual hostility in which he seems to stand to society, and especially to educated society. (*Essays and Lectures*, 63)

Emerson challenged audiences and readers to grasp the authentic meaning of vocation and become better than they had imagined possible. He encouraged them to feel the exaltation of their highest potential, to trust instinct and intuition (the signs of God's presence in persons), and to perceive nature as a source of truths more profound than any that society makes available. On the other side of the true scholar's fear—can I be the true maker of my life?—lay the rewards that Emerson articulated: "He is one who raises himself from private considerations, and breathes and lives on public and illustrious thoughts. He is the world's eye. He is the world's heart" (*Essays and Lectures*, 63).

Emerson and young Thoreau met sometime in the late summer or early fall of 1837 and soon became fast friends. In his journal, February 11, 1838, Emerson wrote: "I delight much in my young friend, who seems to have as free and erect a mind as any I have met." Thoreau had started keeping his own journal in the fall of 1837, prompted by Emerson; the first entry, October 22, is: "'What are you doing now?' he asked. 'Do you keep a journal?' So I make my first entry today." Emerson, fourteen years older, was for Thoreau a teacher, an intellectual and spiritual adviser, and perhaps something of a father and an older brother as well. In 1838 Emerson told his cousin David Greene Haskins: "When Mr. Carlyle comes to America, I expect to introduce Thoreau to him as *the* man of Concord" (cited in Harding, *Days*, 66). Emerson supplied Thoreau with literary direction and tips for reading; the books that Emerson borrowed from Boston and local libraries frequently were the books that Thoreau himself read next (Cameron, *Emerson's Reading*; Sattelmeyer, *Thoreau's Reading*).

In the 1850s Thoreau and Emerson became frustrated by the terms of their relationship; each said that he hoped for intimacy and regretted that the other was not providing it. Thoreau concluded that Emerson was patronizing him, whereas Emerson was baffled by his friend's reclusiveness and failure to cultivate his talents. But the point above all to remember is that these two men loved one another. Long after Thoreau's death, Emerson clung to his feeling for Thoreau and always named him "my best friend."

Emerson led Thoreau to the other strong minds and forthright personalities who took part in the gatherings of the Transcendental Club. Begun in 1836 as Hedge's Club—from F. H. Hedge, a Unitarian minister from Maine—it included Emerson, Brownson, the scholar and reformer Theodore Parker, the feminist writer Margaret Fuller, the teacher-philosopher Amos Bronson Alcott, the poet Jones Very (Thoreau's tutor in Greek at Harvard), and the Boston minister George Ripley, Emerson's cousin and in 1840–1841 the founder of the utopian community Brook Farm, in West Roxbury, Massachusetts.

Transcendentalism represented an effort to break free from the heritage of Calvinism, which emphasized mankind's innate sinfulness, and, furthermore, from philosophical rationalism, which maintained that knowledge was independent of sense experience. Freedom, for the Transcendentalists, meant overcoming the tyranny of everything exterior to the self. Evolving from such prominent German thinkers as Immanuel Kant, Goethe, and the brothers August Wilhelm and Friedrich von Schlegel, and from William Wordsworth, Samuel Taylor Coleridge, Thomas Carlyle, and other English writers whom the Germans influenced and inspired, Transcendentalism in America accented the correspondences between each person and nature and the sheer indwelling presence of the divine in all men and women.

"God is, not was," said Emerson; "he speaketh, not spake." Transcendentalism placed special value on conscience, imagination, and personal autonomy. It called for an openness to and faith in truths that persons could intuit, and an intensive gaze outward to a nature illuminated everywhere by a higher, "transcendent" reality. It connoted breadth and limitless prospect, the possibility that persons could make contact with divinity, and thus it exceeded the respectable boundaries that Unitarianism— the religion upon which Emerson and Thoreau were raised— sought to maintain. "Alone in all history," reflected Emerson in the "Divinity School Address" (15 July 1838),

> [Jesus] estimated the greatness of man. One man was true to what is in you and me. He saw that God incarnates himself in man, and evermore goes forth anew to take possession of his World. He said, in this jubilee of sublime emotion, "I am divine. Through me, God acts; through me, speaks. Would you see God, see me; or, see thee, when thou also thinkest as I now think." (*Essays and Lectures*, 80)

Parker, in "A Discourse of the Transient and Permanent in Christianity" (19 May 1841), stated that Jesus

> was the organ through which the Infinite spoke. It was God that was manifested in the flesh by him, on whom rests the truth which Jesus brought to light, and made clear and beautiful in his life. . . . Exalt him as much as we may, we shall yet perhaps come short of the mark. But still was he not our brother; the son of man, as we are; the son of God, like ourselves? His excellence—was it not human excellence? His wisdom, love, piety,—sweet and celestial as they were,—are they not what we also may attain? (Miller, *Transcendentalists*, 272, 275)

Parker was a minister, and Emerson also had been one until he resigned his office in 1832. Thoreau was not, and he does not describe Jesus in these terms. But for Thoreau, too, human potential is boundless, and the mission of life is striving to perfect oneself. Divinity permeates existence, Thoreau believed, and with dedication and discipline he sought to make the self godly.

Thoreau was a relentless reader, and when gripped by a subject he showed the fervor of a true scholar in his quest for coverage and depth of information. He cherished the Greek and Roman classics (Homer and Virgil in particular); English poetry from Chaucer, Donne, Herbert, and Milton to Coleridge and Wordsworth; seventeenth-century prose writers such as Walter Raleigh (*The History of the World*, 1614), Thomas Browne (*Religio Medici*, 1642), and Francis Quarles (*Emblems*, 1635, and *Hieroglyphikes of the Life of Man*, 1638); treatises on religion and philosophy (a favorite was Ralph Cudworth's Platonist manifesto *The True Intellectual System of the Universe*, 1678); the sacred writings of the Hindus; colonial and local histories and books and pamphlets on the North American Indian tribes; books about exploration and travel; and natural history studies and guidebooks.

Except for Emerson, the Scottish cultural historian Carlyle (author of *Sartor Resartus*, 1836, and *Past and Present*, 1843), and, in the 1850s, Walt Whitman, Thoreau was only marginally attentive to the poets, novelists, and short-story writers of his own time. He was acquainted with the writings of James Fenimore Cooper, Washington Irving, Longfellow, and Herman Melville (the South Seas romance *Typee*, not *Moby-Dick*). But the major English novels by Emily and Charlotte Brontë, Elizabeth Gaskell, and Charles Dickens apparently passed him by. He was no more interested in fiction than Emerson was and seems not even to have been familiar with the novels written by his friend Hawthorne, though he does refer in the journal to Hawthorne's tales. Gaskell and Dickens depicted the effects of poverty, urbanization, and industrialization on English society; so did Benjamin Disraeli in *Coningsby* (1844) and *Sybil* (1845, subtitled "The Two Nations") and Charles Kingsley in *Yeast* (1848) and *Alton Locke* (1850). For Thoreau, however, the novel was not a vehicle for social, economic, and political critique and prophecy. A genuine artist, he felt, composed books about real persons and things and did not dabble in fictions to which readers fled in idle times.

After graduating from Harvard, Thoreau briefly taught public school in Concord, resigning after just two weeks on the job when he was reprimanded for his unwillingness to flog students. He helped out in his father's pencil-making business and then tried unsuccessfully to find a position as a schoolteacher in Maine. In June 1838 he opened a small private school in the Thoreau home but shortly thereafter took over Concord Academy, where his brother John joined him as a fellow teacher in 1839. Enrollment was about twenty-five students per term, and the curriculum included weekly field trips and visits to local shops. The pupils studied formal subjects such as English, mathematics, and foreign languages, but, for the Thoreaus, it was equally important that they learn how to make maps, survey a piece of property, collect Indian relics, and see the landscape with alertness and insight.

In June 1839 Thoreau met an eleven-year-old boy named Edmund Sewall, the grandson of a woman who boarded with the Thoreaus. Edmund became a favorite student at Concord Academy, and through him the Thoreau brothers were introduced to his seventeen-year-old sister Ellen. Both John and Henry fell in love with her; both courted her and, eventually, proposed marriage; and both of their proposals were rejected. Ellen's father, a Unitarian minister in Scituate, south of Boston, did not approve of her marrying one of the Thoreaus, known for their radical and Transcendentalist views. Thoreau never married; neither did his brother or sisters, all of whom lived in the family home. (On Thoreau and sexuality, see Warner.)

The year 1839 also was eventful for a two-week trip that Henry and John took together, August 31 to September 13, traveling along the Concord and Merrimack rivers, an experience that Thoreau made the basis for his first book, published a decade later.

During 1838–1939 Thoreau wrote poems (the best of which, about friendship, is "Sympathy"), and he was active in Concord's intellectual life, especially its lyceum. The lyceum was a society for literary, scientific, and cultural education similar to those established in the 1820s and 1830s in towns and cities throughout the nation. By the mid-1830s there were lyceums in fifteen states—by 1860 the total would reach 3,000—and the lyceum circuit was a popular, and in some cases well-paying, outlet for speakers. Thoreau delivered his first lecture, "Society," to the

Concord Lyceum on April 11, 1838, arguing that "the mass never comes up to the standard of its best member, but on the contrary degrades itself to a level with the lowest." In October he was elected its secretary and, in November, its curator.

To disseminate their work, the Transcendentalists launched a journal, *The Dial*. The first issue, in July 1840, included Thoreau's "Sympathy" and his essay on the Roman satirist Aulus Persius Flaccus. Emerson in particular surmised that the journal would bring Thoreau's writings to the attention of a wider readership. "My Henry Thoreau," he had written in a letter, September 26, 1839, to his brother William, "will be a great poet for such a company, & one of these days for all companies" (Emerson, *Letters*, 2:225). Thoreau's essay "A Natural History of Massachusetts" (July 1842) was just one of his many contributions. During 1842–1843 he assisted Emerson when Emerson replaced Fuller as *The Dial*'s editor, and he edited the April issue himself.

In April 1841, because of his brother's lingering illness from the effects of tuberculosis, Thoreau closed Concord Academy. Having already turned down an invitation to become a Brook Farm resident, at the end of the month he accepted Emerson's offer of room and board at the Emerson home in exchange for doing work as a handyman and gardener.

Both the Thoreau and Emerson families were stricken by tragedy in January 1842. On January 1 John Thoreau cut himself while shaving; the wound became infected; lockjaw set in; and he died on the afternoon of the twelfth in his brother's arms. Thoreau was shattered by his brother's death, and in the following days he suffered psychosomatically from symptoms of lockjaw himself. On January 24 five-year-old Waldo Emerson came down with scarlet fever, and his death on the 27th grievously pained the Emersons and Thoreau, who knew the boy well.

In a letter, March 14, 1842, to Isaiah Williams, a friend and former Concord resident, Thoreau reflected on the lessons about vocation and career that these deaths had taught him. Time is short and must be spent wisely, he explained:

> I must confess I am apt to consider the trades and professions so many traps which the Devil sets to catch men in—and

good luck he has too, if one may judge. But did it ever occur that a man came to want, or the almshouse from consulting his higher instincts? All great good is very urgent, and need not be postponed. (*Correspondence*, 68)

By mid-1842 Thoreau had a new friend in Nathaniel Hawthorne, who was living in Concord in the Old Manse (owned by the Emerson family), where he had moved with his wife after their marriage. Thoreau had planted a garden for them, to be ready when they arrived, and the two taciturn men seem to have gotten along well. In a notebook entry, September 1, 1842, Hawthorne wrote this shrewd description:

> Mr. Thorow [*sic*] dined with us yesterday. He is a singular character—a young man with much of the wild original nature still remaining in him; and so far as he is sophisticated, it is in a way and method of his own. He is as ugly as sin, long-nosed, queer-mouthed, and with uncouth and somewhat rustic, although courteous manners, corresponding very well with such an exterior. But his ugliness is of an honest and agreeable fashion, and becomes much better than beauty. . . . He has repudiated all regular modes of getting a living, and seems inclined to lead a sort of Indian life among civilized men—an Indian life, I mean, as respects the absence of any systematic effort for a livelihood. . . . Mr. Thorow is a keen and delicate observer of nature—a genuine observer, which, I suspect, is almost as rare a character as even an original poet; and Nature, in return for his love, seems to adopt him as her especial child, and shows him secrets which few others are allowed to witness. (166)

Though Thoreau was content with his "Indian life" in Concord, in the first week of May 1843 he moved from Concord to Staten Island, New York, to tutor the oldest son, age seven, of Emerson's brother William. This decision may appear strange, but it was impelled by his own literary aspirations and his friend and mentor Emerson's hopes for him. The move to New York, they believed, would enable Thoreau to make connections with writers, editors, and publishers there.

Thoreau was unhappy in the William Emerson household; and in his journal, September 24, he complained about the bustle and anonymity of the city: "Who can see these cities and say that there is any life in them? I walked through New York yesterday—and met with no real or living person" (cited in Christie, *Thoreau*, 19). In December Thoreau returned to Concord; as he had acknowledged in June in a letter to Emerson's wife Lidian, "I carry Concord ground in my boots and in my hat,—and am I not made of Concord dust?" (*Correspondence*, 103). But he had been at least partially successful in achieving his goals; during his six months in New York he met such notable figures as the utopian theorist Albert Brisbane, author of *The Social Destiny of Man* (1840); the religious philosopher Henry James, Sr.; and the editor and reformer Horace Greeley, who became Thoreau's advocate in the competitive world of newspapers, magazines, and journals. In 1843–1844 Thoreau's writings were published not only in *The Dial* (its final issue was April 1844), but also in the *Boston Miscellany* and the *United States Magazine and Democratic Review*.

In 1844 Thoreau lived with his family and assisted with the pencil business; his research improved his father's product and later led the family to shift from making pencils to supplying graphite to other pencil manufacturers. Thoreau took pleasure as always in the countryside, exploring the woods and rivers with friends. During the summer, he enjoyed rowing and, in the winter, ice skating. In April 1844, however, a trip along the Sudbury River came to a bad end when Thoreau and a companion accidentally set the woods on fire while cooking fish chowder in a dried-out stump. Three hundred acres burned, and Thoreau was rebuked by the town newspaper (he was not named, but everybody knew he was the person referred to)—a deep embarrassment to someone with a reputation as a budding naturalist.

In March 1845 Thoreau began building a cabin near Walden Pond. The idea was not new; in the summer of 1837 Thoreau had spent six weeks sharing with Charles Stearns Wheeler, a friend from Harvard, a shanty, which Wheeler had erected near Flint's Pond in Lincoln, bordering Concord. Named after a town, "Saffron Walden," forty miles from London, Walden Pond is, in Thoreau's words, "a clear and deep well, half a mile long and a mile and three quarters in circumference, and contains about sixty-one and a half acres; a perennial spring in the midst of pine and oak woods, without any visible inlet or outlet except by the clouds and evaporation" ("The Ponds," *Walden*). Thoreau's site was about a mile and a half south of town, on land (a pasture and woodlot, of about fifteen acres) that Emerson had purchased in September 1844.

The subtitle of the book in which Thoreau later wrote about his experiences is "Life in the Woods," and we tend to associate him with forests near a pond and paths between tall trees. But the woods where Thoreau resided were one of the very few forest areas remaining in the Concord environs. Most people made their living from the land; by the first decades of the nineteenth century, not only Concord, but indeed some 60 percent or more of New England was open fields. By the 1840s only about one-tenth of the Concord landscape was wooded, and Thoreau thus was fortunate in being able to find and settle on a good woodland site (see Foster; Brooks). Thoreau took up his new abode during a period of transition, as decade by decade people left the farms and the rural way of life and moved to the cities or journeyed to the Midwest and West. Toward the end of Thoreau's life, the woods where he built his cabin were spreading and filling up the old pastures and farmlands. New England's industrial growth and urban and suburban development since the mid-nineteenth century have been extensive, but, nonetheless, there are far more woods and forest areas in this part of the nation today than there were in Thoreau's lifetime.

Thoreau did not build from scratch but instead bought from an Irishman a hut, which he took apart and then reassembled, fifteen feet long, ten feet wide, sited to allow the morning sun to shine into his doorway. He moved in on the Fourth of July—a fitting date for his declaration of independence, though he says it was simply "by accident" ("Where I Lived . . ."). The cabin contained three chairs, a table, a desk, a small mirror, and a few other items, and it was not until the fall that Thoreau constructed the fireplace and chimney. In May and June, before moving in, he cleared two and a half acres of land and planted beans, corn, and potatoes, so that these crops would be growing when he arrived.

The dwelling that Thoreau built was simple and sturdy because he wanted it that way: it was the right choice for the nature of the new life he had in mind. But his choice also may have derived from a "mountain house" that he had seen and admired on a trip the previous summer to the Catskills and, more broadly, from ideas about the reform of domestic architecture—along the lines of the humble English cottage—that a number of English and American authors had described (see Maynard, "Thoreau's House"). Thoreau was a bookish radical: his thoughts and actions took shape from what he saw around him but as much or more from what he read.

Thoreau's cabin at Walden has been called a utopia of one, in order both to connect it to, and to differentiate it from, the utopian enterprises elsewhere in the country. Two were under way nearby: Brook Farm, begun in April 1841, with Hawthorne as one of its first residents—he would recall his experiences, buoyant at first but soon jaded, in his novel *The Blithedale Romance* (1852); and Fruitlands, in Harvard, Massachusetts, not far from Concord, where Alcott and his family and a few soulmates dwelled with little success from mid- to late 1844.

Like many utopian ventures, Brook Farm and Fruitlands were efforts to construct Christian community on a new basis and had roots that reached back to the revivalism of the Second Great Awakening. The first Great Awakening, which had occurred in the colonies from the 1730s to the 1760s, was marked by intense religious enthusiasm, much of it stimulated by the powerful British preacher and evangelist George Whitefield, who toured the colonies for fifteen months in 1738–1739. The major voice of the second wave was Charles Grandison Finney, who, after experiencing a religious conversion in 1821, conducted revivals and camp meetings in northern New York State.

Finney urged men and women to apply to their lives and communities Christ's words in the gospel: "Be ye therefore perfect, even as your Father which is in heaven is perfect" (Matt. 5:48). This injunction not only kindled individual conversions, but also led to the formation of benevolent and reform groups, associations, networks, and organizations, including the Bible Society, the American Tract Society, and the Home Missionary Society, that were dedicated to "perfecting" social conditions and establishing God's Kingdom—"heaven on earth"—in the present.

More than 100 communities, many religious, some secular, were founded in the period between the Revolution and the Civil War. The most common were the thirty or more across the country that subscribed to the tenets of the French socialist Charles Fourier and his American translator and disciple Albert Brisbane. The largest of these was Red Bank, New Jersey (with a peak membership of 125–150 persons), with seven others clustered in northern Pennsylvania and still more scattered elsewhere in the East and Midwest.

Earlier communities included the Shaker settlement in Mount Lebanon, New York, organized in 1787 and soon replicated elsewhere; the German pietist George Rapp's Harmony Society in western Pennsylvania, begun in 1805; the British reformer Robert Owen and his son Robert Dale Owen's New Harmony, Indiana, established in May 1825, a cooperative settlement intended to replace the competitive, capitalist order and break free from formal religion; and Frances Wright's Owenite community in Nashoba, Tennessee, which started in the fall of 1825 with the goal of educating slaves.

Later examples include Adin Ballou's Hopedale in Massachusetts in the mid-1840s, emphasizing temperance, antislavery, and other reforms; John Humphrey Noyes's communities in Putney, Vermont, in the 1830s, and in Oneida, New York, in the late 1840s, which were based on evangelical Christian principles and were radically perfectionist in spirit and liberated in sexual practices; John A. Collins's no-government/common property community in Skaneateles, New York, in January 1844; Josiah Warren's Modern Times, on Long Island, New York, in 1851; and the Icarian community, keyed to the ideas of Etienne Cabet, a French radical and author of the utopian novel *Voyage en Icarie*, which was first established in Texas in mid-1848 and later relocated to Illinois, Missouri, and Iowa. Perhaps the most successful of all were the communities of Mormons whom Joseph Smith led in Ohio, Missouri, and Illinois in the late 1830s and 1840s, and whom Brigham Young, after Smith was killed by a mob in 1844, brought to their permanent home in the Great Salt Lake Valley in the Utah territory (1846–1847).

Advocates of these utopias challenged custom, tradition, and convention and believed in social progress; they wanted their style of living to function as a model for the society at large— Adin Ballou, for example, referred to Hopedale as "a miniature Christian Republic." To Thoreau, Emerson, and Hawthorne, however, while utopian communities were alluring and admirable to a degree in theory, they were at bottom misconceived and not likely to operate well or last long in practice. In *The Blithedale Romance*, Hawthorne's characters do not become better as a result of membership in the Blithedale community. If anything, they become worse, as the new setting they select for their lives gives them only a different, more dangerous stage upon which to act out their basic personalities. Neither Emerson nor Thoreau accepted invitations to join Brook Farm; to them, it was a form for living that would enclose the individual within the demands and needs of the group and that would lead everyone toward consensus and conformity.

It is a curious fact that the founding of these utopias coincided with the rise of vacation spots and resorts in Newport, Rhode Island; in the Catskills in upstate New York; and in the White Mountains of New Hampshire. When these getaways to nature began, their main purpose was not pleasure but the improvement of health, through bathing in natural springs, taking in the fresh seaside or mountain air, and hiking in the woods and countryside. Some social reformers praised resorts for offering physical and spiritual renewal, but others criticized them as wasteful and extravagant. To the abolitionists, resorts were places where wealthy slaveholders took their families to escape from the heat of the summer months, and where northern businessmen, bankers, and merchants bought luxuries with the money gained from commerce with the slaveowning South. In his journal and in *Walden* Thoreau details the distinctive kind of contact with nature he pursued and the economic independence he maintained to support it, in part to define the difference between his experiment and the tainted types of recreation and renewal to which it might appear akin.

Travel to resorts was made possible by the extension of the railroad, a crucial sign of the technological transformation of

American life to which Thoreau devotes critical analysis in
Walden, where he describes the construction of the track from
Boston to Fitchburg along the western shore of the pond. The
power of the locomotive impressed him, but he hated its effects
on the land and its role in promoting commerce and undermin-
ing personal freedom:

> The whistle of the locomotive penetrates my woods summer
> and winter, sounding like the scream of a hawk sailing over
> some farmer's yard, informing me that many restless city
> merchants are arriving within the circle of the town, or adven-
> turous country traders from the other side. As they come
> under one horizon, they shout their warning to get off the
> track to the other, heard sometimes through the circles of two
> towns. Here come your groceries, country; your rations,
> countrymen! Nor is there any man so independent on his
> farm that he can say them nay. ("Sounds")

The great transportation feat of the 1820s was the completion
in 1825 of the Erie Canal, which connected the Great Lakes region to the Hudson River and New York City. (A popular itiner-
ary for tourists became a trip from New York City up the Hudson
River to Albany, and then westward by way of the Erie Canal to
Niagara Falls.) But soon the expansion of the railway system
showed even more dramatically the American advance in technology. In 1830, when the New York inventor Peter Cooper built
the first locomotive in the United States (speed: 12 mph), there
were twenty-three miles of track. By 1840 the figure had increased to 3,000 miles—nearly twice that of Europe. It reached
9,000 in 1850 and more than 30,000 in 1860, cutting across a nation
that had tripled in size from 1803, the date of the Louisiana Purchase, to the late 1840s, when Mexico ceded vast stretches of land
at the close of the Mexican War. By the 1850s freight trains usually included a dozen ten-ton cars; coal-burning locomotives
were replacing wood-burners; and telegraphs were regulating
train movements. Toward the end of the decade, some passenger lines were making use of the sleeping-car service that the
Chicago industrialist George Pullman had devised.

Many of the laborers on railroad and canal projects were Irish immigrants. They came to the United States in large numbers in the 1840s, particularly in the wake of the terrible Irish famine of 1846. Irish immigration constituted half of the total immigration in the 1840s, and in 1851 it reached a one-year peak of 221,000. Of Concord's total population of 2,249 in the year 1850, 353 (that is, about 15 percent) were foreign-born or were children living in households headed by foreign-born parents. Most were Irish Catholics, and many were single men or women with no property who held unskilled jobs as laborers on the railroad or on farms or as domestics.

By 1860, while Concord's total population had remained steady, the immigrant population had increased from 15 to 21 percent. It is a sign of the transient nature of this group that only a handful of immigrants listed in 1850 also are listed in 1860. Concord was divided along the lines of religion, ethnicity, and class, with a core population of about 30 percent and a large population of persons, many of them immigrants, who lived in the town briefly and then moved on (for these details, see Yanella, "Socio-Economic Disarray").

Boston, twenty miles east, was "the hub of the New England railway system, with lines radiating inland in every direction" (Stover, *Railroads*, 27). Between 1830 and 1835 three railroad lines were built leading out of Boston—to Providence, Lowell, and Worcester; and in 1841 the Worcester line's extension made travel from Boston to Buffalo possible. This building boom was the result of a decision made in the 1830s by Boston's prominent citizens and businessmen, who concluded that railroads, not canals, would be the transportation system of the future. Railroads meant expanded commerce, more markets for goods, increases in land values, and revenues from the delivery of materials and transport of passengers. So many rail lines were laid in New England that some areas were overbuilt; four separate railroads, for example, served a small area of countryside on the Massachusetts and New Hampshire border.

The fifty-mile Boston to Fitchburg Railroad—the target of Thoreau's wrath—had been launched with the expectation that "this would be the beginning of a trans-sectional line to extend the mercantile system of Boston" (Vance, *Railroad*, 69–70). Financed through the sale of stock purchased by those living near the line, and based on the carrying of freight, this highly profitable railroad earned its investors a 10 percent return on capital (Stover, *Railroad*, 69). Hundreds of Irishmen toiled each day to construct the line, which reached Concord in June 1844, thirteen months before Thoreau began living at Walden.

When Thoreau protested, "We do not ride on the railroad, it rides upon us" ("Where I Lived . . . "), his words were thrust at an institution that was making money for many people and that was part of a system already well established and gaining momentum daily—a system that businessmen and manufacturers in Concord welcomed but that was built on the backs of underpaid, overworked laborers. Farmers up to a point welcomed the railroad, too, for, as the scholar Robert A. Gross has shown, it made profitable "the large-scale production of milk, eggs, fruits, and garden vegetables." But, as Gross has pointed out, such production for market as well as for home use made farmers work harder than ever before: work became more time-consuming and burdensome (Gross, "Culture and Cultivation," 50–51).

By the early 1850s nearly every town in Massachusetts with a population of 5,000 or more was linked to a railroad; and the same held true for the majority of towns with a population between 2,500 and 5,000. The railroad expanded markets for raw materials and for farm products and manufactured goods. Through it "the impact of the factory reached into every corner of the state," and the railroad solidified Massachusetts's position as "the state most thoroughly given over to extensive industrial development" (Siracusa, *Mechanical People*, 26, 39).

As Tamara Plakins Thornton has shown in a valuable study, the Boston elite of merchants, manufacturers, financiers, lawyers, and politicans who advocated and supported this turn toward commerce and industry were, at the same time, keenly interested in embracing the virtues of rural life, retreating to nature, and pursuing agriculture. Many of them settled on country estates, seemingly inclined in their own more elaborate way to take up a new form of the simpler life like Thoreau's. During the first decades of the nineteenth century, they even established a range of horticultural and agricultural societies to devise and promote reforms in farming.

But this apparent kinship ultimately points to a dramatic difference between the views and activities of the Boston elite and Thoreau. The elite wanted the best of both worlds, whereas Thoreau's argument was that his life at Walden exposed the destructiveness and folly of the push for industrialization and the ethos of getting and spending that accompanied it. As Thornton notes, by the 1840s, the elite had given up on reforming agriculture, concerning themselves instead with the politer practices of horticulture and stockbreeding. They were now seeking an enjoyable pastime, a diversion for a while from the imperatives of business.

Thoreau cared less about the elite, however, than about the average man and woman, who in ever-increasing numbers were working for others and were subject to the demands and shifts of the marketplace. By 1860 40 percent of America's working population worked for wages—a rise from 12 percent in 1800. Many were women, laboring either in mills and factories or as "outworkers" in the home (making hats or dresses, for instance). Already by 1840, two-thirds of the workers in manufacturing in Massachusetts were women. People everywhere in the state were working harder and more intensively, as if there were no other choice, and this is why Thoreau for his part emphasizes an unhurried, contemplative pace. He addresses his readers in an irritated, mocking tone intended to destabilize the numbing way of life to which many were becoming habituated.

Is Thoreau's argument in *Walden* designed to spur changes in the structure of society as a whole? *Walden*'s point of view and its social and economic criticism are strenuously individualized: this author is speaking to *you*, and it is your life that he tells you must be changed. Thoreau believed that social structures that impair the self must be confronted and resisted. Yet he repeatedly suggests that ultimately these structures do not matter, because we have the capacity to change our lives wherever and however we are situated. Society is an enemy, not an excuse.

In his journal, January 21, 1838, the twenty-year-old Thoreau asserted, "Man is the artificer of his own happiness," adding,

"Let him beware how he complains of the disposition of circumstances, for it is his own disposition he blames" (Princeton ed., 1:125). His reading of the texts of the Roman Stoic philosophers Marcus Aurelius, Cicero, Epictetus, and Seneca reinforced this principle; and the ancient Indian scriptures, such as *The Laws of Menu*, with their sublime ideals of purity, detachment, withdrawal for the sake of personal liberation, inner harmony, and self-discipline, deepened it. When Thoreau professes in *Walden*, "I desire to speak as one not interested in the success or failure of the present economical and social arrangements," he is restating a central tenet of his philosophy ("Visitors").[1]

On no other point is Thoreau so insistent. In a journal entry, for example, he observes: "The true reform can be undertaken any morning before unbarring our doors. It calls no convention. I can do two thirds the reform of the world myself. . . . When an individual takes a sincere step, then all the gods attend, and his single deed is sweet" (Princeton ed., 1:299). Before any "outward" reform can occur, Thoreau contends in an essay on the utopian theorist J. A. Etzler (*Democratic Review*, November 1843), "A moral reform must take place first, and then the necessity of the other will be superceded, and we shall sail and plough by its force alone" (*Reform Papers*, 45–46). In *Walden* he maintains, "The man who goes alone can start to-day; but he who travels with another must wait till that other is ready, and it may be a long time before they get off" ("Economy").

Thoreau responded to social life as a spectacle of human folly, especially the race for riches that reached its height in the Gold Rush days of the late 1840s and 1850s. In an 1849 note to a leaf of the *Walden* manuscript, Thoreau stated, "To show how little men have considered what is the true end of life—or the nature of this living which they have to get—I need only remind you how many have within the last month started for California with the muck rake on their shoulders" (Shanley, *Making of "Walden,"* 107). It was bad enough that many people had surrendered to the grind of tedious work and the pursuit of possessions. But then, to Thoreau's shock and amazement, they mindlessly embarked on get-rich-quick schemes that made matters worse.

Reports of the discovery of gold in California had begun to

appear in newspapers in the East in September 1848, about a year after Thoreau left Walden, and President James K. Polk confirmed them in his December 5, 1848, message to Congress: "The explorations already made, warrant the belief that the supply is very large and that gold is found at various places in an extensive district of country" (J. Richardson, *Compilation*, 4:2486). In 1848 the population of California was about 14,000; by 1852 (statehood was granted in 1850) the non-Indian population alone exceeded 250,000—and this despite the fact that as many as 30,000 persons per year, disappointed that they had found nothing, returned East.

Shed needless things; concentrate on the essential; show loving justice to the self: to Thoreau these were the obvious alternatives to the Gold Rush craze that he denounced. In an angry entry in his journal, February 1, 1852, he wrote:

> The recent rush to California & the attitude of the world, even of its philosophers and prophets, in relation to it appears to me to reflect the greatest disgrace on mankind. That so many are ready to get their living by the lottery of gold-digging without contributing any value to society, and that the great majority who stay at home justify them in this both by precept and example! . . . If I could command the wealth of all the worlds by lifting my finger, I would not pay such a price for it. It makes God to be a moneyed gentleman who scatters a handful of pennies in order to see mankind scramble for them. Going to California. It is only three thousand miles nearer to hell. (Dover ed., 3:265–66; Princeton ed., 4:317)

A few days later, February 9, Thoreau noted, "I did not know that the world was suffering for want of gold. . . . A grain of it will gild a great surface—but not so much as a grain of wisdom" (Dover ed., 3:291; Princeton ed., 4:339), and it is the quest for wisdom, for quiet reflection and self-understanding, that he recounts in *Walden* as he tells of the days he spent by the pond in 1845–1847.

But while he resided at Walden, Thoreau was in truth very hard at work—hard at work on his writing. He was dedicated to writing, and he labored constantly at it. Living at Walden was for him an opportunity for literary production, away from the busy Thoreau home with its boarders and pencil factory.

Aided by two journal volumes he brought along, Thoreau turned first to writing a manuscript about the river trip that he and John Thoreau had taken in 1839. This manuscript became *A Week on the Concord and Merrimack Rivers*, published in 1849, with the invocation "Be thou my Muse, my Brother." He also composed an acute essay on Thomas Carlyle; it was the basis for a lecture he presented at the Concord Lyceum on February 4, 1846, and it appeared in two parts in the March and April 1847 issues of *Graham's Magazine*, a popular, high-quality periodical with a circulation of 50,000. Thoreau also wrote 100 pages on his Maine woods experience, which he turned into a series of articles, July through November 1848, for the *Union Magazine of Literature and Art*.

Thoreau was under way on two lectures about his Walden experiment almost as soon as he had begun it, probably in response to questions from friends and neighbors. By early 1847 Thoreau was making excellent progress on his *Walden* manuscript; he drew from it for a lecture, delivered on February 10, 1847, again at the Concord Lyceum, titled "The History of Myself." In September 1847 the first draft of the *Walden* manuscript was finished.

Thoreau thus was at Walden embarked on a sustained writing project. At one juncture, he was working simultaneously on the first draft of *Walden*, the second draft of *A Week*, and the draft of his trip to Maine that became the first essay in the posthumous book *The Maine Woods* (Adams and Ross, *Mythologies*, 2). Thoreau wrote regularly in his journal as well, which was itself a crafted text that he shaped from notes, drafts, and jottings. In *Walden* Thoreau chooses not to divulge how much time he spent at his writing desk, but he was at Walden less of a sojourner in nature than he was a maker of books, an indefatigable writer who was *always* writing. Writing was his work and life; when he said in a September 17, 1849, letter to Jared Sparks, president of Harvard, *"I have chosen letters for my profession,"* Thoreau was underscoring a decision made and enacted years earlier (*Correspondence*, 249). He went to Walden Pond to write books and to gather experiences for books.[2]

Thoreau resided at Walden for twenty-six months, but, perhaps to relieve the pressure of his acts of writing, he took frequent breaks, and even when he was there his life was not a solitary one. He exaggerated when he told a Harvard classmate, Henry Williams, Jr., on September 30, 1847: "For the last two or three years I have lived in Concord woods alone, something more than a mile from any neighbor, in a house built entirely by myself" (*Correspondence*, 186). Often he walked to town or to the family home a short distance away; he collected specimens for the Swiss naturalist Louis Agassiz, who was in Boston as the guest of the U.S. government and Harvard University; he entertained friends (Emerson and Alcott, for example) and family, including his mother and sisters who brought treats to him on weekends. On August 1, 1846, Thoreau took part in an antislavery meeting, held on his cabin doorstep, at which Emerson and others spoke; and in August–September of the same year he journeyed with a cousin to Maine. Walden "was less of a home and more of a headquarters" (Harding and Bode, in Thoreau, *Correspondence*, 167); Thoreau's friend F. B. Sanborn went further, explaining that Thoreau "really lived at home, where he went every day," while he "bivouacked" at his cabin.

Thoreau also spent a night in jail, the result of his arrest in July 1846 for failing to pay his poll tax, a tax that Thoreau argued meant giving support to the Mexican War. In his antiwar sentiments, he was in the minority, for most Americans supported the war and viewed it as a romantic military adventure that would extend America's democratic ideals. Abolitionists, believing that the real goal was the expansion of slavery south and west, criticized the Mexican War and later condemned the peace treaty, signed in 1848, that gave the United States 500,000 miles of new territory. Thoreau agreed with them; he refused to pay his tax and thought no more about it.

Then one day in late July, on a trip into Concord to have a shoe repaired, Thoreau was stopped by the town constable, Sam Staples, who told him that he needed to pay the tax, several years of which were due. When Thoreau balked, Staples offered to loan him the money. When Thoreau said *no* to that too, the constable led him to jail, where he was placed in a cell with another man. Someone, probably Thoreau's Aunt Maria, paid the tax as soon as the family learned what had happened. Thoreau should have been released, but Staples by then was at home and did not want to go back to the jail.

Thoreau's jailing was, it seems, an accident, and maybe a legal error. The tax that Thoreau refused to pay was a local one, not connected to the state of Massachusetts or to the federal government, and, according to one scholar who has studied the issue, it was unrelated to any funding for the Mexican War (Hoeltje, "Misconceptions"). Another scholar has suggested that Staples's action was illegal; Massachusetts law empowered him to lay hold of Thoreau's goods and disburse them to pay debts, but not to place Thoreau under arrest (Harding, "Thoreau in Jail"). Thoreau was not the first to break this law; his friend Alcott had been arrested for the same reason in January 1843. What made Thoreau special, Staples later said, was that he did not want to leave jail; he was "mad as the devil" that someone had interfered with his gesture by paying the tax for him.

Thoreau departed Walden in September 1847, and for the next ten months he lived again with the Emerson family, helping out while Emerson traveled in Europe. On January 26, 1848, he lectured at the Concord Lyceum on "the relation of the individual to the State," which with the title "Resistance to Civil Government" was published in 1849 in the volume *Aesthetic Papers*, edited by Elizabeth Peabody, an educator, reformer, and Hawthorne's sister-in-law. When it was reprinted after Thoreau's death, it was given the title "Civil Disobedience," by which it is familiarly known.

"Civil Disobedience" was just one of the pieces of literary work that Thoreau produced during this period. In addition to the account of his trip to the Maine woods for *Union Magazine*, he revised extensively the manuscript of *A Week* and started on a second draft of *Walden*. He continued with his journal and began taking notes on the cultures and traditions of the American Indian that by 1861 totaled 3,000 pages of quotations and comments. Thoreau also presented a number of lectures in Maine and Massachusetts, for which he was paid $20 to $25, including two at Hawthorne's invitation in Salem, November 22, 1848, and

February 28, 1849, that described his experiences at Walden Pond. The first, "Student Life in New England, Its Economy," and the second, "Life in the Woods," gave Thoreau the opportunity to try out material for chapters one and two of *Walden*.

A Week on the Concord and Merrimack Rivers was published May 30, 1849, by James Munroe and Company of Boston, but at Thoreau's own expense. The reviews were disappointing, and the book sold poorly. Indeed it was "a commercial disaster, one of the worst-selling books by an eventually-canonized author in American literary history" (Scharnhorst, *Case Study*, 8). Most of the 1,000 copies printed went unsold, with the result that Thoreau accrued a debt to the publisher of $290 that took him many months to pay. The unsold copies were returned to Thoreau four years later; "I have now a library of nearly nine hundred volumes," he wrote in his journal, October 27, 1853, "over seven hundred of which I wrote myself" (Dover ed., 5:459). Thoreau continued to prepare articles for magazines and journals, but the failure of *A Week* showed that he would not make a living from literature.

This failure did not lessen Thoreau's commitment to his writing; for the year 1852, his journal alone totals more than 700 pages. But he was away from his desk more than he liked, spending time working in the family business and making improvements in the science of pencil-making. As the historian Henry Petroski has noted, Thoreau devised a means of refining graphite, combining it with clay, that enabled the Thoreau family to produce the best pencils in the country, pencils of the highest quality manufactured in different degrees of hardness and made for various uses, from writing to drafting and drawing. He did research on pencil-making and reported on the results of his reading to the family; and he made adjustments in the machinery from which the pencils were fashioned.

In 1853 the Thoreaus stopped producing pencils, because the sale of their fine graphite powder had become so profitable in its own right. Thoreau stayed involved in the business, becoming head in 1859 upon his father's death. Thoreau had helped his father to produce "the best pencil in America" (Petroski, *The Pencil*, 115), and it is conceivable that if he had wanted to, he could have become a kindred spirit to William Dean Howells's vigorous title character in *The Rise of Silas Lapham* (1885), a self-made man raised on a farm in Vermont who, after making a fortune from mineral paint, decides to build a mansion in Boston's Back Bay to symbolize his prosperity.

Thoreau wanted to succeed with his books, but he struggled to find the best design for them and too often left his readers perplexed and even a little bored. For its first readers, the problem with *A Week* was its digressiveness, its lack of structure. On one level it does have a controlling form: condensing the two weeks of the trip into one, Thoreau bases each chapter on a day of the week. He describes how the brothers (John is nowhere referred to by name) departed from Concord on Sunday, reached the limit of their canoe journey into New Hampshire by Thursday, and traveled back downstream to Concord on Thursday and Friday. But, along with the sights and sounds of the trip, Thoreau filled his book with all kinds of other material, including much that originally had been published in *The Dial*. He produced a text that is rich and capacious, but not one that stays faithful to its main narrative-line, and readers of his own day found it wandering and disorderly.

The pleasure and peril of *A Week* lie in the variety of things that it includes. For example, Thoreau's first piece in *The Dial*, on the Roman satirist Persius, appears in revised form in the "Thursday" section. He also inserted, in whole or in part, sixty of his poems, twelve of them from *The Dial*. As one of his biographers has remarked, *A Week* is "like a library of the shorter works of Henry Thoreau" (Canby, *Thoreau*, 272). It contains translations, an Indian captivity narrative, bits of local history, comments on other excursions that Thoreau had taken, and essays on Christianity, reading and writing, friendship, Oriental texts and sacred scriptures, Ossian (a Gaelic poet of myth and folk culture, whom the Scottish poet and translator James McPherson claimed in the mid-eighteenth century to have discovered), Chaucer, and other topics.

Emerson had encouraged Thoreau to proceed with publication at the author's expense, and Thoreau blamed Emerson for failing to counsel him on the manuscript, for dispensing bad advice on the terms of its publication, and for failing to review and promote the book. The Emerson/Thoreau friendship had always been intimate yet edgy, uncomfortable, and rivalrous, and now it became more so. In his journal, September 1841, Emerson noted: "I told H. T. that his freedom is in the form, but he does not disclose new matter. I am very familiar with all his thoughts—they are my own quite originally drest. But if the question be, what new ideas has he thrown into circulation, he has not yet told what that is which he was created to say" (Porte ed., 264). These words suggest the burden that Emerson imposed on his young admirer; and they bear witness to the struggle for originality and independence that Thoreau waged even as he took pride in Emerson's friendship. During his stay at Walden, Thoreau beautifully praised Emerson:

> Emerson has special talents unequalled—The divine in man has had no more easy methodically distinct expression. His personal influence upon young persons greater than any man's. In his world every man would be a poet—Love would reign—Beauty would take place—Man & Nature would harmonize. (*Journal,* Dover ed., 1:432-33; Princeton ed., 2:224)

But in the 1850s Thoreau complained about the treatment he received from Emerson and, more pointedly, about the type of person—complacent and conventional—he believed that Emerson now was. On October 10, 1851, Thoreau wrote in his journal: "When I consider what my friend's relations & acquaintances are—what his tastes & habits—then the difference between us gets named. I see that all these friends and acquaintances & tastes & habits are indeed my friend's self" (Dover ed., 4:61–62; Princeton ed., 4:137). Emerson was an astute critic of his own behavior, and in his journal, July 1852, he observed: "Thoreau gives me, in flesh & blood & pertinacious Saxon belief, my own ethics. He is far more real, & daily practically obeying them, than I; and fortifies my memory at all times with an affirmative experience which refuses to be set aside" (Porte ed., 436).

Emerson's and Thoreau's grievances were similar. Thoreau, in his journal, May 23, 1853, wrote: "Talked, or tried to talk with

R. W. E. Lost my time—nay, almost my identity. He, assuming a false opposition when there was no difference of opinion, talked to the wind—told me what I knew—and I lost my time trying to imagine myself somebody else to oppose him" (Dover ed., 5:188). In his own journal, February 1856, Emerson stated:

> If I knew only Thoreau, I should think cooperation of good men impossible. Must we always talk for victory, & never once for truth, for comfort, & joy. Centrality he has, & penetration, strong understanding, & the higher gifts—the insight of the real or from the real, & the moral rectitude that belongs to it; but all this and all his resources of wit & invention are lost to me in every experiment, year after year, that I make, to hold intercourse with his mind. Always some weary captious paradox to fight you with, & the time & temper wasted. (Porte ed., 465)

Verbal gamesmanship and self-distancing, not revelation of self: each man protested against this tendency in the other, and their mutual disappointment intensified through the 1850s.

In this decade Thoreau also was a surveyor; he bought books and tools and prepared a handbill that advertised his skill. Surveying was the occupation listed for him in the 1860 U.S. Census, and records of his work can be found in the Concord town archives for 1850–1860 (his survey in June 1850, for example, of the lot for the new Concord courthouse). He studied and took notes, too, on a host of books about the Indians, including *Jesuit Relations*, a series of annual reports (in French) by the Jesuits, 1633–1672, on their missionary activities in the New World. He seems to have envisioned writing a big book like Henry Rowe Schoolcraft's *Historical and Statistical Information Respecting the History, Condition, and Prospects of the Indian Tribes of the United States* (1851–1857) or Lewis Henry Morgan's *League of the Iroquois* (1851). In addition, he worked diligently on his natural history studies, collecting specimens, keeping records of the arrival of birds and the appearance of flowers, and examining the stages of growth of trees.

More than anything else, in the 1850s Thoreau continued to

write and, despite the failure of *A Week*, struggled to get his work into print. In 1852 he published a section of his work-in-progress on the Maine woods in *Sartain's Union Magazine*; and his report on his travels, "A Yankee in Canada," appeared in three installments, from January through March 1853, in *Putnam's Monthly Magazine*.

The most important literary event of the 1850s for Thoreau was the publication on August 9, 1854, of *Walden; or, Life in the Woods*. Thoreau had finished a draft of the book while he was still living at Walden, and a note included in *A Week on the Concord and Merrimack Rivers* indicated that *Walden* would be published "soon." But the poor sales of *A Week* made the publisher unwilling to proceed with the second book—a misfortune for Thoreau, to be sure, but also a stroke of literary good luck since it allowed him to revise and expand the *Walden* manuscript and to test this material on lecture audiences. If *A Week* had been successful, *Walden* would have been a shorter, less enthralling book; it would have been a supplement to *A Week*, not—as we now view it—the masterpiece for which writing *A Week* was preparation.

Thoreau worked on *Walden* from 1846 to 1849, with an intense period from the middle of 1848 through 1849 when he produced most of the pages that went into the first seven chapters. At some point he inserted at the top of the first page of the first version: "Walden or Life in / the Woods by Henry Thoreau / Addressed to my Townsmen." Apparently he pretty much set the manuscript aside from late 1849 to late 1851 or early 1852, though he did weave into it passages from Hindu and Chinese texts. In the first months of 1852 and thereafter Thoreau added the material that became chapters eight through eighteen. It was during this time that he included such famous passages as the description of the owl ("Sounds"), the battle of the ants ("Brute Neighbors"), the fishermen on the ice ("The Pond in Winter"), and the thawing of the sand banks and the melting of the pond ("Spring").

Thoreau inlaid chapter titles and reworked and linked chapters to draw special notice to the cycle of the seasons. The cyclical rhythm was crucial, because it unified a book that was pieced together, assembled and built up over the span of the first draft and six revisions, plus the final copy for the printer, during seven years of work. The scholar J. Lyndon Shanley offers this summary of the major differences from the first to the final versions:

> The version he wrote at the pond [i.e., the first draft] was only about half as long as the final text. . . . [It] represents various parts of *Walden* very unevenly. It contains approximately 70 per cent of the first half—"Economy" through "The Bean Field"; a little less than 30 per cent of "The Village" through "Higher Laws"; less than 50 per cent of "Brute Neighbors" through "Spring"; and none of "Conclusion." (*Making*, 25, 94)

The text as experienced may feel like the flow of a river, but, as far as its composition is concerned, Thoreau constructed the book piece by piece like a mosaic; it is the product of countless acts of revision, large and small. As Thoreau later stated in the journal, March 11, 1859, his main literary principle was: "Find out as soon as possible what are the best things in your composition, and then shape the rest to fit them. The former will be the midrib and the veins of the leaf" (Dover ed., 12:39). The best-known sentence in the book, "The mass of men lead lives of quiet desperation" ("Economy"), first appears in a draft of *A Week*; after being cut from that text, and after much reworking of context, Thoreau placed it in *Walden*.

For this book about his Walden experiences of the mid-1840s, Thoreau even included, as Shanley has noted, material from his journals for the 1830s and early 1840s. When, for instance, he describes playing his flute in his boat ("The Ponds"), he is drawing on a journal entry for May 27, 1841. A piece of his account of the growth of new life ("Spring") comes from an entry, September 29, 1843, that Thoreau wrote while he was on Staten Island. And the first paragraph of "Conclusion" takes shape from a journal entry for March 21, 1840.

Walden hence is a *work* of art; in the best sense, it is highly artificial. It is not the story of Thoreau's life, but a story that represents that story, that recreates it for emblematic and symbolic purposes. Even as Thoreau leads us to perceive *Walden* as autobiographical—a book about his period of residence in 1845–

1847—he undercuts this expectation, violating the genre he seems to have adopted. His shifts in chronology are sometimes startling, all the more so because he appears unfazed by them. "But the pond has risen steadily for two years, and now, in the summer of '52," he writes in "The Ponds." "One pleasant morning after a cold night, February 24th, 1850," he reports in "Spring"; and, in the next paragraph: "In 1845 Walden was completely open on the 1st of April; in '46, the 25th of March; in '47, the 8th of April; in '51, the 28th of March; in '52, the 18th of April; in '53, the 23rd of March; in '54, about the 7th of April." He makes sure that the book is up-to-date, in this case bringing it to within several months of its publication, seven years after he left the cabin.

Thoreau's publisher was Ticknor and Fields, the prestigious Boston firm that published Longfellow and Hawthorne. The first edition of 2,000 copies, each retailing for a dollar and with a 15 percent royalty to the author, included with the text two illustrations: on the title page, a sketch of the cabin by Thoreau's sister Sophia (he later groused about its inaccuracies); and in the chapter "The Pond in Winter," a chart that Thoreau made of Walden Pond. *Walden* sold 1,750 copies during the first year of publication. Most of the sales occurred within the first month; and much of this total came from the Boston area. The reviews were fairly good. "By the end of August 1854," *Walden* had "been praised in over thirty magazines from Maine to Ohio. . . . Of the sixty-six contemporary reviews that have been located, forty-six were strongly favorable" (Dean and Scharnhorst, "Contemporary Reception," 293). Horace Greeley ran a prominently placed review in the *New York Tribune*, as well as extracts from the text itself. Complimentary reviews by Lydia Child (*National Anti-Slavery Standard*, 16 December 1854) and George Eliot (*Westminister Review*, January 1856) showed Thoreau's impact on readers of keen judgment and understanding. The first edition sold out in 1859; it was reprinted (280 copies) in March/April 1862, and again (another 280 copies) in November/December of this same year.

Thoreau's writing in *Walden* is wonderful from beginning to end, in, for example, his gruff, satiric account of how and why he launched his Walden enterprise, built his cabin, and simplified his needs, and in his stunning descriptions of the pond as it both changes and remains faithful to itself, different yet the same through the passage of the seasons. But the book can also be misleading, as Thoreau himself realized. *Walden* promotes love of nature and energizing contact and communion with it, but the specific life that Thoreau describes is not intended as a model for others. As he emphasizes in the chapter "Economy," "I would not have any one adopt *my* mode of living on any account. . . . I would have each one be very careful to find out and pursue *his own* way, and not his father's or his mother's or his neighbor's instead." The full title of the first edition is *Walden; or, Life in the Woods*; but for the reprint, Thoreau chose the simpler title *Walden*, in order to forestall if he could a reader's tendency to conclude that personal transformation required a life in the woods.

On July 4, 1854, about a month before *Walden's* publication, Thoreau presented an address, "Slavery in Massachusetts," at an abolitionist meeting in Framingham, Massachusetts. It was published in *The Liberator* on July 21, the *New York Tribune* on August 2, and the *National Anti-Slavery Standard* on November 12. *Walden* says little about slavery, in large measure because the book had been so long in the making and derived from so many different textual sources. But when *Walden* appeared, many readers, especially those in Boston and Concord, no doubt identified the author as an uncompromising abolitionist. In "Slavery in Massachusetts" Thoreau presented an irate moral indictment and was far more bitter and fiery in his tone than he had been in "Resistance to Civil Government."

The slavery crisis had intensified with the Compromise of 1850, by which point there were in the South 3.2 million slaves. Supported by the distinguished U.S. senators Henry Clay, Stephen A. Douglas, and Daniel Webster, the compromise was intended to resolve the sectional strife that slavery had engendered. But its chief provision, a stricter Fugitive Slave Law, enraged many in the North, for it mandated that all citizens assist in the capture of runaways from slavery and set penalties of fines and imprisonment for anyone who harbored, rescued, or concealed fugitives. Emerson called the law a "filthy enactment," adding, "I will not obey it, by God" (Porte ed., 429). Thoreau's family had been committed to the antislavery cause since the 1830s, and he now began to shelter fugitive slaves and aid them in their safe passage to Canada.

The compromise was followed in January 1854 by the Kansas-Nebraska Act, which allowed settlers in the Kansas and Nebraska territories to choose for themselves whether to allow slavery. This was Illinois senator Douglas's tenet of "popular sovereignty." "Let the people living in the territory decide" would be the basis, according to Douglas, through which to resolve the sectional dispute over slavery expansion. But this policy meant that slavery could expand westward, and not be limited to the boundaries of the states in which it existed. Three years later, in 1857, the Supreme Court's *Dred Scott* decision gave even greater protection to slavery, by affirming that: (1) slaves were not and could not become U.S. citizens; (2) blacks had no rights that white persons were bound to respect; and 3) Congress had no power to exclude slavery from any territory belonging to the United States.

These developments on the national scene angered abolitionists like Thoreau and his family and prompted many to call for and to engage in the violent measures that they had at first rejected. Not only did white and black abolitionists resort to law-breaking violence to free fugitive slaves—for example, the rescues of the fugitive Shadrach in Boston in February 1851 and the fugitive Jerry in Syracuse, New York, in October 1851—but some of them endorsed or defended slave revolt and rebellion. William Lloyd Garrison, Wendell Phillips, and other Boston-area abolitionists were aware of the moral ambiguity of standing firm against violence in theory and yet accepting or at least condoning it in practice. But their willingness to do so grew as they witnessed the tragic failure of legal measures to prevent the return to slavery of two fugitives in Boston, Thomas Sims (1851) and Anthony Burns (1854).

Thoreau opposed slavery but in general stayed away from abolitionist rallies and antislavery organizations. In the aftermath of the Burns case, however, he did take part in the July 4th outdoor meeting of the Massachusetts Anti-Slavery Society, held in

Framingham. Garrison, who presided, possessed a great sense of theater and knew exactly how to shock the public and publicize the antislavery campaign. He scheduled the meeting for the day on which America celebrated its independence and proclaimed its ideal of equality for all. Garrison's purpose was to dramatize the contrast between the nation's principles and the recent return of the fugitive Burns to Richmond, Virginia, where he was manacled and jailed, and the passage of the Kansas-Nebraska Act.

The platform was draped in black crepe. Behind the rostrum was hung the insignia of Virginia, which was decorated with ribbons of triumph, and next to it was the seal of the Commonwealth of Massachusetts, inscribed with the words "Redeem Massachusetts" and decked in "the crepe of servitude." Above the rostrum flew two flags, on which were the names "Kansas" and "Nebraska." In the background was the American flag, upside down and bordered in black. After his introductory comments to the several thousand in attendance, one of whom was Thoreau, Garrison read from Scripture and then closed his Bible and lit a candle.

Garrison told the audience that he would "now proceed to perform an action which would be testimony of his own soul, to all present, of the estimation in which he held the proslavery laws and deeds of the nation." He burned copies of the Fugitive Slave Law and the documents that ordered Burns back to Virginia, in each instance asking the audience to answer "Amen" in line with the formula in Deuteronomy (27:15–26). Finally he burned a copy of the Constitution, alleging as he held it high that it was "a covenant with death, an agreement with hell." "So perish all compromises with tyranny," to which the audience uttered "Amen" as Garrison ground the ashes under his heel.

Thoreau delivered "Slavery in Massachusetts" on this highly dramatic occasion, taking his stand with other abolitionists as they denounced the government. On one level his address is consistent with the Transcendentalist principles by which he had always abided. It is wrong, he insists, to permit the laws of the land to take priority over conscience. Right principle is felt strongly within, and it clarifies for us whether we should defer to a state or federal statute. To the argument that slavery is protected by the Constitution and that all persons, however opposed they might be to slavery, are obliged to accept that fact, Thoreau replied:

> The question is, not whether you or your grandfather, seventy years ago, did not enter into an agreement to serve the devil, and that service is not accordingly now due; but whether you will not now, for once and at last, serve God,—in spite of your own past recreancy, or that of your ancestor,—by obeying that eternal and only just CONSTITUTION, which He, and not any Jefferson or Adams, has written in your being. (*Reform Papers*, 103)

On another level "Slavery in Massachusetts" takes issue with the life that Thoreau himself had been leading—and is at odds with the commitment to withdrawal and contemplation that his book *Walden* would in a month make known. The Burns case has struck him, he says, "with the sense of having suffered a vast and indefinite loss":

> I did not know at first what ailed me. At last it occurred to me that what I had lost was a country. I had never respected the government near to which I lived, but I had foolishly thought that I might manage to live here, minding my private affairs, and forget it. . . . I dwelt before, perhaps, in the illusion that my life passed somewhere only *between* heaven and hell, but now I cannot persuade myself that I do not dwell *wholly within* hell. (*Reform Papers*, 106)

Thoreau claims that he realizes he cannot be a private person; the crime of slavery, he implies, has made the Walden experiment—soon to be defined and celebrated in a glorious book—invalid, impossible to cling to. But while Thoreau remained an abolitionist, he did not now enter the public movement with the intensity of a Garrison or a Phillips. His instinct was always to return to his "private affairs"; however much he hated slavery, he was above all a writer and was determined to stay faithful to this vocation.

Thoreau's main tie to antislavery during the 1850s was the militant abolitionist John Brown. Thoreau met Brown in March 1857 and in May 1859 heard him speak in Concord about his battles with proslavery forces in the Kansas territory. Like many Transcendentalists and reformers, Thoreau admired Brown as a plain but passionate man of principle. Amos Bronson Alcott described the community's response in his journal, May 8, 1859:

> This evening hear Captain Brown speak at the Town Hall on Kansas affairs and the part taken by him in the late troubles there. He tells his story with surpassing simplicity and sense, impressing us all deeply by his courage and religious earnestness. Our best people listen to his words—Emerson, Thoreau, Judge Hoar, my wife—and some of them contribute something in aid of his plans without asking particulars, such confidence does he inspire with his integrity and abilities. . . . Though sixty years of age, he is agile and alert, resolute, and ready for any audacity in any crisis. I think him just about the manliest man I have ever seen, the type and synonym of the Just. (315–16)

Brown and twenty-one followers attacked the federal arsenal in Harpers Ferry, Virginia, on October 16, 1859. His intention was to liberate and arm slaves, establish strongholds in the mountains, and stir up insurrections, striking against slavery in the heart of the South. But his grand design fell apart the next day, when a number of Brown's men were killed and he was wounded and captured by U.S. troops under the command of Robert E. Lee, later the Confederacy's foremost general. Portrayed by abolitionists as a selfless martyr for the antislavery cause, Brown was executed on December 2, 1859.

For many writers, including Thoreau, Brown's raid, trial, and execution were historically momentous—and a magnificent subject for literature. One writer after another strove to express Brown's significance more brightly than others had done and to give it a compelling form in poetry or prose. Emerson, Parker, Phillips, Child, Garrison, Douglass, and the clergyman and editor Henry Ward Beecher wrote and spoke about him in 1859–1860, and in later years they and other reformers, intellectuals, and authors, including Hawthorne, Walt Whitman, and Herman Melville, further explored the meanings of Brown's exploits.

In one remarkable sentence after another in journal entries and speeches after the raid, Thoreau seems to be competing not only with his contemporaries but also with himself. Above all in "A Plea for Captain John Brown," presented in Concord on October 30, and then again in Boston on November 1, and in Worcester, two days later, Thoreau testified to Brown's greatness as a Transcendentalist champion, exerting himself to make his literary resources measure up to the majesty and gravity of this heroic figure. There is a strong element of self-description and self-justification in Thoreau's portrait, too, as he hails the moral courage of a spare, rigorous, dedicated man, a New England surveyor like himself.

Brown "could not have been tried by a jury of his peers, because his peers did not exist," Thoreau says. His example "has already quickened the public pulse of the North; it has infused more, and more generous, blood into her veins and heart than any number of years of what is called commercial and political prosperity could. How many a man who was lately contemplating suicide now has something to live for!" Connecting Brown to the crucified Christ, Thoreau concludes, "He is not Old Brown any longer; he is an Angel of Light." Thoreau's "Plea" was included in the collection *Echoes of Harper's Ferry*, edited by James Redpath, which by February 1860 had sold 33,000 copies (*Reform Papers*, 125, 135, 137; see also *Journal*, Dover ed., 12:408, 438–39, 406).

Thoreau's involvement in antislavery was profound but sporadic, and for the most part his life in the 1850s and early 1860s was private and uneventful. He enjoyed visits with friends, including William Ellery Channing, a Concord poet; Daniel Ricketson, a Quaker poet and historian from New Bedford; Thomas Cholmondeley, an English author and traveler who shipped to him from England a present of forty-four volumes of Oriental religious, historical, and philosophical texts; and F. B. Sanborn, an educator, reformer, and abolitionist. Thoreau took trips to Maine in September 1853 and to Cape Cod in 1855. In 1856 he went to New York and New Jersey, where he and Alcott met briefly with Whitman, who gave Thoreau an inscribed copy of the second edition, 1856, of *Leaves of Grass*, a book that Thoreau termed "a great primitive poem,—an alarum or trumpet-note ringing through the American camp" (*Correspondence*, 445).

There were trips to Cape Cod again and Maine in 1857, the White Mountains of Vermont and New Hampshire in 1858, and Minnesota in 1861. Thoreau savored nature walks, undertook forays in quest of Indian relics and materials, and made scientific studies and collected botanical specimens. Emerson provides a vivid description:

> [Thoreau] was of short stature, firmly built, of light complexion, with strong, serious blue eyes, and a grave aspect; his face covered in the late years with a becoming beard. His senses were acute, his frame well-knit and hardy, his hands strong and skillful in the use of tools. And there was a wonderful fitness of body and mind. He could pace sixteen rods more accurately than another man could measure them with rod and chain. He could find his path in the woods at night, he said, better by his feet than his eyes. He could estimate the measure of a tree very well by his eye; he could estimate the weight of a calf or a pig, like a dealer. From a box containing, a bushel or more of loose pencils, he could take up with his hands fast enough just a dozen pencils at every grasp. He was a good swimmer, runner, skater, boatman, and would probably outwalk most countrymen in a day's journey. ("Thoreau," 422)

"His whole figure," said Thoreau's friend Ellery Channing,

> had an active earnestness, as if he had no moment to waste. The clenched hand betokened purpose. In walking, he made a short cut if he could, and when sitting in the shade or by the wall-side, seemed merely the clearer to look forward into the next piece of activity. Even in the boat he had a wary, transitory air, his eyes on the outlook,—perhaps there might be ducks, or the Blanding turtle, or an otter or sparrow. (*Poet-Naturalist*, 33)

But where Thoreau went matters less than what he wrote in his journal and in the manuscripts over which he labored. The manuscript later published as *Cape Cod* (1865) was completed by September 1855; articles from it appeared in the June, July, and August issues of *Putnam's Monthly Magazine*. Another essay, on his experiences in Maine, was published in the *Atlantic Monthly* in 1858. He was as persistent as ever in his craft as a writer.

In December 1860 Thoreau caught a severe cold while conducting a nature experiment near Concord. It turned into bronchitis and then tuberculosis. His western trip to Minnesota, which lasted two months, was an effort to find a climate with dry, crisp air that might improve his health. But Thoreau's condition grew worse, and he died in Concord on May 6, 1862. The clerk in Concord town hall recorded: "Henry D. Thoreau. 44 years, 9 months, 24 days. Natural Historian." He was buried May 9 in Concord; Emerson read the eulogy, and others in attendance included Hawthorne and Louisa May Alcott.

With the aid of his sister Sophia, Thoreau had worked on his manuscripts and papers until the day of his death. A series of his nature articles, "Walking," "Autumnal Tints," and "Wild Apples," appeared in the *Atlantic Monthly* in 1862, and a distilled statement of his beliefs, "Life without Principle" (the title punned on the economic term "principal"), came out in the same magazine in 1863, followed by other pieces in the 1860s and 1870s. *Excursions*, edited by Sophia and Emerson, was published in 1863; *The Maine Woods*, edited by Sophia and William Ellery Channing, in 1864; *Cape Cod*, also edited by Sophia and Channing, in 1864; *Letters to Various Persons*, edited by Emerson, in 1865; and *A Yankee in Canada, with Anti-Slavery and Reform Papers*, edited by Sophia and Channing, in 1866.

A revised edition of *A Week*—yet another of Thoreau's projects in 1862—was published in 1868. In the 1880s four volumes of excerpts from Thoreau's journals appeared, selected by Harrison G. O. Blake, a friend and his literary executor after Sophia's death. The Boston publisher Houghton Mifflin issued its "Riverside" edition of Thoreau's writings, eleven volumes, in 1894, and in 1906 the "Manuscript" or "Walden" edition, comprising twenty volumes, including fourteen volumes of the journals, was published. As Lawrence Buell has noted, this publication of the journal made Thoreau "the first American person of letters to have his diary published in full" ("Thoreau Enters," 26).

The journals will never replace *Walden* and "Resistance to Civil Government" in importance, but they are a fascinating treasure-trove of insights, ideas, and observations. Some of the journals are missing sections, however, especially from 1837 to 1850, when Thoreau took clippings to use in drafts of books and essays. There is nothing, or else only fragments, for 1844, the first half of 1845, 1847, and the first half of 1848. Of the journals we do possess, some are short, sixty pages or so, while others are extremely long, as many as 500 pages. At first Thoreau perceived the journal as a storehouse of materials for books and articles; later, it evolved for him into a major enterprise in its own right, amounting in the end to twenty-one volumes. For the final eight years of his life, Thoreau's journal runs to sixteen volumes, 4,000 pages, 1 million words. The journal overall totals 2 million words.

It is an astonishing achievement—an act of disciplined literary production, sustained year after year, that few American authors have rivaled. "I have always been surprised," said Ellery Channing, "at the pertinacity with which Henry kept to the writing of his journal. This was something truly heroic" (cited in Howarth, 7). In the words of the critic Alfred Kazin, Thoreau's journal "became the most unflagging example—even among American writers—of a man's having to write his life in order to convince himself that he had lived it. Thoreau came to shape his life by the fiercest control words could exert. He hoped these words would be taken for his life. He was the first reader he had to convince" (*Procession*, 64).

Kazin's point acquires still greater force when one realizes how much Thoreau produced in the 1850s in addition to the journals: twelve notebook volumes, totaling 3,000 pages, on Native Americans; 700 pages of notes, records, and charts on the flora and fauna of Concord; 631 pages on "wild fruits"; and 354 pages on "the dispersion of seeds." Thoreau was a cultural historian, an anthropologist, and, in this decade, a scientist—and a scientist as keen on the act of writing up his experiments as in conducting them. He enjoyed studying nature but, even more, delighted in the opportunity to write about it when he felt it had saturated his consciousness. In his journal, May 10, 1853, Thoreau observed:

> He is the richest who has most use for nature as raw material of tropes and symbols with which to describe his life. If these gates of golden willows affect me, they correspond to the beauty and promise of some experience on which I am entering. If I am overflowing with life, am rich in experience for which I lack expression, then nature will be my language full of poetry,—all nature will *fable*, and every natural phenomenon be a myth. (Dover ed., 5:135)

For Thoreau, writing was the fundamental fact of existence, and everything else he made secondary to it; even nature, which he cherished, was in essence raw material for his literary imagination. Showing extraordinary dedication and resolve, Thoreau created and shaped his life on page after page of text. In the journals, notebooks, essays, and books he lived, a consummate artist.

NOTES

1. See, for example; Marcus Aurelius, *Meditations* (bk. 3, sec. 5): "A man should be upright, not be *kept* upright"; and the *Bhagavad Gita* (3:35): "Better one's own duty, though imperfect, / Than another's duty well performed." Thomas Carlyle was one of the first nineteenth-century intellectuals to dramatize this principle, stating in *Signs of the Times* (1829; first published in *Edinburgh Review*, no. 98): "To reform a nation, no wise man will undertake; and all but foolish men know, that the only solid, though far slower reformation, is what each begins and perfects on *himself*" (18).

2. As these details indicate, the date of publication of Thoreau's writings is one thing, and their period of composition is another. For example, *Cape Cod* was published in 1864, two years after Thoreau's death. But Thoreau wrote nearly all of it in 1849–1852 (with some material added in 1855), which places it close to the publication of *A Week* and before the final work on and publication of *Walden*. See Adams and Ross, *Mythologies*, 128, 130.

WORKS CITED

Adams, Stephen, and Donald Ross, Jr. *Revising Mythologies: The Composition of Thoreau's Major Works*. Charlottesville: University Press of Virginia, 1988.

Alcott, Amos Bronson. *Journals*. Edited by Odell Shepard. Boston: Little, Brown, 1938.

Brooks, Paul. *The People of Concord: One Year in the Flowering of New England*. Chester, Conn.: Globe Pequot, 1990.

Buell, Lawrence. "Henry Thoreau Enters the American Canon." In *New Essays on "Walden,"* edited by Robert F. Sayre, 23–52. New York: Cambridge University Press, 1992.

Cameron, Kenneth Walter. *Concord Literary Renaissance*. Hartford, Conn.: Transcendental Books, 1984.

———. *Ralph Waldo Emerson's Reading*. Hartford, Conn.: Transcendental Books, 1962.

———. *Thoreau's Harvard Years*. Hartford, Conn.: Transcendental Books, 1966.

Canby, H. S. *Thoreau*. Boston: Houghton Mifflin, 1939.

Carlyle, Thomas. *Signs of the Times*. *Edinburgh Review* 98 (1829). Rpt. in *Victorian Prose*. Edited by Frederick William Roe. New York: Ronald Press, 1947. 5–18.

Channing, William Ellery. *Thoreau, the Poet-Naturalist, with Memorial Verses*. New ed., enlarged. Edited by F. B. Sanborn. Boston: Goodspeed, 1902.

Christie, John Aldrich. *Thoreau as World Traveler*. New York: Columbia University Press, 1965.

Conway, Moncure Daniel. *Emerson at Home and Abroad*. Boston: Osgood, 1882.

Dean, Bradley P., and Gary Scharnhorst. "The Contemporary Reception of *Walden*." In *Studies in the American Renaissance 1990*, edited by Joel Myerson, 293–328. Charlottesville: University Press of Virginia, 1990.

Emerson, Edward Waldo. *Henry Thoreau, as Remembered by a Young Friend*. Boston: Houghton Mifflin, 1917.

Emerson, Ralph Waldo. *Emerson in His Journals*. Edited by Joel Porte. Cambridge: Harvard University Press, 1982.

———. *Essays and Lectures*. Edited by Joel Porte. New York: Library of America, 1983.

————. *Letters*. Edited by Ralph L. Rusk. 6 vols. New York: Columbia University Press, 1939.

————. *Miscellanies*. Boston: Houghton Mifflin, 1904.

————. "Thoreau." *Atlantic Monthly* 10 (August 1862): 239–49. Included (newly edited) in Myerson, *Emerson and Thoreau*, 419–30.

Foster, David R. *Thoreau's Country: Journey through a Transformed Landscape*. Cambridge: Harvard University Press, 1999.

Gross, Robert A. "Culture and Cultivation: Agriculture and Society in Thoreau's Concord." *Journal of American History* 69 (June 1982): 42–61.

Harding, Walter. *The Days of Henry Thoreau: A Biography*. 2d ed. New York: Dover, 1982.

————. "Thoreau in Jail: Was It Legal?" *American Heritage* 26 (August 1975): 36–37.

Hawthorne, Nathaniel. *The American Notebooks*. Edited by Randall Stewart. New Haven: Yale University Press, 1932.

Hoeltje, H. H. "Misconceptions in Thoreau Criticism." *Philological Quarterly* 47 (1968): 563–70.

Howarth, William L. *The Book of Concord: Thoreau's Life as a Writer*. New York: Viking, 1982.

Johnson, Linck C. *Thoreau's Complex Weave: The Writing of "A Week on the Concord and Merrimack Rivers," with a Text of the First Draft*. Charlottesville: University Press of Virginia, 1986.

Kazin, Alfred. *An American Procession*. New York: Knopf, 1984.

Lincoln, Abraham, *Speeches and Writings*. Edited by Don E. Fehrenbacher. 2 vols. New York: Library of America, 1989.

Lowell, James Russell. "Thoreau's Letters." *North American Review* 101 (October 1865): 597–608. Included in Myerson, *Emerson and Thoreau*. 437–45.

Maynard, W. Barksdale. "Thoreau's House at Walden." *Art Bulletin* 81, no. 2 (June 1999): 303–25.

Meltzer, Milton, and Walter Harding. *A Thoreau Profile*. New York: Crowell, 1962.

Miller, Perry, ed. *The Transcendentalists: An Anthology*. Cambridge: Harvard University Press, 1950.

Myerson, Joel, ed. *Emerson and Thoreau: The Contemporary Reviews*. New York: Cambridge University Press, 1992.

Petroski, Henry. *The Pencil: A History of Design and Circumstance*. New York: Knopf, 1990.

Richardson, James D. *A Compilation of the Messages and Papers of the Presidents.* 11 vols. New York: Bureau of National Literature, 1897–1911.

Richardson, Robert D., Jr. *Henry Thoreau: A Life of the Mind.* Berkeley: University of California Press, 1986.

Salt, Henry S. *Life of Henry David Thoreau.* 1890, rev. 1908. Reprint, edited by George Hendrick, Willene Hendrick, and Fritz Oehlschlaeger, Urbana: University of Illinois Press, 1993.

Sattelmeyer, Robert. *Thoreau's Reading: A Study in Intellectual History, with Bibliographical Catalogue.* Princeton: Princeton University Press, 1988.

Scharnhorst, Gary. *Henry David Thoreau: A Case Study in Canonization.* Columbia, S.C.: Camden House, 1993.

Shanley, J. Lyndon. *The Making of "Walden," with the Text of the First Version.* Chicago: University of Chicago Press, 1957.

Siracusa, Carl. *A Mechanical People: Perceptions of the Industrial Order in Massachusetts, 1815–1880.* Middletown, Conn.: Wesleyan University Press, 1979.

Stover, John F. *American Railroads.* Chicago: University of Chicago Press, 1969.

Thoreau, Henry David. *Correspondence.* Edited by Walter Harding and Carl Bode. New York: New York University Press, 1958.

———. *Early Essays and Miscellanies.* Edited by Joseph J. Moldenhauer and Edwin Moser, with Alexander C. Kern. Princeton: Princeton University Press, 1975.

———. *Faith in a Seed: "The Dispersion of Seeds" and Other Late Natural History Writings.* Edited by Bradley P. Dean. Foreword by Gary Paul Nabhan. Introduction by Robert D. Richardson, Jr. Washington, D.C.: Island Press, 1993.

———. *Journal.* Edited by Elizabeth Hall Witherell, William L. Howarth, Robert Sattelmeyer, and Thomas Blanding. 5 vols. to date. Princeton: Princeton University Press, 1981–.

———. *The Journal of Henry D. Thoreau.* Edited by Bradford Torrey and Francis H. Allen. 1906. Rpt. 2 vols. New York: Dover, 1962.

———. *Reform Papers.* Edited by Wendell Glick. Princeton: Princeton University Press, 1973.

———. *Walden.* 1854. Reprint, edited by J. Lyndon Shanley. Princeton: Princeton University Press, 1971.

Thornton, Tamara Plakins. *Cultivating Gentlemen: The Meaning of Country Life among the Boston Elite, 1785–1860.* New Haven: Yale University Press, 1989.

Vance, James E., Jr. *The North American Railroad.* Baltimore: Johns Hopkins University Press, 1995.

Warner, Michael. "Thoreau's Bottom." *Raritan* 11 (Winter 1992): 53–79.

———. "Walden's Erotic Economy." In *Comparative American Identities: Race, Sex, and Nationality in the Modern Text,* edited by Hortense J. Spillers, 157–74. New York: Routledge, 1991.

Woodbury, Charles J. *Talks with Ralph Waldo Emerson.* New York: Baker & Taylor, 1890.

Yanella, Philip R. "Socio-Economic Disarray and Literary Response: Concord and *Walden.*" *Mosaic* 14 (1981): 1–24.

THOREAU IN HIS TIME

Thoreau, Manhood, and Race

Quiet Desperation versus Representative Isolation

Dana D. Nelson

In the opening passages of *Walden's* first chapter Thoreau sets up his arguments about "Economy" through a complex of images: desperate man (laboring men), mastered man (slaves), and primitive, or natural, man (the Indian basket-weaver). Readers generally take these "men" as figures for timeless truths—and they do so for good reason. Thoreau consistently pushes such images toward general, or representative, rather than specific meaning. The direction of his opening reflections is resonantly symbolic in these pages, where even apparently locally drawn images (such as the Indian basket-weaver) point the way toward larger, universal truths for our modern world.

The first image in this complex stands as a gathering point for the others. Thoreau's argument that "men labor under a mistake" highlights the way modern men are captive to their enterprise in ways they may not apprehend, and not just those who live in cities or work in factories. Thoreau points out that everyone is in bondage—even pastorally located farmers have become "serfs of the soil."[1] Thoreau's glancing mention of slavery utilizes that American institution as a metaphor for a more broadly conceptualized argument about self-enslavement: free men's mental bondage to peer pressure and career recognition. In the same way, the Indian basket-weaver stands not as a particular person, but as a nostalgic marker for an outdated, simpler conception of labor, where the value of production is not conceptualized through competition, "industry," and the least common denominator of mass appeal but through trained craft and individually particular care. These symbolic "men" suggest to readers the logic of turning away from the rushed pace of modern life, the necessity of stepping out of the frenetic economy of the business world and into nature. There one will find, through a return to life's most basic rhythms, a new birth of freedom and an alternative philosophy to the contemporary world:

> To anticipate, not the sunrise and the dawn merely, but, if possible, Nature herself! How many mornings, summer and winter, before yet any neighbor was stirring about his business, have I been about mine! . . . It is true, I never assisted the sun materially in his rising, but, doubt it not, it was of the last importance only to be present at it.[2]

Thoreau's alternative economy revises the industrious aim of Benjamin Franklin's equally timeless adage, "Early to bed, early to rise, makes a man healthy, wealthy and wise," placing the emphasis less on *wealth* and more on health and wisdom. This is advice that has appealed to readers—however difficult they may have found it to implement—from Thoreau's time into our own.

But it is possible to read these images differently, less in the terms of timelessness and more as historically specific, responding to recent and local economic, political, and social developments that may have been affecting everyone, but in vastly different ways. This interpretive approach can actually offer more help for understanding Thoreau's legacy for our own time because such historical contextualizing permits us more carefully to analyze the particular effects of Thoreau's response to similar issues in his own day. For instance, Thoreau's discussion of desperate men is loaded with references to poor men and also to men who are persistently overworked and despairing of escaping from an increasingly long day devoted to work-for-profit. If we resist the impulse to read these men symbolically and transhistorically, we can understand Thoreau's comments as referencing what was during his lifetime a newly generalized and still developing cultural imperative for men to accommodate themselves to strenuous economic competition as the nation made its transition from a subsistence economic culture (or "competence" economy) to market capitalism.

This shift entailed gigantic financial swings, panics, and depressions (not just for the nation's economy but for the people who had to live within it), with one of the severest coming in 1837, just as Thoreau had quit his first job teaching at the public school in Concord. The accelerating market economy, both as economic fact and cultural ethic, was increasingly impacting everyone on the eastern seaboard: for instance, Robert A. Gross has detailed extensively the "agricultural revolution" that was increasingly drawing in Concord farmers during the middle years of the nineteenth century, a rapid shift from a cooperative, largely subsistence agriculture to a rationalized agricultural capitalism:

> Had a visitor come to Concord around 1800 and lived through the 1850s, he or she would certainly have been unprepared for the ways things changed. . . . To participants in the process, who did not know the outcomes, the transition must have been at times a deeply unsettling experience. It challenged old habits and practices, demanded new responses while promising only uncertain rewards, and swept up those who wanted only to be left alone, comfortably carrying on in their fathers' ways. Even those farmers and entrepreneurs who successfully rode the tide must have had their doubts. Those who resisted or just plain failed said little about their fate, succumbing to what Thoreau saw as lives of "quiet desperation."[3]

By paying specific attention to the local economic, social, and political developments of Thoreau's lifetime, we can better appreciate the kinds of carefully traced connections Thoreau's writings helped his readers to make in their own day. He asked them to see connections between groups of people and labor conditions that would seem to them entirely different, in the case of *Walden* between working-class drudgery and the supposedly emancipatory professions and careers of the emerging middle classes. His is a counterintuitive and even radical argument that asks his middle-class readers to re-envision something their culture valued highly as a certain route to not just financial security but personal happiness—"industry"—and to see it in almost opposite terms, as a regimen that was destroying and not at all enhancing their basic human dignity and happiness. One of Thoreau's greatest analytical gifts came in the way he identified the myriad ways national identity was being conceptualized less democratically than capitalistically. Repeatedly he described how this capitalist citizenship curtailed men's ability to conceptualize genuinely effective democratic self-governance.

Using this historicist method also can help us appreciate the ways in which Thoreau's syncretic intellectual habit could sometimes decrease rather than increase the political acuity of his analysis. For example, in utilizing a metaphor comparing actual African-descended slaves to white laborers, entrepreneurs, and farmers, Thoreau is drawing on and extending a familiar political argument of the day among such groups as the Workingman's Party. These labor activists countered increasingly aggressive abolitionist arguments on behalf of racial equality with their own demand that these philanthropists first turn their attention toward what "workeyists" regarded as an even more brutal form of enslavement. "Wage slavery" was a term they used to describe industry's accumulating practices of long days, low wages, structured dependence on company housing and stores, and a spiraling cycle of poverty for workers. Insisting that *white* equality had to come before cross-racial equality, "workeyists" galvanized working-class activism *and* anti-black riots in cities across the North in the 1830s and 1840s.

Recognizing this, we might want to think about how, in positing an image that makes equivalent the slavery of African Americans and poor (often immigrant and frequently Irish) whites with the compulsive industrious habits of his (largely) middle-class audience, Thoreau despecifies the political import of *both* abolitionist and workeyist critiques against economic practices from which the middle classes were *both* benefiting and (as Thoreau rightly insisted) suffering. Instead his generalizing metaphor encourages his readers not to act politically or philanthropically but to respond to such arguments through a kind of sympathetic collapse critics have long tended to ascribe only to middle-class women writers in the nineteenth century: to "feel the pain" of slaves by "recognizing" it as *their own*.

This is neither to ignore Thoreau's abolitionist writings (for instance, his essays on John Brown and on "Slavery in Massachusetts") nor activism (he sheltered at least one fugitive slave on the Underground Railroad) but to insist that we pay some attention to the complex and even contradictory tendency of arguments that public intellectuals like Thoreau formulated in response to some of the most pressing issues of their day. It is clear that the economic transitions of the early nation affected men in general. But it is also clear that it affected them in highly particular ways, ways that even brutally differentiated them one from another: the difficulties faced by an enslaved man on a South Carolina plantation are *not exactly* the same as the difficulties faced by an overworked and underpaid Irish immigrant dockworker in New York City, whose difficulties are *not exactly* the same as the difficulties of a young white clerk with no savings trying to compete his way with twenty other clerks into a single managerial position in Cincinnati, Ohio. Thoreau's slave metaphor reaches for a way to identify and legitimate the very real anxieties and suffering his middle-class male readers were experiencing in market and career competition, redescribing capitalist citizenship's ideal of Industrious Manhood as Enslaved Manhood. But his overgeneralization about men's very particular experiences and traumas here obfuscates, rather than creates, helpful routes for effective political understanding and change.

As Michael Warner recently has pointed out, "It is child's play to show the limit of Thoreau's critique" of the economic system of his day.[4] But exploring specific aspects of his reaction to the social, political, and economic developments in his own day can be very useful to our own thinking process for similarly complex issues today as well as for understanding more carefully the ongoing appeal of Thoreau's writings. The remainder of this chapter provides a historical base that helps contextualize Thoreau's work more broadly on the very topic that seems most central in these opening images: Thoreau's effort to critique and redefine "manhood."

Ideas about "manhood" were changing drastically during Thoreau's lifetime—how to conduct oneself as a man was a topic much debated in political, economic, and social advice literature.[5] In the New England colonies under British rule, "manhood" was a patriarchal, corporate ideal grounded in hierarchical practices of communitarian reciprocity; in the Revolutionary era, "manliness" was the husbandly, patriotic response of the citizenry to the outrages committed by England against a symbolically feminine "America." During Thoreau's lifetime, "manliness" came to mean something different, not so much as a group ideal than as an individual discipline. This new man, the "individual," stood as an emblem of a basic American ideal: freedom.

A carefully contextualized reading of Thoreau helps us see something different in that ideal manly individual. Thoreau shows us how men were being taxed with and atomized by the contradictory demands of democratic relations and capitalist citizenship. Developing ideas about democracy taught men to see themselves as equals in a new space of civic fraternity. But expanding capitalism needed those same men to compete against each other—to discipline themselves for and to learn to "enjoy" not equality but inequality. In the early United States, tensions men registered in the transition between competence cultures and market relations, and in the dissonances between capitalism and democracy, were negotiated (and not always, as Thoreau underscores, to men's own advantage) by developing notions of manhood and citizenship. In the next three sections of this chapter, I outline the contexts, strengths, and limitations of Thoreau's response. In section 1, I turn to two key texts from the early nation to offer some background for the historical changes in practices of manhood that Thoreau so insistently targeted. Section 2 turns directly to Thoreau's work and carefully reads his analysis of civic manhood's developing attachment to whiteness. Finally, section 3 holds up Thoreau's desire for an equalitarian space of friendship—a space where men could fully appreciate each other's individual particularity—against the concrete outline of his remediative strategy for redeeming manhood from market competition.

Changing Manhood

When St. John de Crèvecoeur defined "this new [American] man" in his *Letters from an American Farmer* (1782), he put three categories at the heart of his definition: European-descent, land-ownership, and fatherhood. In response to the question, "What, then, is the American?" Farmer James narrates the development of a "new race of men":

> I could point out to you a family whose grandfather was an Englishman, whose wife was Dutch, whose son married a French woman, and whose present four sons have now wives of four different nations. *He* is an American, who, leaving behind him all his ancient prejudices and manners, receives new ones from the new mode of life he has embraced, the new government he obeys and the new rank he holds.[6]

The availability of land for purchase in the American colonies creates expanded opportunities for experiencing successful manhood: "Wives and children, who before in vain demanded of him a morsel of bread, now fat and frolicsome, gladly help their father clear those fields whence exuberant crops are to arise to feed and clothe them all."[7] The purchase of land does not just make men better parents, it literally remakes them as free, independent, American men:

> From nothing to start into being; from a servant to the rank of a master; from being the slave of some despotic prince, to become a free man, invested with lands to which every municipal blessing is annexed! What a change indeed! It is in consequence of that change that he becomes an American. This great metamorphosis has a double effect: it extinguishes all his European prejudices, he forgets that mechanism of subordination, that servility of disposition which poverty had taught

him; and sometimes he is apt to forget it too much, often passing from one extreme to another.[8]

Passing from one extreme to another is not exactly a good thing
in Farmer James's estimation. When he describes the "industriousness" that characterizes the new American man, he is not
using the word in the more modern sense that it would shortly
assume, as a methodical work routine that ideally results in the
rapid accumulation of lands and goods as wealth, but in its older
and more basic sense of "hard work." For James, industriousness
marked the ability of men to achieve an independent (or free-
holding) subsistence, what in the terms of the day was known as
a "competency."

Farmer James sees free-hold farming and good fathering as
inextricably linked. Having inherited a farm from *his* father,
Farmer James relates how "when my first son was born, the
whole train of my ideas was suddenly altered; never was there a
charm that acted so quickly and powerfully . . . my excursions
since have not exceeded the bounds of my farm and all my principal pleasures are now centred [*sic*] within its scanty limits."[9] For
his passionate devotion to farm *and* family, James is labeled a
"farmer of feelings." He judges good and evil in his world (pre-
Revolutionary and Revolutionary America) by the standard of
how it impacts on men's ability to be good farmers. The farming
he idealizes allows men to provide for their family while also
spending time with them. This ideal teaches him that slavery is
bad because it interrupts the "natural" relation of "paternal fondness" between fathers and their children (see Letter IX). And
Farmer James appeals to readers to see negative aspects of the
Revolution both in the way that it causes citizens to question
their ties to the "patria" or Fatherland and in the way that battles,
raids, and property seizures leave men unable to protect their
families (see Letters III and XII). The emotional and physical dan-
gers of the Revolution "unman" Farmer James, where international crisis manifests itself as a threat to the agency and security
of "manhood."

In Farmer James and in the Revolutionary era more generally,
we can see the passing of an older model for manhood and ges-

tures toward its newer manifestations in the early United States. In, for instance, the episode of Letter III (the famous "What is an American?" letter), where Farmer James helps Andrew the Hebridean become financially established in the colonies, we see the vestiges of an ideal of manhood grounded in reciprocity and communal obligation. In colonial New England, as Anthony Rotundo summarizes, "manhood" was conceptualized as "an area of compromise between communal ideal and individual desire," where "duty" and "usefulness" were more important to manliness than "self-assertion."[10] And in the *kind* of life that Farmer James idealizes and helps Andrew purchase for himself, we can see an ideal of "happy competence," where American land provided access to a farming life of comfort and independence formerly inconceivable for most European immigrants. Farm production was largely limited by the amount of family labor, and so this was a "comfort" associated not with the accumulation of excess profits and goods, but with easy subsistence.[11] Increasingly during the Revolutionary era, the leisure time that was associated with such an easy subsistence was used, as Farmer James demonstrates, to cultivate an emotionally fulfilling domestic circle. Good men were, as James underscores again and again, husbands and fathers who made sure their wives and children were not just well fed, but also *happy*.

Another shift we can see beginning but not completed in *Letters from an American Farmer* is a new correlation between manliness and "whiteness." "This new race" of American men is formed politically and socially through an appeal to European (note that he does not say "white") descent. What was formerly imagined in the terms of "difference" (where being Dutch was nothing like being Scottish) was now increasingly reimagined as commonality—and that *American* commonality was metaphorically conceptualized as whiteness. The import of this newer conceptualization of patriotic, common, "white" manliness shows up even more clearly in Royall Tyler's 1787 play *The Contrast*. In a key moment of this drama (where the hero's name *is* "Manly") the character Jonathan voices his objection to being labeled a "servant" (his preference is to be called a "waiter") by exclaiming, "What, will you take me for a nagur?" Jonathan claims dignity for a traditionally demeaning form of labor by calling attention to his "racial" status as a *white*: he wants his interlocutor to recognize from his "whiteness" that his service to Manly is voluntary or *independent,* quite differently from "blacks" whose slave labor is forced and who are thereby marked as "dependents." Jonathan's "contrast" calls attention to the way citizenship and political entitlement in the early United States were "democratically" expanding for white men across class divides in the same moment it was antidemocratically contracting for other members of society. While African-descended blacks stood from the first moment of the Revolution as patriots alongside European-descended whites, after the war's end free blacks watched those colonial and state rights they did have begin radically to erode along with their political hopes. The First Act of Naturalization (1790) identified eligible citizens as white men, and by the 1810s, beginning in New Jersey, states in both the North and South began revoking the rights of free blacks to vote (free blacks could vote as late as 1835 in North Carolina and 1837 in Pennsylvania).

If new "democratic" relations between white men promised to smooth over formerly insuperable class barriers, other forces were working to countermand the fraternal experiences that this new democratic expansion seemingly promised to those same white men. Tyler's play is helpful for seeing this transition as well. *The Contrast* advertises itself in its prologue as a portrait of distinctive American equality, "where proud titles of "My Lord! Your Grace!" / To humble *Mr.* and plain *Sir* give place." We are promised a portrayal of fraternal equality, but what we get is characterological ranking as the play sorts "real" men from the dross. "The Contrast" between men is drawn most emphatically in its comparison of how Billy Dimple, an elite "gentleman," and Colonel Henry Manly, a Revolutionary War veteran, treat women in the play. Dimple strings them along variously for their looks or their money. Manly, as his name announces, is straightforward and honorable. The audience knows he will treat women with the same dignity that he gives to the men he describes as "my late soldiers[,] my family."[12] For Henry Manly (as for John Jay, whose sentiments in *Federalist Paper* Number 2 he echoes), the "brother[hood of] soldiers" provides an American ideal, where citizens, like families, are "united by a similarity of language, sentiment, manners, common interest, and common consent in one grand mutual league of protection."[13]

The play holds out this relationship as its model of equality. But careful readers will notice that this "grand mutual league" is really something more accurately described as benign hierarchy, a model of "representation" founded on an ideal of American "sameness" that is vertically ordered. Manly is in New York City to petition Congress for funds for the soldiers *under his command* who were wounded in battle. His heroically protective relation to the men suggests him as a good protector for the romantic Maria, who is unhappily engaged to the foppish Dimple. Manly lectures Dimple about romance, defining it as an act of protection: "In our young country, where there is no such thing as gallantry, when a gentleman speaks of love to a lady, whether he mentions marriage or not, she ought to conclude either that he meant to insult her or that his intentions are the most serious and honorable."[14] His ability to assume such responsibility marks him as the ideal type for American men, indeed as America's representative.

Curiously, though, this representative man has no equal in the play; indeed, one of the play's laments is for the loss of the spirit of patriotic brotherhood in the (supposedly effeminate) scramble for "luxury." Though brother veterans remember each other (as Manly notes, "Friendships made in adversity are lasting"[15]), brotherhood seems in danger of being forgotten *by* American men. Though the play directs us to blame this fraternal atomization on a growing fascination with European manners and consumer goods (a consumer interest figured as both unmanly and unpatriotic), the play's structure suggests something different, revealing that there are no practical grounds for experiencing brotherhood in the post-Revolutionary United States. In *The Contrast*, the training-ground for brotherhood—the Revolutionary battlefield—is now a fading memory. The play's staging of civic engagement seems unlikely to provide Manly the equal he deserves—there are no men with whom Manly might forge civic brotherhood or friendship, only men whose silly notions his role is to correct. Instead, his emotional energy will now be channeled away from his friendships with "brother soldiers" and into his marriage with Maria, as he learns to "mind the main chance"—that is, to compete economically with those very "brother" soldiers and citizens.

Manly's civic isolation thus constitutes his competitive, capitalist edge. The play asks us both to admire this and to laugh about it. But it is worth thinking a little more carefully about what such a shift meant for the men who lived it. As the historian Charles Sellers has emphasized, there were profound experiential differences between "competence" economies and market practices, and the rapid paced transition between the two was difficult for people in ways historians and cultural critics have long tended to overlook. He points out that the "capitalist revolution of life did not convert Americans overnight into the self-confident enterprisers of liberal mythology" and summarizes the accumulating effects of the market revolution overtaking the United States in the early nineteenth century as a "stressful passage from resistance through evasion to accommodation":

> Traditional patterns of communal cooperation weakened, and agricultural reformers derided old-fashioned farmers who "cannot bear to work alone," and were always having to "call in a neighbor to change work." While it might be "very pleasant" to "have our neighbours to work with us," said advocates of the new capitalist order, "it tends to lounging and idleness, and neglect of business."[16]

The developing emphasis on men's *individual* "industry" and the need for "self-making" made it more difficult for men to conceptualize a political response to the rapid national generalization of market capitalism and the often whiplashing personal effects this transition entailed in peoples' lives. Instead, this new ideal of competitive manhood encouraged men to see such general phenomenon as the wildfire of bankruptcies that crossed the nation as a result of market swings in 1819 and 1837 not as a problem delivered by the economic system, but as their own *personal* failure—as a lack of initiative, work ethic, or market savvy.

In *Walden*, Thoreau offers a compelling critique of the disciplinary effects of "industry" (one that continues to appeal to readers today). But we also can see ways in which he too was conditioned by competitive individualism to undervalue collectivist political models and even to reject community-based response to the social ills he identified (as he puts it in "Life without Principle": "The community has no bribe that will tempt a wise man"[17]). His corrective scheme in *Walden* as well as in other writings, including "On Civil Disobedience" and "The Last Days of John Brown," is to emphasize an ideal of manliness that appeals to isolationist heroism. It is in this light that we might understand the broader social context for Thoreau's impatient dismissal of community elders in the opening passages of *Walden*: "I have lived some thirty years on this planet, and I have yet to hear the first syllable of valuable or even earnest advice from my seniors."[18] Rotundo describes the way men in the early nation learned to stop thinking of themselves as "part of an organic community from which they drew personal identity," instead re-envisioning society as "a collection of atoms—unranked humans without assigned positions of any sort" where each man was now "free of the cord of generations that had given his forefathers a place in historical time." For this new man, the "past did not weigh him down. . . . The individual was now the measure of things and men were engrossed with themselves as *selves*. The dominant concerns were the concerns of the self—self-improvement, self-control, self-interest, self-advancement."[19]

Whiteness and Competing Manhoods

Thoreau is not aiming at discrediting his elders so much as he is aiming to debunk the supposed superiority of their "experience" to his own: "Here is life, an experiment to the great extent untried by me; but it does not avail me that they have tried it. If I have any experience which I think valuable, I am sure to reflect that this my Mentors said nothing about."[20] He emphasizes that experiential equality among men is achieved through practical and intellectual independence. His comments underscore even as they suggest a critique of a larger cultural trend toward a particular conception of democratic practice emerging in the 1830s and 1840s. This is a period known as "the era of the common man" because it marks the time during which suffrage was "universalized" for adult white men regardless of wealth. Politics became popularized, political parties developed, and the first national presidential election day was established on November 7, 1848. And, though the label won't help us know it, this was also a period, as Edward Pessen has carefully detailed, of growing inequalities in wealth and an actual decrease in the rate of upward economic mobility.[21]

The kind of democratization that came through the popularization of politics in the Jacksonian era appears to have worked powerfully to blunt men's ability even to recognize growing economic inequality among white American men. Describing how "during the 1820s and 1830s American politics became a mass ritual for the expression of popular culture," historians Alan Dawley and Paul Faler observe that:

> In contrast to several European countries, political democracy did not arise in the United States from the class demands of dispossessed workers against the propertied interests that controlled the state. Instead it arose from an interclass movement that included both propertyless workers and small entrepreneurs, and was dominated by property-owning artisans and farmers.

This shared, celebratory popularization of political conventions, parades, rallies, electioneering, and voting days seemed to have papered over growing discrepancies in access to wealth. As Dawley and Faler summarize, "Just as inequality waxed in economics, it seemed to wane in politics."[22]

The apparent political equality that men achieved in the universalization of white male suffrage accelerated the possessive claiming *of* whiteness and an increasingly aggressive effort to demarcate whiteness's boundaries as a claim not just to political but also to economic entitlement. Thoreau was good at resisting this "democratic" impulse in some important ways. In *Walden*, he makes fun of the habit of ranking people by metaphors of skin color. His portrayal of African-descended slaves and freemen re-sists his white readers' habitual emphasis on "seeing" black. For instance, in the passage on the runaway slave, Thoreau does not much dwell on the fugitive as a physical human being except to assert that he or she is "real."[23] Thoreau was opposed to his cul-ture's growing predilection for correlating a person's basic value with skin color, and his insistence on the fundamental ("real") humanity of the runaway slave is in keeping with his wry de-scription of Brister Freeman's grave marking: "'a man of color,' as if he were discolored."[24] His own refusal to "color" the hu-manity of the African Americans he describes thus strives to counter the racial spectacularization that was becoming so im-portant to white U.S. culture from the 1830s through the 1850s, through intensifying slave practices, abolitionist activism, and the explosively popular entertainment form, blackface minstrelsy.

Revolutionary rhetoric had relied extensively on abolitionist rhetoric to appeal to colonists to take up the patriotic cause. With regard to the actual practice of legally institutionalized slavery, Michael Goldfield observes:

> At the time of the American Revolution, slavery in North America was a contradictory, frequently unprofitable institu-tion, with the dramatic exception of certain large enclaves—the sugar-growing areas of Louisiana [not yet part of the United States] and the rice, indigo, and Sea Island cotton areas of South Carolina and Georgia. In most places, tobacco (the once-dominant cash/export crop) was becoming increasingly difficult to grow profitably. This situation underlay the open-ness of the Virginia Founding Fathers to ending slavery, the enormous increase in manumissions in the Upper South at that time, and the feeling that slavery would eventually die out. But it was not to be.[25]

With the invention of the cotton gin in 1793, slavery was soon legally and socially re-entrenched. Cotton production in the United States, which increased nearly a hundredfold in the first forty years of the nation's existence, more than tripled again in the years between 1830 and 1850. As cotton became fundamental to the nation's export economy, both for plantation culture in the South and textile manufacture in the North, slave codes and practices intensified. After the Denmark Vesey conspiracy (1822) and the Nat Turner uprising (1831), slaveholding states rigidified anti-literacy and assembly laws. Slave "management" practices became even harsher, with slaveholder advice literature counseling, for instance, that it was more profitable to "replace" slaves every seven years or so than to support them well clothed and fed through a longer and healthier life. Scientists like Charles Caldwell, Samuel George Morton, and Josiah Nott began justifying these more draconian practices by offering "evidence" that whites and blacks were separately created species and that blacks were hopelessly and permanently inferior to whites.

As slavery and racism intensified in the 1830s and 1840s, a newly energized abolitionist movement sprang up following the publication of David Walker's eloquent and revolutionary essay *Walker's Appeal . . . to the Colored Citizens of the World* (1829) and the first issue of William Lloyd Garrison's newspaper *The Liberator* (January 1, 1831). At first supported primarily by free blacks, the movement and its proponents were attacked nearly as violently in northern communities as in the South. Meetings were broken up by mob violence, and prominent abolitionists were threatened, harassed, arrested, and sometimes murdered. In the South, postmasters began an unwarranted search of U.S. mails, destroying abolitionist literature, newspapers and pamphlets. The U.S. government was not much better: abolitionist petitions were initially "gagged" (remaining unheard) in Congress. But by the late 1830s abolition was drawing thousands of white supporters in the North, and their newspapers, pamphlets, and books, from the *National Anti-Slavery Standard*, to Frederick Douglass's 1845 *Narrative*, to Harriet Beecher Stowe's 1852 *Uncle Tom's Cabin*, were becoming bestsellers and effectively focusing the nation's attention on racial slavery as *the central* political issue of the day.

While many northern whites came to support abolition, this did not always—or even frequently—signify their commitment to racial equality. Abolitionist appeals, such as the parlor room drama sheets for guests to reenact beloved scenes from *Uncle*

Tom's Cabin, drew on the widespread popularity of blackface minstrelsy, practiced as mass entertainment among the northern urban working class and quickly adopted in form and spirit by whites all over the nation. Ironically, the entertainment that reinforced white supremacy and racist exclusion grew out of white attendance at and participation in black-led and African-influenced rituals and entertainments like Negro Election Day and Pinkster celebrations.[26] Cultural historian and critic Eric Lott has highlighted the early nineteenth-century proliferation of whites "blacking up" with burnt cork to play "Jim Crow" and "Sapphire" as a "historically new articulation of racial difference," a cultural practice that marks the white working classes' ambivalent desire to claim whiteness as a supra-class category for "independence" and civic (as well as economic) entitlement: "The insecurity that attended class stratification [in the 1830s through the 1850s] produced a whole series of working-class fears about the status of whiteness."[27] Minstrelsy's cultural roots, as well as performances that "exposed" the threat of interracial "amalgamation," simultaneously registered growing white racism and whites' fascination with black cultural forms, black bodies, black humanity, and even the possibility of interracial class solidarity.[28] Lott helps us remember the way minstrelsy replays—in twisted form—the human possibilities that institutionalized racism suppresses. But it is also important not to lose sight of the way that, as Roediger summarizes:

> blackface performances tended to support proslavery and white supremacist politics. Certainly some songs evoked the horrors of slavery, especially of being sold and taken away from home. But countless others painted a paternal plantation and contented slaves. . . . When political chips were down, minstrelsy could speak directly for specific anti-Black policies in a way that it could not for egalitarian ones.[29]

It is precisely Thoreau's repudiation of the racial spectacularization of "blacks" rehearsed variously by abolitionism and minstrelsy that allowed him to develop some of his best insights about the way institutionalized slavery helped to rationalize other, seemingly different forms of labor victimization. In other words, refusing to see "racial" difference enabled him to see important connections between practices of enslavement and the kinds of ideological enlistment that teach people to choose their own subordination to a system that does not represent or perhaps even benefit them. For instance, in his well-known essay "Resistance to Civil Government," Thoreau redescribes the notion of "good citizen[ship]" not in familiar terms of liberty and responsibility, but as a self-diminishing embrace of mindless subordination to an invidious power structure:

> Behold . . . such a man as an American government can make, or such as it can make a man with its black arts, a mere shadow and reminiscence of humanity . . . The mass of men serve the State thus, not as men mainly, but as machines, with their bodies. They are the standing army, and the militia, jailers, constables, *posse commitatus*, &c. In most cases there is no free exercise whatever of judgment or of moral sense; but they put themselves on a level with wood and earth and stones, and wooden men can perhaps be manufactured that will serve the purpose as well.[30]

Thoreau understands that racial slavery encouraged "white" people to feel relieved by the differences of political, social, and economic condition that skin color rationalized. But he wanted his readers to see something altogether different: the complement of (black) slavery in the United States is not (white) "freedom" but voluntary self-enslavement to a system that is built on differentiated models of exploitation.

Analyzing the institution of slavery helped Thoreau make arguments about reforming manhood. But talking about black *people* never seemed to provide Thoreau with useful examples of manhood. For instance, in his encounter with the runaway slave, he does not describe the fugitive's but rather his own capability: "One real runaway slave, among the rest, whom I helped to forward toward the northstar."[31] Thoreau scholar Robert F. Sayre emphasizes a striking dynamic in Thoreau's habits of racial representation. For Thoreau:

The slave was a pathetic figure, the Indian a tragic one. . . . Both images, however distorted, provoked strong responses in Thoreau. In his abolitionism and his refusal to pay his tax, his hiding of escaped slaves and championing of John Brown, he indeed did help slaves. But the near absence of anything in his writing *about* the slaves which he helped reveals how little interest he had in them. Their pathos was a call on his manhood, but they were not his manly equals. Towards Indians he was exactly the opposite. He scarcely did a thing *for* them, but he read, thought and wrote about them throughout his adult life.[32]

Sayre points out that in his Walden project, Thoreau "enacted the white fantasy of living like an Indian"[33]—even to the point that he appropriates Samoset's welcome to the Puritans in his address to his Walden "pilgrims" (visitors), "Welcome Englishmen! welcome Englishmen!"[34]

Thoreau's fascination with Indians—a fascination that extends from his *Maine Woods* and *Week on the Concord and Merrimack Rivers* through *Walden* and eventually to his voluminous notes on Native Americans in a collection he called his "Indian Books"—was a manifestation of a habit developing more generally in the nineteenth-century United States. The habit began with the reduction of more than 2,000 diverse indigenous cultures and nations to one stereotype: the Indian. This Indian was invested with European-based cultural beliefs both positive and negative: about romanticized primitivism (look at the simple bucolic life they live and we used to live) and about intolerable savagism (they are heathen barbarians who will never assimilate to our civilized way of life).[35] The flip-flopping values of this reductive stereotype can tell us very little about the diverse cultures of Native Americans in North America. But it can tell us a great deal about the values and anxieties of the culture producing it. For example, historian Michael Paul Rogin has helpfully analyzed the way in which "the Indian" was used as a symbolic demon that helped to articulate the values of emergent liberal society in the new nation:

Liberalism insisted upon work, instinctual repression, and acquisitive behavior; men had to conquer and separate themselves from nature. Indians were seen as playful, violent, improvident, wild and in harmony with nature. Private property underlay liberal society; Indians held land in common. Liberal relations were based, contractually, on keeping promises and on personal responsibility. Indians, in the liberal view, were anarchic and irresponsible. Americans believed that peaceful competitiveness kept them in touch with one another and provided social cement. They thought the Indians, lacking social order, were devoted to war. [36]

Rogin investigates the way the stereotype of "the Indian" helped negotiate economic issues for white America. His observation here points us toward considering the ideological fiction of the "peaceful competitiveness" of early U.S. capitalism against its experientially anxious, potentially devastating cultural and material results. Analyzing Thoreau's and his culture's developing obsession not just with Indians but with *playing* the Indian can help us understand the ambivalence white men felt about emerging models of competitive manhood.

This new manhood, requiring individual men to internalize in the terms of personal responsibility the political and economic vicissitudes of the early nation, propelled a substantially intensified need for the articulation and management *of* manliness. It is possible to see how "playing Indian" could serve such a project. First of all, it was a way for white men to claim a "primitive" manliness that marketplace competition might have made them long for and feel deprived of. In this sense, the imagined community between manly Indians and manly (white) Americans invited white men, much like Robert Bly and Shepherd Bliss invite men today, to beat their drums and reject the "feminizing" effects of "civilization" (imaginatively and temporarily) for the pure, primitive spaces of manly affiliation. This idealized, imaginary "interracial" male community, then, offers us some insight into the mid- to late-century exploding popularity of such secret fraternal organizations as the International Order of Red Men (whose supposed founding came in 1492), such fictions as James Fenimore Cooper's *Last of the Mohicans* (1826), or such "health-cures" as Francis Parkman's 1846 trip to the frontier, detailed in his book *The California and Oregon Trail* (1849).

Second, playing Indian allowed white men a way to voice anxieties about and critiques of the demands of competitive manhood and in the very same moment to disavow those anxieties and critiques. No better a place to think about this second effect than in Thoreau's presentation of the Indian basket-weaver in *Walden*. There are a few layers here to unpack that, taken together, diagram the multidirectional usefulness of racial projection for negotiating issues that emerge in competitive market relations among white men. Most apparently, the image of the basket-weaver works like a stock comedy figure whose gaffs we laugh at, thus giving us pleasure in our own superior knowledge. An earnest naïf, the Indian is eager to participate in sales for economic gain. But he just doesn't get it: "What!" he accuses the seemingly uncooperative trader/purchaser who does not want his baskets: "Do you mean to starve us?" Operating out of "primitive" expectations of community and reciprocity, the Indian is unable to "get" capitalism. He cannot conceptualize capitalism's fundamental tenet of manipulating *imbalance*; his business mistake comes as he banks on reciprocity: "He would have done his part, and then it would be the white man's to buy them."[37]

In the next layer the Indian stands, in an increasingly loaded way in the nineteenth-century United States, for the "communist" antithesis/supplement to capitalism.[38] That is to say, Thoreau's naive Indian (who can't see he's a failure as a capitalist because he's a commun[al]ist) is a necessary symbol that supplements the logic of capitalism, making a way for the capitalist system and individual capitalist actors to externalize its/their own multiple ambivalences about living inside of capitalism. The Indian as savage-savant, whose befuddlement implicitly critiques without challenging the acommunal logic of market relations, holds open a cultural space for white men to voice ambivalence about its destructuring of community and even critique market brutality while disavowing responsibility for that critique by appearing to be strong boosters. It is important to recognize that such disavowal had political ramifications that went well beyond laughing at such supposedly "silly Indians." Labeling Indians as enemies of capitalism buttressed white claims to Native lands, provided logic for breaking treaty agreements with indigenous nations, and provided rationales for the brutal enforcement of Indian removal that began in the late 1830s. And these actions provided an arena, almost always violent, for the rehearsal of white men's claims to independent, competitive manhood.

In yet another layer, Thoreau-the-artist stands in as his own version of that Indian, peddling a beautiful and refined "basket"—his writing—for which he, like the Indian, is ultimately unwilling to cultivate (base) market desire because it would diminish the higher spiritual value, and indeed the manliness, of his work. As he puts it in "Life without Principle," if "you must be popular . . . you are paid for being something less than a man."[39] In this way Thoreau stands in as the Indian to make a pedagogical (and double-fisted) argument to his reading public, that they should buy his work not because it is marketable but because the book's very refusal to make concessions to readers' desires will mark their own manly resistance to market values in their act of purchasing and contemplating those arguments. It is worth looking at the way this posture—and his project in *Walden* more generally—replicates what we might term Revolutionary Red-Face, popular from the Boston Tea-Party forward, where white men strike the pose of independent manhood by playing Indian.[40] A careful analysis of Thoreau's fascination with Indians helps us pay attention to the ways such white performances of independent (red) manhood were always complexly loaded up with competitive capitalist claims *and* anticapitalist, communitarian longings.

It is easier for us to think about constructions of white manhood in relation to "black" African Americans and "red" Native Americans. It is less easy for us to analyze the way "whiteness" was consolidated also against groups we now think of as being included in that category. That is precisely what scholars like Noel Ignatiev, in his study of *How the Irish Became White*, have been helping us to do. As he notes, the position of the Irish Catholic peasantry in mid-century Ireland was materially comparable to that of American slaves. Once in the United States, the Irish:

> commonly found themselves thrown together with free Negroes. Irish and Afro-Americans fought each other and the police, socialized and occasionally intermarried, and developed a common culture of the lowly. They also both suffered the scorn of those better situated. Along with Jim Crow and Jim Dandy, the drunken, belligerent and foolish Pat and Bridget were stock characters on the early stage. In antebellum America it was speculated that if racial amalgamation was ever to take place it would begin between those two groups.[41]

Because of their economic association in the lowest tiers of the working class with free blacks, mid-century Irish immigrants became "racially" suspect in the middle-class Protestant mainstream, regarded as perhaps being "beyond the pale" of white civilization. Thus the Irish offered yet another symbolic means where "independent manhood" could be counterposed to "other types"—both through cultural representation and through violent actions like Philadelphia's 1843 and 1844 Kensington riots, or Boston's 1854 riots, where Nativists excited anti-Irish rallies and rioting, and even burned down Catholic churches.

If Thoreau was good at resisting the (white) democratic habit of stereotyping African Americans, he was far less able to resist the bribe when it came to the Irish. It is possible to argue that Paddy stereotypes provide the key contrast against which Thoreau stakes his own economic sensibility and manliness throughout *Walden*. As literary critic Timothy Powell observes, "In stark contrast to Native Americans (who are 'almost exterminated'), African-Americans (a 'race departed') and women (who are almost textually non-existent), the Irish are everywhere throughout *Walden*"[42]—as dirty squatters, impecuniary laborers, and drunken ghosts. Thoreau, who depicts his residence on his friend Ralph Waldo Emerson's property as "squatting," assembles his cabin from the disassembled home of the Irish railroad laborer James Collins. Thoreau's own claim to superior economy comes not only in his thrifty avoidance of the expense of new boards, but also through the detailed contrast of his "tight, light, clean"[43] reconstruction of Collins's squalid "shanty."

Later, building from this lesson, Thoreau undertakes to instruct another spendthrift Irishman, John Field, who by Thoreau's estimation enslaves himself to overlaboring because he insists on squandering an excess of his income on frivolities like tea, coffee, and meat. Different from the naive Indian basketweaver, in whose place Thoreau can stand to make an argument for his higher economy, the dull Field and his wife cannot even comprehend the basic operations of the economy Thoreau wants them to transcend. At Thoreau's suggestion that they give up eating expensive meat and go "a-huckelberrying" in the leisure time they would gain from their reduced expenses, "John heaved a sigh . . . and his wife stared with arms a-kimbo, and both appeared to be wondering if they had capital enough to begin such a course with, or arithmetic enough to carry it through." Field, "with his inherited Irish poverty and poor life, his Adam's grandmother and boggy ways," becomes an essential contrast to the "only true America" that Thoreau more capably and wisely represents.[44]

And as we learn in the passage on "Former Inhabitants," it is exactly Thoreau's philosophical economism that constitutes *his* competitive edge. Coming after not only the free blacks who used to reside in Walden Woods but also the drunk Irishman Hugh Quoil (who dies of delirium tremens), Thoreau's philosophical musings "repeople" the now deserted woods. Thoreau defines his presence there as a kind of natural succession: "Alas! how little does the memory of these human inhabitants enhance the beauty of the landscape! Again, perhaps, Nature will try, with me for a first settler, and my house raised last spring to be the oldest in the hamlet."[45] His advantage leaves him literally alone in the field.

Representative Isolationism, or Natural Manhood

In proliferating contrasts to poor Irish laborers, Thoreau insists on his "squatter" status, as though he is simply a more philosophical and presumably dry-footed version of these men with their "wading webbed bog-trotting feet.[46] Only once does his superior-class status show up for the readers to see, in Thoreau's speculation about what John Field might think of *him*: "I wore light shoes and thin clothing, which cost not half so much, though he might think I was dressed like a gentleman."[47] Thoreau gives his readers a glimpse of class contrast but dismisses its significance quickly: ". . . (which, however, was not the case)." But despite this quick repudiation, as Powell observes, Thoreau's "philosophy of 'self-reliance' is haunted by the question of class privilege."[48] Thoreau's symbolic deployment of Irish characters to stake his own individual claim to a more effectual economic sensibility reflects two aspects of a larger cultural trend. First, as middle-class historian Stuart Blumin observes, "The massive migration of the antebellum era—so closely linked with industrial development, changes in work and the changing scale and structure of the big city—contributed to the distinctiveness of classes and the power of class identity" by mid-century.[49] Second, this new middle class recognized itself not in the terms of a group identity, but through a lexicon of individual merit, universal order, and basic common sense. As Burton Bledstein summarizes, "In America, the middle-class person insisted that individual attainment at a fleeting moment in a career, and not class structure, allowed for the observable diversity in standards of living."[50] This is a precise diagram of Thoreau's stance in *Walden*. Even as he critiqued the ideology of industriousness, Thoreau asked readers to see his own supposedly superior economic "success" at Walden not as the result of his class advantage—in, for example, the form of family and community support, education, and vocational expectations—but of his own special wisdom and industry: "I am convinced, both by faith and experience, that to maintain one's self on this earth is not a hardship, but a pastime, if we will live simply and wisely."[51] But his assertion here and his didactic contrasts with Irish immigrants Collins and Fields elsewhere ask readers to overlook, as Powell concisely summarizes, "the kind of class privilege that allowed Thoreau to go from living among the Irish in Walden Woods to living in Emerson's spacious home on Lexington Road when his 'experiment' was over."[52]

The middle decades of the century—roughly Thoreau's adult lifetime—mark the rise to public dominance of the modern middle classes. As Sellers has detailed, one way middle-class culture marshaled resources and centered itself societally came in its successful campaign to transfer what had previously been private expenses—burial, fire company insurance, and schooling for example—to the public domain.[53] Another way that it did so was in its creation of and rise to economic and social managerial dominance. The middle-class logic of manhood described by Bledstein became the organizing rationale for the emergence of white-collar work and professional work more generally:

> The middle-class person attempted to eliminate wasteful competition and to establish universal standards for moral and civil behavior. He was the world's organizer, punctual, industrious, mathematical, and impersonal. He sharpened his mind into an analytic knife. He sought accurate information, acted with the coldest prudence, and built a more perfect institutional order.[54]

As the "world's organizer," a middle-class intellectual could claim to stand as the culminating example and the natural, meritocratic representative for public order. In *Walden*, Thoreau positions himself as an anti-representative for public or, more specifically, market order, and instead as a philosopher-representative of a more natural order, drawing on the middle-class logic of individual representivity even as he critiques middle-class aims and values. His posture as an organizer preaching simplicity and solitude provides an alternative model for national manliness in the "only true America" but suggests also a key counterproductive turn in his thinking on the subject.

Thoreau critiques the nation's market order and its middle-class social logic as forces that attack and deprive men of their natural integrity. In "Life without Principle," Thoreau scoffs that "I see advertisements for *active* young men, as if activity were the whole of a young man's capital."[55] Near the beginning of *Walden*, he describes this modern disorder and its antidote with a sensitivity that is almost breathtaking. The mistaken discipline of "industriousness" so occupies men "with the factitious cares and superfluously coarse labors of life that its finer fruits cannot be plucked by them," he asserts.[56] The finer fruits, he then suggests, are actually *other men*: his next image offers the "finer qualities of our nature" as the metaphorical referent for that fruit. It is *men* whose bloom fades in transit to market, the proper appreciation of which requires "only the most delicate handling." Yet, he comments, "We do not treat ourselves nor one another thus tenderly."[57] Thoreau's image concisely renders the affective tolls of market economy, which has for Thoreau not to do only with the personal costs of "industriousness" but also the interpersonal costs for men in constantly competitive relations.

In this image, Thoreau fleetingly posits a world of deliberate care and friendship among men. But there is precious little of this imagined tender exchange in the world of *Walden*. Indeed, Thoreau seems almost entirely unable to imagine a productive, working alternative. Shortly, describing his own philosophy of what we might call natural manhood, he summarizes its ultimate rule: "Above all . . . the man who goes alone can start today; but he who travels with another must wait till that other is ready, and it may be a long time before they get off."[58] Thoreau's alternative to market competition among men is not a remodeled political or emotional engagement but a principled withdrawal from the messiness of such interaction. But we might read Thoreau's arguments about a manly isolationism in *Walden* and elsewhere with that early image in mind: Thoreau's rigorous solitude is fueled by a longing and a nostalgia for connectedness, for a kind of equalitarian, caring manly community that we get only glimpses of in his writings, with, for instance, Alex Therien in *Walden,* with his brother in *A Week,* with his "Indian" guides Joseph Aitteon and Joe Polis in *Maine Woods,* and in such poems as "Lately, Alas, I Knew a Gentle Boy." Thoreau seems ultimately unwilling to elaborate on those possibilities,[59] choosing to represent imagined rather than actual relations between men as the most satisfactory ones (as he concludes his poem, "Distance, forsooth, from my weak grasp hath reft / The empty husk, and clutched the useless tare, / But in my hands the wheat and kernel left"[60]). He redeems his carefully cordoned, contemplative manhood by outlining it as the heroic posture of nature's philosopher, nature's representative.

Or we might say that he redeems his aloneness by imagining he somehow stands *for* all those men with whom he might otherwise long to have such tender relationships. Thoreau turns to science to find a rationale (or a moral) for the affective foreclosure of manly community and describes the absence of other men in his world not as his choice, but as nature's process of selection. His *Walden* chapter on "Former Inhabitants" provides the most concise overview of this strategy, where the dearly departed slave and free blacks who had inhabited Walden Woods along with the fatally alcoholic Irishman leave the ground vacant for Thoreau's experiment. Thoreau describes the vacated/abandoned sites he discovers as the "germ of something more," suggesting that somehow its former inhabitants failed to take root because of a certain failure on their part properly to cultivate their opportunity. The land remains "unimproved" because their self-indulgence (for instance, he speculates, they used the water supply only to "dilute their glasses" of whiskey) and want of proper industry disselects them from Walden's natural history, leaving finally only Henry. His moralizing appeal to the logic of science allows Thoreau counterintuitivly to confirm the communitarian value of the philosophical economy of natural manhood *in* his very disconnection, where nature "herself" selects the solitary poet/philosopher not to interact with but to represent others in their absence, with his "reminiscences" to "repeople . . . the woods."[61]

So we could say that Thoreau recuperates the very isolation he earlier lamented by pretending he is not alone. We can laugh at him for this or sadly shake our heads. But even better we can use Thoreau's ironic recuperation to probe the limits of his imagination on the subject of white manhood's political possibilities. In Thoreau's vision for the "only true America," men stand philosophically, heroically, quietly alone—they do not engage in the messy negotiations required for a search for effective democratic alternatives to capitalist citizenship. In his poem "Lately, Alas, I Knew a Gentle Boy," the persona describes friendship with another boy as complete identification: "We two were one while we did sympathize / So could we not the simplest bargain drive."[62]

Thoreau argues that friendship must be protected from the market. But his work here and elsewhere indicates that he cannot imagine an alternative to the sympathetic collapse of identity he associates with friendship on the one hand, or the competitive imbalance among men structured by the market on the other.

What he most needs, and seems unable to imagine or unwilling to contemplate, is a third position where men might disagree and differ from each other in politically and socially productive ways. Thoreau is allergic to capitalist citizenship, and for good reason. It divides men from each other and separates them from the best parts of themselves. But his "corrective" model does not counter the quiet desperation, it actually *heightens* it by lending heroic stature to men's emotional and political isolation under capitalist citizenship. Reading Thoreau in his historical context helps us conceptualize how representivity works as a kind of practical wrong turn, because it just as fully fails to provide the emotional exchange he accuses capitalist citizenship of denying to men. The representative posture is iconically available for Thoreau through both civic logic and through the natural-succession scientific logic I have been outlining above. It serves well theoretically and intellectually to redeem the enormous loneliness that "industriousness" and market competition entailed for men in Thoreau's understanding. But however abstractly satisfying, natural manhood doesn't get him any closer to those longed-for sympathetic exchanges with men. Philosophically substituting scientific models of natural succession for the messy work of political and emotional negotiation determines that Thoreau must describe as heroic the solitude he might otherwise have been able to identify as an imaginative dead end. But instead of seeing that dead end, he is left attempting to deny its effects, as we can see in the chapter "The Pond in Winter." There, he tries to discard his feelings as so much pondscum: "Why is it that a bucket of water soon becomes putrid, but frozen remains forever sweet? It is commonly said that this is the difference between affections and the intellect."[63] It's worth noting that he never does succeed at his project of replacing emotions with cold thought, no matter how hard he projects them away from himself. As he queries (of the pond!) in the closing chapter of *Walden*: "Who would have suspected so large and cold and thick-skinned a thing to be so sensitive?"[64] Indeed.

NOTES

1. Henry David Thoreau, *Walden*, ed. J. Lyndon Shanley (Princeton: Princeton University Press, 1971), 5.

2. *Ibid.*, 17.

3. Robert A. Gross, "Culture and Cultivation: Agriculture and Society in Thoreau's Concord," in *Material Life in America, 1600–1860*, ed. Robert Blair St. George (Boston: Northeastern University Press, 1988), 520–21.

4. Michael Warner, "*Walden's* Erotic Economy," in *Comparative American Identities: Race, Sex and Nationality in the Modern Text*, ed. Hortense Spillers (New York: Routledge, 1991), 173.

5. Leonard N. Neufeldt provides a careful study of *Walden's* dialogue with the advice literature for young men that was so explosively popular during Thoreau's lifetime. See Neufeldt's *The Economist: Henry Thoreau and Enterprise* (New York: Oxford University Press, 1989), especially section 2, "*Walden* and the Guidebook for Young Men."

6. J. Hector St. John de Crèvecoeur, *Letters from an American Farmer and Sketches of Eighteenth-Century America* (New York: Penguin, 1981), 69–70.

7. *Ibid.*, 70.

8. *Ibid.*, 83.

9. *Ibid.*, 53.

10. Anthony Rotundo, *American Manhood* (New York: Basic Books, 1993), 15, 12–14.

11. Daniel Vickers summarizes this concept in his essay "Competency and Competition: Economic Culture in Early America," *William and Mary Quarterly* 47, no.1 (1990): 3–29: "To early modern readers, the idea connoted the possession of sufficient property to absorb the labors of a given family while providing it with something more than a mere subsistence" (3). Noting the cultural "tension between [household] independence and capitalism," Christopher Clark elaborates that:

The pursuit of household "independence," while it rarely produced a literal self-sufficiency, strongly influenced rural culture, farming practices, and attitudes toward land and accumulation. In New England and in many upcountry regions elsewhere, there was a substantial degree of local self-sufficiency and poor integration with distant, international markets. Accounting practices were devoted to keeping track of local debts and credits, not to accumulating profits. ("Rural American and the Transition to Capitalism," in *Wages of Independence: Capitalism in the Early American Republic*, ed. Paul A. Gilje [Madison, Wisc.: Madison House, 1997], 66, 68)

12. Royall Tyler, *The Contrast*, repr. in *The Heath Anthology of American Literature*, 2d ed. vol. 1, ed Paul Lauter (Lexington, Mass.: Heath, 1994), 1122.

13. Ibid., 1116.

14. Ibid., 1117–1118.

15. Ibid., 1122.

16. Charles Sellers, *The Market Revolution: Jacksonian America, 1815–1846* (New York: Oxford University Press, 1991), 28–29; 19.

17. Thoreau, "Life without Principle," in *Reform Papers*, ed. Wendell Glick (Princeton: Princeton University Press, 1973), 159.

18. Thoreau, *Walden*, 9.

19. Rotundo, *American Manhood*, 19–20.

20. Thoreau, *Walden*, 9.

21. Edward Pessen, *Riches, Class and Power before the Civil War* (Lexington, Mass.: Heath, 1973).

22. Alan Dawley and Paul Faler, "Working-Class Culture and Politics in the Industrial Revolution: Sources of Loyalism and Rebellion," *Journal of Social History* 9 (1976): 474–75.

23. Thoreau, *Walden*, 152.

24. Ibid., 258.

25. Michael Goldfield, *The Color of Politics: Race and the Mainsprings of American Politics* (New York: New Press, 1997), 84.

26. See David Roediger, *The Wages of Whiteness: Race and the Making of the American Working Class* (New York: Verso, 1991), 100–111.

27. Eric Lott, *Love and Theft: Blackface Minstrelsy and the American Working Class* (New York: Oxford University Press, 1993), 70.

28. See Ibid., 134–35.

29. Roediger, *Wages of Whiteness*, 124.

30. Thoreau, "Resistance to Civil Government," in *Reform Papers*, ed. Glick, 66.

31. Thoreau, *Walden*, 152.

32. Robert F. Sayre, *Thoreau and the American Indians* (Princeton: Princeton University Press, 1977), 24–25.

33. Ibid., xi.

34. Thoreau, *Walden*, 154.

35. For more on the nineteenth-century ideological construction of the Indian stereotype, see Robert F. Berkhofer, Jr., *The White Man's Indian: Images of the American Indian from Columbus to the Present* (New York: Vintage, 1979).

36. Michael Paul Rogin, *Fathers and Children: Andrew Jackson and the Subjugation of the American Indian* (New Brunswick, New Jersey: Transaction Publishers, 1975, repr. 1991), 8.

37. Thoreau, *Walden*, 19.

38. For example, the state of Colorado has almost no reservation land within its territory because of the incredible efficacy of Denver editor and politician William B. Vickers, who literally began a red-scare aimed at the Utes in the late 1870s. Beginning with an editorial for the *Denver Tribune*, Vickers described the Utes as "practical Communists" and encouraged white readers to drive them out of the state, reminding them that "the only good Indian is a dead one." See Dee Brown, *Bury My Heart at Wounded Knee: An Indian History of the American West* (New York: Washington Square Press, 1981), 356–67.

39. Thoreau, "Life without Principle," 158.

40. For a useful historical survey of this practice, see Philip J. Deloria's *Playing Indian* (New Haven: Yale University Press, 1998).

41. Noel Ignatiev, *How the Irish Became White* (New York: Routledge, 1995), 3.

42. Timothy Powell, *Ruthless Democracy: A Multicultural Interpretation of the American Renaissance* (Princeton: Princeton University Press, 2000), 94.

43. Thoreau, *Walden*, 205.

44. Ibid., 209, 205.

45. Ibid., 264.

46. Ibid., 209.

47. Ibid., 206.

48. Powell, *Ruthless Democracy*, 97.

49. Stuart Blumin, *The Emergence of the Middle Class: Social Experience in the American City, 1760–1900* (New York: Cambridge University Press, 1989), 253.

50. Burton Bledstein, *The Culture of Professionalism: The Middle Class and the Development of Higher Education in America* (New York: Norton, 1976), 21.

51. Thoreau, *Walden*. Edited by Stephen Fender (New York: Oxford University Press, 1997), 70.

52. Powell, *Ruthless Democracy*, 97.

53. See for example, Sellers, *Market Revolution*, 365–69.

54. Bledstein, *Culture of Professionalism*, 27.

55. Thoreau, "Life without Principle," 159.

56. Thoreau, *Walden*, 6.

57. Ibid.

58. Ibid., 72.

59. My reading here differs substantially from Henry Abelove's compelling argument in "From Thoreau to Queer Politics," *Yale Journal of Criticism* 6, no. 2 (1993): 17–27, where he asserts that the text positions all readers, like Alex Therien (in the passage where he sounds out *The Iliad* in Greek and listens to Henry translate it), as "the object of a homosexual seduction . . . regardless of our gender or sexual taste" (22–23). Abelove argues that *Walden* positions itself as an "anti-novel," in the sense that it refuses to focus on the "news" of bourgeois family life (23). Positing an affective life outside both competitive capitalism and middle-class family forms, *Walden* rejects "love . . . as firmly" as "the ideals of fame, money and compassion" (24).

60. Thoreau, "Lately, Alas, I Knew a Gentle Boy," *The Portable Thoreau*. Edited by Carl Bode (New York: Viking Penguin, 1947), 232.

61. Thoreau, *Walden*, 264.

62. Thoreau, "Lately, Alas," 232.

63. Thoreau, *Walden*, 297.

64. Ibid., 302.

Domesticity on Walden Pond

Cecelia Tichi

> I kept Homer's Iliad on my table through
> the summer.
>
> Henry David Thoreau, *Walden*, 1854

Much is made of the *Iliad* in Thoreau's experiment in living at Walden Pond, but very little of the table on which it sat. The volume of Homer's epic on the three-legged table inside Thoreau's ten-by-fifteen-foot house is just one of the *Iliad*ic references that leads scholars of *Walden* to research Thoreau's studies in classical Greek at Harvard College, to note his favorite edition and his enthusiasm for a heroic Homeric life, and to search out the many citations in *Walden* in order to debate the extent to which the text might be deliberately heroic and/or epic (Sattelmeyer, *Thoreau's Reading*, 6, 8, 9, 23; Johnson, "Revolution and Renewal," 216–18). Thoreau's table, however, has gone unremarked, though it too recurs in *Walden*, both in Thoreau's inventory of furniture (which also includes his bed, desk, three chairs, and looking-glass), and again when he enjoys the table anew when placing it outdoors in the sunlight (*Walden*, 111–12). Indoors, we learn, the table occupies the single room that serves as kitchen, chamber, keeping-room—and parlor (242).

That table in the parlor may seem insignificant to literary scholars, but students of material culture know that a table and parlor are signposts of domesticity. Studies of material culture in nineteenth-century America require an identifcation of Thoreau's table as a rustic version of the middle-class center parlor table, a "shrine within the ritual space of the parlor" and "site of carefully edited selections of familial possessions—family Bibles and other important books" (Grier, *Culture and Comfort,* 87). From this viewpoint, Thoreau's tabletop *Iliad* becomes not only a secular scriptural enshrinement of Homer but also an artifact contributing to the composition of the middle-class, mid-nineteenth-century American parlor. Framed by the terms of material culture studies, that is, the cherished book on the parlor table is a domestic convention, the *Iliad* domesticated by its very site, and the entire subject of Thorovian homemaking in *Walden* open for revaluation.

This discussion seeks to open *Walden* (1854) to the world of nineteenth-century domesticity, a site of decades-long feminist and material culture scholarship. It revisits *Walden* in order to consider its engagement with issues often thought synonymous with the largely middle-class, nineteenth-century American female domain. This is essentially a discussion mandated by the vocabulary of *Walden*, including Thoreau's numerous observations on contemporary American quotidian life, on foodways, hospitality, rituals of calling cards, interior furnishing, and housekeeping.

Juxtaposed particularly with Catherine Beecher's *Treatise on Domestic Economy* (1841) and the Catherine Beecher–Harriet Beecher Stowe *American Woman's Home* (1869), *Walden* emerges as Thoreau's own "Treatise on Domestic Economy" and insists on joining the colloquy on nineteenth-century American domestic culture, proving to be a text affirmative of an essentialist, ideal domesticity and simultaneously vexed about the market economy's deformation of it. In this regard, *Walden* critiques a warped domesticity in ways that prove consistent with the very contemporary women's texts against which it has been assumed to stand in "radical" and "diametric opposition," to parody, to play "off," or to "appropriate" for a Transcendentalist poetics (Gleason, "Re-Creating *Walden*," 680–86; Johnson, "Revolution and Renewal," 221–23; Taketani, "Thoreau's Domestic Economy," 65, 66).

Walden, in fact, models a "primitive" domesticity based upon fundamentals of food, shelter, and clothing as exhibited, in Thoreau's view, by a past of edenic and colonial households and by the natural world in the ongoing present (with Native Americans treated as integral with nature). These are contrasted with an increasingly middle-class, mid-nineteenth-century "extravagant" consumerist life of the market economy, which is critiqued substantially not only by Thoreau but also by the Beecher sisters and by Lydia Maria Child as well, notably in her *The Frugal Housewife* (1829).

It is useful to reflect briefly upon why, thus far, *Walden* has been excluded from, or found to be alien to, the world of domesticity, beginning with acknowledgement of Thoreau's apparently overt and thoroughgoing hostility to that domain. *Walden* scorns unnecessary "domestic comforts," remarks ominously that "our lives are domestic in more senses than we think," and lauds Walden's "deficiency" of such "domestic sounds" as the churn, spinning wheel, and kettle (24, 27, 28, 127). One recalls the lamentation that "we worship . . . Fashion," a Thorovian female figure who "spins and weaves and cuts with full authority," while ladies weave toilet cushions as a trivial distraction from serious reflection on their "fate" (25, 8). Sewing in *Walden* is a postlapsarian occupation, introduced as "a kind of work which you may call endless," a woman's dress exemplified as work "never done" (23). With these kinds of barbs at female domestic activity, and with gender serving as a major and continuous heuristic since the late 1960s, it has not seemed useful to ask what connects *Walden* with the "Cult of True Womanhood?" (Welter, "Cult of True Womanhood").

In later twentieth-century Americanist feminist criticism, Thoreau's domesticity doubtless would be examined had he not become a problematic literary "other" in the male cohort of Hawthorne, Melville, Emerson, and, to a lesser extent, Poe. Feminist criticism, which is arguably an outgrowth of 1960s social movements that embraced Thoreau as a counterculture exemplum, located him, perhaps inevitably, in the pantheon of male writers who virtually monopolized nineteenth-century American literary studies into the 1970s via a largely male professoriat who were self-identified with New England as the synecdoche for the entire nation (see Baym, *Feminism*). In her pathbreaking *Sensational Designs* (1985), Jane Tompkins recalls Thoreau's position within a male grouping "celebrated as models of intellectual daring and honesty," while their female counterparts were known for "dishing out weak-minded pap to nourish the prejudices of an ill-educated and underemployed female readership" (*Sensational Designs,* 124). Tompkins and numerous other scholars involved themselves in work of feminist recovery, remediation, and theory and were largely uninterested in exploring ways in which the "classic" male canon converges with that of the "d———d mob of scribbling women" (Hawthorne's notorious phrase), even though Thoreau's countercultural example *per se* enabled feminist argumentation based on oppositionality in relation to culturally centrist accommodation.[1]

Gendered domains of scholarly investigation, meanwhile, have also carried their covert anti-domesticity prohibitions on the masculinist side. Philip Fisher's *Hard Facts* (1985) broached the notion of a crucial affiliative nexus between *Walden* and Catherine Beecher's *Treatise on Domestic Economy,* but the linkage has been rejected even as analysts pursued other, male-related topics that are treated in *Walden* as caustically as is domesticity (Fisher, *Hard Facts,* 88). *Walden* is a forum for complaints that authentic work has been supplanted by the palsy of "St. Vitus's dance," that civilization now turns "somersaults" from a "spring-board" of "bankruptcy and repudiation," and that the typical farmer is "crushed and smothered" as he pushes a barn before him down the road of life (92, 32, 5).[2] All these, however, have evidently served, not as a deterrent but as an invitaton to scholarly pursuit of Thoreau's complex—and notably complicitous—relation to conditions of work, to contemporary agriculture, and to the market economy, plausibly because they involve explicitly masculine domains, or, in post-1960s feminist critics' usage, spheres.

Thoreau's relation to domesticity, when acknowledged, has been characterized, however, as hostility across barricades of gender, as an ideological antithesis to it, and as a "guerilla" attack in which the very terms of domesticity are turned against it in

Thorovian warfare (Johnson, "Revolution and Renewal," 223). Thoreau's own critique of domesticity, that is, has been taken at face value and reinforced in critical discussion. Critics concede that he "adopted some of Beecher's aims and method," echoed her "exuberant" tones in the "Conclusion" to *Walden*, and endorsed her views on diet and care of the body and her utilitarian approach to clothing as well as her ethos of economy in house building. Yet Thoreau by no means "threw in his lot" with female domestic reformers, these critics hasten to say, finding instead that he rejected Beecher's "ethic of enterprise," her Americanist chauvinism, and her "twinned ideologies of deference and standardization" (Johnson, "Revolution and Renewal," 222; Gleason, "Re-Creating *Walden*,"680–86). Such positions preserve the essential masculine Thoreau by locating ideology beyond and above the exigencies of quotidian life, which is drastically subordinated and thereby dismissed as an issue of minor interest and importance.

The longtime identity of Thoreau as a nature writer, of course, has also operated to exclude *Walden* from material culture studies of domesticity, and, here again, statements in the text appear to claim an environmental aesthetic by rejecting that of the domestic: "A taste for the beautiful is most cultivated out of doors, where there is no house and no housekeeper" (*Walden*, 38). Such a statement has been read as a signpost directing readers away from domestic spaces into the natural world out-of-doors.[3] Though the subject area of *Walden*—including home life and domestic architecture—is germane to issues of domesticity, Thoreau's name does not appear in such major studies as *The American Family Home, 1800–1960* (1986), by Clifford Clark, Jr., or in *Our Own Snug Fireside: Images of the New England Home, 1760–1860*, by Jane Nylander (1993), or in *Culture and Comfort: People, Parlors, and Upholstery, 1850-1930*, by Katherine C. Grier (1988), or Stephen Mintz's study of American antebellum reformers, *Moralists and Modernizers* (1995). Even a folklorist's comment on Thoreau's involvement in traditionally female domestic life avoids focused argument on its nineteenth-century particularities. Henry Glassie, who notes Thoreau's reluctant respect for wallplaster and a closed stove, subordinates these observations to the general statement that, for Thoreau, "culture is enslaving—and necessary" ("Meaningful Things," 73).

The domestic vocabulary of *Walden*, however, indicates that culture is a matter of considerable intricacy, that it resists such generalization, and that we might usefully turn to scholarship on nineteenth-century American domesticity and material culture, not to rescue or liberate Thoreau from the contagion or taint of domesticity but in order to contextualize *Walden* within it. The moment is opportune, as scholarship seeks to move beyond constricting binary formulations such as the hegemonic versus minority or, for that matter, male versus female spheres, or Thorovian nature versus civilizaton. Lora Romero's *Home Fronts: Domesticity and Its Critics in the Antebellum United States* (1997), for example, calls for a rejection of these attenuated binarisms, urging instead a consideration of "the possibility that traditions, or even individual texts, could be radical on some issues (market capitalism, for example) and reactionary on others (gender or race, for instance). Or that some discourses could be oppositional without being downright liberating. Or conservative without being downright enslaving" (*Home Fronts*, 4). This new summons calls for an examination of multiple subject positions held concurrently within narrative worlds, to which this discussion adds the *Walden* narrative in its relation to the literature of nineteenth-century domesticity.

The province of *Walden*, as Thoreau indicates, includes the village of Concord with its "shops, offices, fields . . . the depot, the post-office, the bar-room, the meeting-house, the school-house, the grocery, . . . court-house, . . . jail, . . . dwelling house," the "tavern and victualling cellar," the "barber, the shoemaker, the tailor," and the "bank" (*Walden*, 4, 133, 96, 168–69). Thoreau recounts his impromptu visits to "some bright village parlor or lecture room" (168–69). His *bona fides* are those of a writer knowledgeable at firsthand about the interior spaces of work, commerce, civic culture, education, recreation, and ranging from affluence to poverty's degradation.

Reviewing the particulars of Thoreau's critique of the contemporary dwelling house, it is useful to consider his derogation as an

act of reformist engagement, not as a guerilla attack nor sepa-
ratist's or secessionist's manifesto when he denounces the contemporary mid-1800s house as easily synonymous with "a work-
house, a labyrinth . . . a museum, an almshouse, a prison, a
splendid mausoleum," a demonic site of burnishing doorknobs
and scouring tubs, an impoverishing and spuriously affluent scene
of "paint and [wall]paper, [closed stove] Rumford fireplace, back
plastering, Venetian blinds, copper pump, spring lock, commodi-
ous cellar . . . superfluous glow-shoes [galoshes] and umbrel-
las" in an atmosphere of fear that sunlight will damage furniture
and fade the carpeting (*Walden*, 28, 33, 223, 31, 36, 66).

The very particulars of Thoreau's critique suggest how carefully he has scrutinized the domestic furnishings and housekeeping practices of the moment, how attentive to the "modern
drawing room, with its divans, and ottomans, and sunshades, and
a hundred other oriental things," which he (and Harriet Beecher
Stowe) critiqued as effeminate and emasculating (*Walden*, 36, 37;
Stowe qtd. by Hedrick, 313). The "family tomb" matches the
"family mansion," and Thoreau writes, "I wonder that the floor
does not give way under the visitor while he is admiring the gewgaws upon the mantel-piece" (*Walden*, 37). (His scrutiny extends
to the poor shanty-Irish Collins family whom he believes to be in
bondage to a market economy, their household containing not
only a stove and bed and seating arrangement, but also the consumerist burdens of "a silk parasol, gilt-framed looking glass,
and a patent new coffee mill" [43].) Thoreau enjoys the paradox
of impoverished wealth: "Furniture! Thank God, I can stand
without the aid of a furniture warehouse. . . . Indeed, the
more you have of such things, the poorer you are" (65–66).

Such statements, culled from *Walden* and viewed in the aggregate, can sound like a focused diatribe. Encountered desultorily
as the text proceeds, they can feel like a leitmotif played against
the ostensibly more important issues of Nature's metaphysics or,
as one recent study argues, against an economy of nature's su-
perabundant extravagance (Grusin, "Thoreau, Extravagance").
The writer so much celebrated for his exaltation of the wild ("we
need the tonic of wilderness" [*Walden*, 317]) appears to make the
domestic household his foil, and the reader of *Walden* may find

these recurrent barbs argumentively supportive of a radically alternate ontological locus of Nature.

The world of *Walden*, however, is not wild, but benevolent and domestic—as Fisher aptly terms it, "suburban," "park-like," and of the "back yard" (*Hard Facts*, 80, 81). Accordingly, it provides the environ for domesticity throughout the text (80, 81). Thoreau's "wildness is held in a domestic embrace" (Tichi, *New World*, 167). In his study of the nineteenth-century origins of the American suburb, John Stilgoe remarks that "*country* to Thoreau meant a borderland place, a place—like Concord—in the borderlands" between city and farmland (*Borderlands*, 98). Critics have acknowledged the attraction of such places in an era when the expansion of marketplace capitalism intensified the alienation between the individual and work, and Gillian Brown has gone further to link domesticity to Thoreau's Walden experiment, explaining that domesticity's "ideal of creating a sphere apart from the marketplace" coincided with the reformist's goal of relocation to "the fringes of society, [or to] the woods in vanishing rural America" (*Domestic Individualism*, 105). "Conceived as withdrawn to himself, the individual shares the definitive principle of domesticity: its withdrawal from the marketplace," which itself "signifies what is beyond the individual," being "either the freedom the disenfranchised want, or the disenfranchisement or risk [which] the already entitled individual fears" (*Domestic Individualism*, 105, 7, 59). In this sense, then, Thoreau calls himself "the home-staying, laborious native of the soil," his situation a "country seat," his bean field "the connecting link between the wild and the civilized fields" (Brown, *Domestic Individualism*, 157, 158).

This claim to a domesticated liminal landscape has long interested scholars of Thoreau, but typically in connection with American pastoralism. Thoreau is seen as the "Harvard graduate, heir of a complex urban civilization, who deliberately chooses to recover the natural" (Marx, "Pastoralism," 56). Yet the borderland or, as Leo Marx terms it, the middle landscape can and ought to be redirected to its domestic "home-staying" identity, with such terms as "suburban" and "back yard" working as directional signals that point not only to Vergil's *Eclogues* or Spenser's *Shepheardes Calender* but also to the making of the home. We note Catherine Beecher's suburban design ethos of the borderland in which trees are to be planted in "clumps" rather than straight rows, house paint to be "stone color," portico pillars "made simply of the trunks of small trees . . . with the bark taken off, and their knots projecting a little" (*Treatise*, 291). Thoreau tells us he "shingled the sides of [his] house . . . with imperfect and sappy shingles made of the first slice of the log, whose edges [he] was obliged to straighten with a plane" (*Walden*, 48). These passages are appositional, the "home-staying" Thoreau and the "rural" Beecher advancing an ethos of the dwelling site within a domesticated nature and material or built environment referential to it yet ideologically secure as "a place apart from market conditions and competition," one in which labor would be spiritualized (Brown, *Domestic Individualism*, 106, 109).

Issues of mutuality between *Walden* and the household advice texts, as critics of Thoreau reluctantly admit, include clothing, household equipment, hygiene, health, recreation, privacy, and others too, but this discussion will consider three areas in some detail. These are the dwelling house, the parlor, and housekeeping, starting with an apparently desultory, ephemeral remark in *Walden*, when Thoreau (who describes Concord's dwelling houses arranged "in lanes and fronting one another") rejects time spent earning an income for "a house in the Grecian or the Gothic style" (*Walden*, 168, 70).

This prepositional phrase on architectural styles sounds at first merely like a casual dismissal of the value of popular mid-nineteenth-century Greek Revival and Neo-Gothic architectural fashion. (It is noteworthy that in her *Treatise on Domestic Economy*, Catherine Beecher illustrates the "large and genteel house[s]" with line drawings in Greek-Roman Revival and in Gothic styles [286–87].) In fact, both "Grecian" and "Gothic" styles were deeply involved in issues of American middle-class morality, education, and civil and religious duty. The Grecian or Greek Revival style, popular in the mid-nineteenth century in the Northeast and Midwest, incorporated such elements as Greek and Roman columns, windows, and doors in order to reaffirm "the classical ideals in which Greece and Rome had been built" and thereby to separate the Republican heritage of the United States from Europe (Clark, *American Family Home*, 6–9).

As for a "Gothic style" dwelling, here again, Thoreau's reference is keyed to a contemporary sociopolitical issue, the Christian home movement, begun in the later 1840s, in which architects responded to ministerial calls for what Horace Bushnell titled *Christian Nurture* (1847), wherein a child "breathes the atmosphere of the [Christian] house" (qtd. in Clark, *American Family Home*, 25). As Clifford Clark, Jr., says in his study of American house design, "The result was the conception of the house as a church, an idea that reached its fullest development in the Gothic Revival style" (25). "The pattern-book writers in the 1840s and 1850s," writes Clark, "touted the rural Gothic house as the perfect place for Christian nurture" (25).

Material culture studies enlarge the scope of Thoreau's reference because the apparently casual phrase really positions *Walden* in an adversarial posture over and against a middle-class architectural social vocabulary of Republicanism and Protestant Christianity. *Walden* argues, contrarily, that these value systems, encoded in styles of domestic architecture, are undergirded by a destructive economic system likely to destroy those enmeshed in it. To desire a "Grecian or Gothic" dwelling and commit oneself to its acquisition is thus actually to forfeit one's life to the market economy as it infiltrates domestic life. Republicanism and Christianity become the false consciousness in which one subjects oneself to incessant labor, "always on the limits, trying to get into business and trying to get out of debt," the civic self compromised in a network of "lying, flattery, voting, contracting yourselves into a nutshell of civility," and sycophantism in the courtship of customers (*Walden*, 6–7). This is a state of things in which any time passed in other activities, such as reading, is defined economically as "borrowed or stolen," and Thoreau trumps the Republicanism and the Christian Home movement with this indictment: a dwelling house ostensibly expressive of Republican or Christian values really manifests the most extreme form of enslaving statist and market economy oppression (5, 8, 6, 32). The most interesting dwellings in America are, says Thoreau, the "humble log huts and cottages of the poor," while the "suburban box" of the middle class awaits the enrichment of the inner life to render its architecture "agreeable to the imagination" (47).

Log huts and humble cottages versus Grecian and Gothic houses and the suburban box may sound like a simple binary opposition, the former a lever to discredit the latter, which is to say that the formulation might seem like a Thorovian renunciation of contemporary, domestic, middle-class ways of life. Yet Thoreau's extensive commentary on housing suggests that his effort is reformative rather than renunciative and that *Walden* forwards an ideal of domesticity in its statement on domestic interior design. We are not concerned here with the much-discussed carpentry or acquisition of building materials for the Walden dwelling but of Thoreau's envisioned domestic household and its space. In "House-Warming," he eschews Victorian "gingerbread work" and describes his ideal "dream" house, a "primitive" house, this key word invoked repeatedly in *Walden* to mean essential, utilitarian, simple, and identified with a previous "golden age" marked by "enduring materials" and spatial openness (243–44; cf. 62, 64, 70). Such house "shall consist of only one room" that is "vast, rude, substantial . . . without ceiling or plastering, with bare rafters . . . supporting a sort of lower heaven over one's head" (243). It contains "all the essentials of a house . . . where you can see all the treasures of the house at one view," the single space combining "kitchen, pantry, parlor, chamber, store-house, and garret" (243–44).

Thoreau's open floorplan rejects the spatial subdivision of the Victorian house in which he feels "hospitality is the art of *keeping* you at the greatest distance" and in which the injunction to "make yourself at home" is a hypocritical euphemism for "solitary confinement" (244). *Walden* instead projects a communal, shared space in which the entire dwelling and its occupants are visible and accessible to one another, an ideal of authenticity that was enunciated in Harriet Beecher Stowe's series of "House and Home Papers" in the *Atlantic Monthly* (1864), in which an ideal parlor open to family, friends, and pets on a drop-in basis is dubbed a "library, study, nursery, greenhouse, all combined . . . a sort of log-cabin" (41). (One might say that the *American Woman's Home* advocates a Gothic or Greek Revival exterior with the spiritual essence of the log cabin within; indeed, the interior of Uncle Tom's and Aunt Chloe's cabin had already provided Stowe the opportunity to endorse middle-class material culture as correlative with occupants' self-respect, dignity, kindness, and benevolence [*Uncle Tom's Cabin*, 68].) The Thoreau-Stowe "log-hut" or "log-cabin" ideal would find full statement in John Greenleaf Whittier's nostalgic "Snow-Bound" (1864–1866), a celebration of "simple life and country ways" in which extended family, boarders, guests and pets gather around a central hearth during a winter snowstorm to enjoy "food and shelter, warmth and health, / And love's contentment more than wealth" (*Complete Poetical Works*, 401, 405).

Thoreau's projection, of course, is far less direct than Stowe's and Whittier's, plausibly because his own family life, like Herman Melville's, had been sufficiently difficult that the autobiographical model personally would not serve to authenticate the domestic ideal (see Lebeaux, *Young Man Thoreau*, 29–62). Just as the pod of whales instances roseate family life in *Moby-Dick*, so do *Walden*'s animal families—e.g. the partridges in "Brute Neighbors"—suggest the basis for Thoreau's implied model family eligible for occupancy of his capacious "dream" house. Not surprisingly, the natural world provides the domestic model for both dwelling house and occupants because it is "a house whose inside is as open and manifest as a bird's nest" (*Walden*, 244). ("Manifest" may exploit the embedded pun on maleness in order to insist that the presumptively maternal nest be occupied by a paternal principle too.)

Catherine Beecher, likewise, advised that house design be simple. For economy of labor, she, like Thoreau, warned against "brasses demanding labor" and rejected "filigree ornaments" on "casings and mantelpieces" (*Treatise*, 271). Of a floorplan, she wrote, "*A perfect square* encloses more rooms, at a less expense, than any other shape" (271). Her square differs from Thoreau's rectangle, but both advised a four-sided rectilinear floorplan for the sake of economy. And though Beecher's interior is subdivided into rooms, a series of sliding pocket doors can be opened to enable the mother to "have her parlor, nursery, and kitchen, all under her eye at once" (271, 278).

Thoreau's emphasis on a household economy of sufficiency over and against one of unaffordable extravagance also positions *Walden* in accord with the domestic advice texts, which, like *Walden*, hearken to an American past of frugal self-sufficiency more identified with Benjamin Franklin than the capitalist market economy (Taketani, "Thoreau's Domestic Economy," 66–68). Lydia Maria Child, in *Hints to Persons of Moderate Fortune* (1832), warned that "the prevailing evil of the present day is extravagance. . . . It is too plain that our present expensive habits are productive of much domestic unhappiness. . . . Do not let the beauty of this thing, and the cheapness of that, tempt you to buy unnecessary articles. . . . Buy merely enough to get along with at first. . . . Begin humbly" (qtd. in Nylander, *Our Own Snug Fireside*, 73). Three of Child's novels, as we know, were checked out of the Harvard College library by Thoreau in his student days, and it is a fair assumption that he was familiar with her highly successful *The Frugal Housewife* (1829), retitled *The American Frugal Housewife* (1831), a how-to advisory on the salvaging and reuse of household goods, home manufacture of goods (e.g., soap) available in shops, and "Cheap Common Cooking" (Sattelmeyer, *Thoreau's Reading*, 24, 152). The Thoreau who salvaged his favorite kinds of chairs, to be had for the asking from Concord garrets where they were stored because newer fashion superseded them, is compatible with the Child of *The Frugal Housewife* (*Walden*, 65). It is noteworthy that Child's advice is not gender-specific, that its needs-based criterion of value includes the male provider as well as mistress of the household, that domestic happiness or its opposite is the basis for the advice. The household of Child's "frugal housewife" is to be found in the Thorovian "humble . . . cottage" and is projected from the Walden house to its larger "dream" version.

The architectural example draws us further into Thoreau's stance toward contemporary material culture and its diverse social meanings, and the parlor provides a most useful case study. "Parlor," a word repeatedly invoked in *Walden*, is itself a tremendously pressured term, denoting a range of moral values, as scholarship has revealed. "Architectural advice books published in the middle decades of the nineteenth century reveal that parlors became an important aspect of space and room use planning even in very modest structures" (Grier, *Culture and Comfort*, 65). Calvert Vaux's *Villas and Cottages* (1864) included a parlor "accessible to visitors" in the most modest designs, and houseplan books profliferated from the 1850s, "inexpensive advice books aimed at respectable members of the lower and middle classes" (Clark, *American Family Home*, 40; Grier, *Culture and Comfort*, 65).

A drawing-room or "parlor consciousness" developed in America from the mid-nineteenth century, when a "parlor" was defined as "a room in a private house set apart for the conversational entertainment of guests" (Grier, *Culture and Comfort*, 64). Karen Halttunen notes that "geographically, [the parlor] lay between the urban street where strangers freely mingled and the back regions of the house where only family members were permitted to enter uninvited" and was thus the borderland site of highly ritualized behavior constantly negotiating private and public space (*Confidence Men*, 59–60; 104–23). The parlor was used for a range of activities, from games (parlor games with printed rules) to the laying out of the deceased for visitation. An 1850 *Godey's* article, "New Furniture," itemized the requisite furniture for the contemporary household and listed parlor furnishings, including "sofas and ordinary chairs" with rosewood frames, "covered with satin damask, crimson and black, deeply tufted or knotted" or with "velvet, plush, or haircloth." The "center tables" became "shrines within the ritual space of the parlor, the sites of carefully edited selections of familial possessions," such as family Bibles, other "important" books and calling cards—thus Thoreau's table as graced summerlong with the *Iliad* (Grier, *Culture and Comfort*, 66, 87).

Beecher's *Treatise* devotes an entire chapter "On the Care of Parlors," guided by principles of economy of acquisition and maintenance. This "largest and handsomest room" in use "only when the family are dressed to see company" elicits Beecher's advice on wall finishes (common plaster the cheapest, preferably finished with oil paint "of a light and sober cast"), on curtains and carpets ("Brussels carpets do not wear so long as the three-ply ones"), on mirrors and pictures ("they should be placed so that the lower parts are not above the eye of an observer"), on the selection of mahogany furniture ("mahogany furniture made in Winter is very likely to crack"), and miscellaneous tips (e.g., "a large brick, covered with carpeting, is good to hold doors open" (*Treatise*, 337, 338, 339, 342, 343, 340).

Students of material culture cite the descriptors and names of such objects as those cited above as a "vocabulary" of furnishing, meaning that the objects themselves comprise a language on status, morality, ethics, and gender, a language spoken by the household and understood by its occupants and visitors. The American parlor, accordingly, has been decoded according to its status in the second half of the nineteenth century (Grier, *Culture and Comfort*, 81–102). For the householder, the jeopardy of the parlor was its potential to degenerate into a site of social ambition, excessive gentility, and the triviality and caprice of market-driven fashion—this last, as we noticed, the basis of Thoreau's own complaint. "It would seem," he writes, "as if the very language of our parlors would lose all its nerve and degenerate into *parlaver.* . . . In other words, the parlor is so far from the kitchen and workshop" (*Walden*, 245).

With household production centered in kitchen and workshop, the remote parlor (abetted by Calvert Vaux's designs, which positioned kitchen and parlor at the antipodes of the household) degenerates to the production of conversational trivia, with language itself ennervated. Stowe, moreover, warned that if bachelors and boys were excluded from parlor home life, they would flee the home, and Stowe's critique of the parlor of the 1860s exactly matches Thoreau's—"a museum of elegant and costly gewgaws" (qtd. in Hedrick, 313–14; see Stowe, "House and Home Papers," 40–47).

But the parlor also promised to be what its ideal expressed, a center of family cohesion, moral virtue, social accord, and spiritual devotion. The parlor of Stowe's "House and Home Papers" instances this ideal, being "wide-spread, easy-going, and jolly," a room in which "everybody there was to do just as he or she pleased" and in which "everything was strong and comfortable" ("House and Home Papers," 41). Stowe had so furnished Tom's and Chloe's homey cabin with a "table, somewhat rheumatic in its limbs . . . drawn out in front of the fire, and covered with a cloth" in anticipation of an evening meal, the dining table in the novel collapsed with that of the parlor (*Uncle Tom's Cabin*, 68).

A key term in this formulation is parlor "comfort," explained by Caroline Kirkland, among others, in *A Book for the Home Circle* (1853): "Comfort is one of those significant and precious words that are apt to be much abused. . . . It is so good a word, in its true character, that none but honest people can use it with propriety" (*Home Circle*, 144–61). Thoreau evidently understood this when he admitted that his house was "more comfortable" when plastered and when he located the ideal of shelter in terms of "comfort" in the biblical era of Adam and Eve, when "man wanted a home, a place of warmth, or comfort, first of physical warmth, then the warmth of affections" (*Walden*, 27–28). Beecher cites "*economy of comfort*" in a house made comfortable for domestic workers as well as the family and "company" (*Treatise*, 273, 274). Thoreau fairly boasts of the "twenty-five or thirty souls" occupying his room quite comfortably on occasion, the room functioning as parlor not only then, but also at other times when two or three of his household chairs are occupied for "friendship" or "society" (*Walden*, 140). "Comfort" and its economy are crucial to domesticity. In Kirkland's usage, the term is sacralized, the parlor itself at its best a kind of sacred space.

Readers of *Walden* are probably most familiar with Thoreau's "parlor of the fishes," which he observes through the pond ice in "The Pond in Winter" (*Walden*, 283). Such a scene, in combination with his denunciation of "domestic comforts" and warning that "our lives are domestic in more senses than we think," seems directed at the kind of overscrupulous maintenance manual that Beecher and others compiled for the furnishing and care of the parlor, as if to suggest that this one room both consumes and trivializes the vast human energy expended on its behalf (283, 28). Thoreau's ichthyological reference seems to mock women's ethos of domesticity, to turn it into aquarial spectatorship or voyeurism, miniaturized and sealed in ice.

But only if *Walden* is thought to repudiate the objects of its critique. If *Walden* is analyzed, instead, as a serious counterculturist critique of errant domestic life, one intended not to repudiate but to reform it, then Thoreau's commentary on housekeep-

ing opens itself to a rereading of domestic life framed as an appreciative, if reformist, statement. His critique is prompted by
the ways in which the material arrangements of actual domestic
practices fail manifest spritual ideals. For Thoreau, it is the current praxis of domesticity that is objectionable but subject to remediation. It is useful to review Thoreau's full description of the
fish in their parlor:

> I cut my way first through a foot of snow, and then a foot of
> ice, and open a window under my feet, where, kneeling to
> drink, I look down into the quiet parlor of the fishes, per-
> vaded by a softened light as through a window of ground
> glass, with its bright sanded floor the same as in the summer;
> there a perennial waveless serenity reigns as in the amber twi-
> light sky, corresponding to the cool and even temperament of
> the inhabitants. Heaven is under our feet as well as over our
> heads. (282–83)

This parlor, with its "quiet," its pervasive "softened light" perpetual summer "serenity," and "cool and even temperament
of the inhabitants," models the ideal parlor of the *economy of
comfort.* Beecher provided a chapter on the "Domestic Manners" able to sustain such social "serenity" as Thoreau admires
(Beecher, *Treatise,* 120–34). In context of the parlor literature, this
passage sounds reverentially idealized. It is one of numerous
places in *Walden* in which the natural world provides the exemplum for an appropriate domesticity. The Thorovian parlor is not
cluttered with furniture and protected by blinds and heavy
draperies but furnished with light. It is not the consumerist parlor marketed aggressively by merchants and manufacturers but
the essence of simplicity, comfort, serenity, and the free circulation of lives in social relation—and referential to the Walden
house parlor of his twenty-five or thirty "souls, with their bodies,
at once, under [Thoreau's] roof" (*Walden,* 140).

The parlors of Thoreau's own household and of the pond
model an economy of comfort detached from a market economy,
though Beecher also worried that the excessive outlay for parlors
in "this Country" was one of "the poorer" examples of expense

and of the "economy of comfort." Beecher and Stowe regretted expensive parlors achieved by "money which did not produce either beauty or comfort" (Beecher, *Treatise*, 337; Beecher and Stowe, *American Woman's Home*, 84). The sisters' guidance, scrupulously keyed to a budget as rigorous as Thoreau's (albeit one of $80 rather than his entire house construction and furnishings budget of 28.12^1/_2$), is meant to enable the householder successfully to negotiate the treachery of the market economy to achieve the moral, virtuous, democratic home whose quintessence is the parlor—which is to say, the parlor ideal as Thoreau represents it in the pond, a version of "heaven under our feet," a claim fully consonant with the parlor ideal.

Consider yet another of Thoreau's statements on domesticity:

My "best" room . . . my withdrawing room, always ready for company, on whose carpet the sun rarely fell, was the pine wood behind my house. Thither in summer days, when distinguished guests came, I took them, and a priceless domestic swept the floor and dusted the furniture and kept the things in order. (*Walden*, 141–42)

The passage not only tweaks the householder's anxiety over solar carpet fade but also pointedly critiques a vexed issue in nineteenth-century American middle-class life, namely, the role of domestic servants responsible for household maintenance, dusting and sweeping, and a host of other duties. Their "price" was a sensitive issue in the literature of domesticity. Beecher warned against "making penurious savings by getting the poor to work as cheap as possible" and noted that "many amiable and benevolent women have done this . . . without reflecting on the want of Christian charity thus displayed" (*Treatise*, 181). She suggests that the daughters of the household, "enfeebled" by sedentary habits, be obliged to exercise in daily household tasks requiring "stooping, bending, and change of position," and she notes as well the household monetary savings to "mothers who [otherwise] will hire domestics to take away all these modes of securing to their daughters health, grace, beauty, and domestic virtues" (116–17). (Beecher is silent on the question of depriving

poorer women of the work necessary for their own livelihoods.)
This ideological stance has been noted by Dolores Hayden, who
recognizes Beecher's effort to position housework as a means toward women's power and skill across all class lines (*Grand Domestic Revolution,* 56).

Thoreau's example of the "priceless" domestic, of course,
models a circumvention of the problem of class bias and exploitation of the poor in the "Christian" and "Democratic" home
(Beecher, *Treatise,* 2–14). He simply renders its domestic support
as literally without price, removing it from a wage economy. But
he thereby reverts, once again, to nature as expressive of a domestic ideal propounded by the women's guidebooks. His floor
is swept, his furniture dusted, the "things" in his room kept in or-
derly arrangement, and his designation of a "best . . . withdrawing room" respected. Additionally, Thoreau argues that
kindness to the poor might best be shown by self-employment of
heads of household in the kitchen (*Walden,* 76). He assents to
Beecher's notion that housework can be a "pleasant" pastime and
offers his own guide to simplified cleaning:

> When my floor was dirty, I rose early, and, setting all my fur-
> niture out of doors on the grass, bed and bedstead making
> but one budget, dashed water on the floor, and sprinkled
> white sand from the pond on it, and then with a broom
> scrubbed it clean and white. (*Walden,* 112–113)

The white wood floors, as Jane Nylander explains in her study
of New England households, were those left unfinished, with
sand the favored abrasive cleaning agent into the early nineteenth century. One New Hampshire woman recalled that in
the 1830s, "It was all so very clean, the chairs, table, floor and all
the woodwork was unpainted and was kept white by being
scoured with sand" (Nylander, *Our Own Snug Fireside,* 118–19).
Thoreau's sand scrub implicitly rejects the latter days of carpeting and of paint (the latter surface easier to maintain, according
to Beecher), and his example of housekeeping argues for a simpler domesticity practiced in the recent past, once again up-
holding the ethos of cleanliness. His parlor of the fishes, we re-

call, featured a "bright sanded floor" against the notion of Brussels or three-ply carpets.

The "best withdrawing room" situated outdoors in a pine grove also calls readers to the scene of Thoreau's housekeeping, when his furniture is moved outdoors while Thoreau scrubs his floor. Enjoying the sight of sunshine on his "three-legged table" with its books, pen, and ink, and a bird on the next bough, he muses on the defamiliarized pleasures of these objects in the outdoors, then notes the blackberry vines running round the table legs and the ambient strewing of pine cones, chestnut burrs, and strawberry leaves (*Walden*, 113). "It looked as if this was the way these forms came to be transferred to our furniture, to tables, chairs, and bedsteads,—because they once stood in their midst" (113).

Readers of *American Woman's Home* will note a kind of indoors-outdoors cross-referencing of scenes of nature and artifice, when the mistress of the house is advised to bring the outdoors indoors to furnish the rooms. The house whose occupants lack money need never be "condemned" to bareness nor its mistress feel like a "disinherited child of nature . . . so long as the woods are full of beautiful ferns and mosses, while every swamp shakes with tremulous grasses" (*American Woman's Home*, 94). *Walden* recalls the "bower" shelter that preceded bodily clothing, and the Beecher sisters promote a naturalism in home decor, including wall-mounted hanging baskets of ferns and swamp grasses, their containers covered with bark, pine cones, and moss (95). "Rustic frames" made of hard, seasoned branches and garnished with acorn clusters, or frames cut to resemble "a rough break" in the wood contribute to "an effect of grace and beauty" exceeding that of "expensive cabinet furniture" (91–93). Entire windows can become floral bowers, vegetable cuttings sprouted into indoor plants, and entwined roots varnished to serve as flower stands. Stowe depicted an ideal "great, large, airy parlor" that "seemed a trap to catch the sunbeams" and in whose "bow-window were canaries always singing, and a great stand of plants always fresh and blooming, and ivy which grew and clambered and twined about the pictures" ("House and Home Papers," 41, 42). Beecher and Stowe advise that such an outdoors atmosphere

requires "no investment . . . than a hammer and an assortment of tacks, and beautiful results will be produced" (*American
Women's Home*, 96–99).

Thoreau would doubtless comment with acerbity on all of
this, urging those concerned simply to go outdoors and spare
themselves the foolish task of tacking branches into frames and
varnishing roots. Thoreau scorns as unnecessary many of the domestic practices Beecher and Stowe demystify for a readership
whose size he would have envied. A hypothetical exchange between the two parties might well include a Stowe-Beecher retort
that Thoreau shuttled between his Concord family home and his
cabin home, the latter a dwelling for just two years, its occupant
alone and the structure itself empty much of the time.

And one can readily identify domestic issues on which *Walden*
disagrees with the Beechers and Child and all other domestic advice texts—on the felicity of curtains, on partitioned rooms, on
various cleaning compounds and the very lubricant of social conversation. The opposition, however, has been long presumed, the
points of convergence largely unacknowledged or rejected.[4] It is
well to bear in mind Gillian Brown's statement: "The fact that
domestic ideology helps form cultural coherence does not mean
that it represents a monolithic design. . . . No single system
emerges in the operations of the domestic" (*Domestic Individualism*, 8–9). The Beechers, accordingly, revert in their household
advice books to principles of Protestant Christianity while
Thoreau looks to domestic paradigmatic nature in and around
the pond and hearkens to housekeeping practices waning or vanished from the Concord of his era. Thoreau's *sine qua non* is seasonal comfort, Beecher's and Beecher-Stowe's an atmosphere of
Christian benevolence.

It must be acknowledged, however, that despite their collective efforts to posit a world separate from that of the market
economy, that world nonetheless makes its incursions into *Walden*, into *The Frugal Housewife*, into *A Treatise on Domestic Economy*
and the *American Woman's Home*. The very adoption of the account book for domestic purposes, both in Child and in Thoreau,
brings mercantile practices into the realm from which both at-
tempted to exclude them. Precise knowledge of the degree of

Thoreau's household frugality is blocked by the "lack of access to the mercantile code that regulated prices and commodity in 1840's Concord," but Thoreau's mercantile mentality is evinced in the presentation of outlays for food in a business ledger entry identical in format to that for the construction of the Walden house (Taketani, "Thoreau's Domestic Economy," 68; *Walden*, 59, 49). Beecher's very rubric of "domestic economy," moreover, parallels Thoreau's credentialing of himself as "real-estate broker" and land speculator, all such terms seeking legitimation in terms of the market-economy that both writers sought to repudiate (*Walden*, 81, 82).

Issues of production and consumption in the new era of relentless machine-manufactured "superfluities" also appear in the literature of domesticity. Beecher grasped the extent to which American economic livelihoods were enmeshed in and dependent on the acquisition and retention of products "not absolutely necessary to life and health," and she advised readers that consumerism must be regarded as a form of philanthropy: "the use of superfluities . . . is . . . indispensable to promote industry, virtue, and religion" (*Treatise*, 161).

Walden repeatedly rejects such consumption as impoverishment but nonetheless celebrates nature's "economy of extravagance," which valorizes unbounded production in terms of nature's propagation. Citing the natural world, once again, as exemplary, Thoreau idealizes nature's and primitive man's riddance of superfluities via the *natural* destruction (fire, predation) that eliminates problems of consumption capacity, and it has been noted that this ethos is informed by "the capitalist ideology of antebellum America" (Grusin, "Thoreau, Extravagance," 45, 47).

Framed by the natural world and Protestant Christianity, respectively, all these texts nonetheless mutually honor and reinforce ideals of domesticity. Just as the Beecher and Stowe *American Woman's Home* maneuvers a gender reversal from the New Testament to state that "every girl should be trained to be a 'wise woman' that 'buildeth her house' aright" (Matt. 7:24), so is *Walden* arguably a manual for the siting, construction and maintenance of a morally principled house and household (Beecher and Stowe, *American Woman's Home,* 430). Beecher's *Treatise* exalted domesticity in millennial terms as the "building of a glorious temple, whose base shall be coextensive with the bounds of the earth, . . . whose splendor shall beam on all lands, . . . with new rejoicings of the morning stars" (*Treatise,* 14). *Walden's* ecstatic conclusion that "the sun is but a morning star" is premised on Thoreau's equally grandiose "brag for humanity" that his "house had its site in such a . . . forever new and unprofaned, part of the universe" [*sic*] (*Walden,* 333, 49, 88). His bragging rights are based in great part on *Walden's* investment in domesticity.

NOTES

1. Tompkins, *Sensational Designs* (1985), for instance, employs a counterculturalist ethos to argue that the popular domestic novel presents "a critique of American society far more devastating than any offered by better-known critics such as Hawthorne and Melville" (and surely Thoreau) (124, 144). David Leverenz, in *Manhood in the American Renaissance* (1989), working within a similar kind of argumentive framework, locates the valorized countercultural "alienated imagination" in the roster of the male writers, including Emerson, Melville, Hawthorne—and Thoreau—in juxtaposed opposition to the domestically mainstream women writers valorized in *Sensational Designs* (172). In vigorous disagreement, both critics nonetheless participate in the same post-60s project of canon reformation, both operating within the culture versus counterculture model.

2. See Nicholas K. Bromell, *By the Sweat of the Brow: Literature and Labor in Antebellum America* (1993); Michael T. Gilmore, *American Romanticism and the Marketplace* (1985); and Robert A. Gross, "Culture and Cultivation: Agriculture and Society in Thoreau's Concord" (1982; reprint 1988).

3. Recent such studies include Lawrence Buell, *The Environmental Imagination: Thoreau, Nature Writing, and the Formation of American Culture* (1995); Roderick Frazier Nash, *The Rights of Nature: A History of Environmental Ethics* (1989); and Laura Dassow Walls, *Seeing New Worlds: Henry David Thoreau and Nineteenth-Century Natural Science* (1995).

4. At the turn of the twenty-first century, Thoreau's housekeeping principles "near the bone" (329) can be termed minimalist and seen as objectified in the nineteenth century in the functional and largely rectilinear Shaker furniture collected and displayed by art museums in the twentieth century, just as the Beecher-Stowe interior naturalism would be considered to be codified in the Arts and Crafts movement, whose productions have also been bought for display in major museums—with reproductions of both styles available commerically for home consumption. Both traditions, it must be recalled, address the terms of American domestic life and, much to the point here, both operate conjunctively to affirm it

REFERENCES

Baym, Nina. *Feminism and American Literary History: Essays*. New Brunswick, N.J.: Rutgers University Press, 1992.

Beecher, Catherine. *A Treatise on Domestic Economy*. 1841. Reprint. New York: Source Book Press, 1970.

Beecher, Catherine, and Harriet Beecher Stowe. *An American Woman's Home*. 1869. Reprint, Hartford, Conn.: Harriet Beecher Stowe Center, 1975.

Bromell, Nicholas K. *By the Sweat of the Brow: Literature and Labor in Antebellum America*. Chicago: University of Chicago Press, 1993.

Brown, Gillian. *Domestic Individualism: Imagining Self in Nineteenth-Century America*. Berkeley: University of California Press, 1990.

Buell, Lawrence. *The Environmental Imagination: Thoreau, Nature Writing, and the Formation of American Culture*. Cambridge: Harvard Univeresity Press, 1995.

Child, Lydia Maria. *The Frugal Housewife*. Boston: Marsh & Capen, and Carter & Hendee, 1829.

Clark, Clifford, Jr. *The American Family Home, 1800–1960*. Chapel Hill: University of North Carolina Press, 1986.

Fisher, Philip. *Hard Facts: Setting and Form in the American Novel*. New York: Oxford University Press, 1985.

Gilmore, Michael T. *American Romanticism and the Marketplace*. Chicago: University of Chicago Press, 1985.

Glassie, Henry. "Meaningful Things and Appropriate Myths: The

Artifact's Place in American Studies." In *Material Life in America, 1600–1860,* edited by Robert Blair St. George, 63–94. Boston: Northeastern University Press, 1988.

Gleason, William. "Re-Creating Walden: Thoreau's Economy of Work and Play." *American Literature* 65, no. 4 (December 1993): 673–701.

Grier, Katherine. *Culture and Comfort: People, Parlors, and Upholstery, 1850–1930.* Rochester, N.Y.: Strong Museum. Distributed by the University of Massachusetts Press, 1988.

Gross, Robert A. "Culture and Cultivation: Agriculture and Society in Thoreau's Concord." In *Material Life in America, 1600–1860,* edited by Robert Blair St. George, 519–34. Boston: Northeastern University Press, 1988.

Grusin, Richard. "Thoreau, Extravagance, and the Economy of Nature." *American Literary History* 5, no. 1 (Spring 1993): 30–50.

Halttunen, Karen. *Confidence Men and Painted Women: A Study of Middle-Class Culture in America, 1830–1870.* New Haven: Yale University Press, 1982.

Harding, Walter. *The Days of Henry Thoreau.* New York: Knopf, 1970.

Hawthorne, Nathaniel. *Letters, 1853–1856.* Vol. 17 of the Centenary Edition of the Works of Nathaniel Hawthorne. Edited by Thomas Woodson. Columbus: Ohio State University Press, 1987.

Hayden, Dolores. *The Grand Domestic Revolution: A History of Feminist Designs for American Homes, Neighborhoods, and Cities.* Cambridge: MIT Press, 1981.

Hedrick, Joan D. *Harriet Beecher Stowe: A Life.* New York: Oxford University Press, 1994.

Johnson, Linck. "Revolution and Renewal: The Genres of *Walden.*" In *Critical Essays on Henry David Thoreau's "Walden,"* edited by Joel Myerson, 215–35. Boston: Hall, 1988.

Kirkland, C[aroline] M. *A Book for the Home Circle.* New York: Scribner, 1853.

Lebeaux, Richard. *Young Man Thoreau.* Amherst: University of Massachusetts Press, 1977.

Leverenz, David. *Manhood in the American Renaissance.* Ithaca, N.Y.: Cornell University Press, 1989.

Marx, Leo. "Pastoralism in America." In *Ideology and Classic American Literature,* edited by Sacvan Bercovitch and Myra Jehlen 36–69. Cambridge: Cambridge University Press, 1986.

Matthiessen, F. O. *American Renaissance: Art and Expression in the Age of Emerson and Whitman.* 1941. Reprint, New York: Oxford University Press, 1968.

Mintz, Stephen L. *Moralists and Modernizers: America's Pre–Civil War Reformers.* Baltimore: Johns Hopkins University Press, 1995.

Nash, Roderick Frazier. *The Rights of Nature: A History of Environmental Ethics.* Madison: University of Wisconsin Press, 1989.

Nylander, Jane C. *Our Own Snug Fireside: Images of the New England Home, 1760–1860.* 1993. Reprint, New Haven: Yale University Press, 1994.

Pease, Donald. *Visionary Compacts: American Renaissance Writings in Cultural Context.* Madison: University of Wisconsin Press, 1987.

Romero, Lora. *Home Fronts: Domesticity and Its Critics in the Antebellum United States.* Durham: Duke University Press, 1997.

Sattelmeyer, Robert. *Thoreau's Reading: A Study in Intellectual History, with Bibliographical Catalogue.* Princeton: Princeton University Press, 1988.

Stilgoe, John. *Borderland: Origins of the American Suburb.* New Haven: Yale University Press, 1988.

Stowe, Harriet Beecher. "House and Home Papers." *Atlantic Monthly* 13 (January 1864): 40–47.

———. *Uncle Tom's Cabin, or, Life among the Lowly.* 1852. Reprint, New York: Penguin, 1981.

Taketani, Etsuko. "Thoreau's Domestic Economy: Double Accounts in *Walden.*" *Concord Saunterer* 2, no. 1 (Fall 1994): 65–76.

Thoreau, Henry David. *Walden.* 1854. Reprint, edited by J. Lyndon Shanley, Princeton: Princeton University Press, 1971.

Tichi, Cecelia. *New World, New Earth: Environmental Reform in American Literature from the Puritans through Whitman.* New Haven: Yale University Press, 1979.

Tompkins, Jane. *Sensational Designs: The Cultural Work of American Fiction, 1790–1860.* New York: Oxford University Press, 1985.

Walls, Laura Dassow. *Seeing New Worlds: Henry David Thoreau and Nineteenth-Century Natural Science.* Madison: University of Wisconsin Press, 1995.

Welter, Barbara. "The Cult of True Womanhood." In *History of Women in the United States,* vol. 4; *Domestic Ideology and Domestic Work;* pt. 1, edited by Nancy Cott, 48–89. Munich: Saur, 1992.

Whittier, John Greenleaf. *Whittier's Complete Poetical Works.* Cambridge: Houghton Mifflin, 1894.

Romancing the Real

Thoreau's Technology of Inscription

Laura Dassow Walls

> That a delicate shuttle should have
> woven together the heavens, industry,
> texts, souls and moral law—this re-
> mains uncanny, unthinkable, unseemly.
> . . . Is it our fault if the networks are
> simultaneously real, like nature, nar-
> rated, like discourse, and collective,
> like society?
>
> Bruno Latour
> *We Have Never Been Modern*

Thoreau in our day would never be recognized as a "scien-tist"—indeed, use of the term would be anachronistic. Trou-bled by the lack of a word that might unify all the various work-ers in the physical and natural sciences, William Whewell, the British polymath of science, coined it in 1834 by analogy with "artist." The novel term caught on only slowly, however, and would not come into popular usage until much later in the cen-tury. So Thoreau wrote instead of "the man of science," and in his early journal entries he envisions the "true man of science" as brave and vital, with "a deeper and finer experience" and possessed of "a more perfect Indian wisdom" ("Natural History," 29)—someone who could unite earth and heaven under one higher law.

Thoreau's own search for a foundation to ground that vision led him to read widely and intently throughout his lifetime in natural philosophy and science. More particularly, his personal quest for an effective way to braid together the physical facts of the natural world and the truths of transcendental "higher law" moved toward a working solution around 1850, when he began to immerse himself in the writings of explorer-naturalists such as the German Alexander von Humboldt and England's Charles Darwin. Humboldt, who was hailed in Thoreau's day as the very symbol of science itself, had earned his fame as the first scientific explorer of South America. His dozens of books and his active patronage of promising young men of science made him central to the work and careers of many who followed, including Darwin, who was inspired by Humboldt to take up natural history and to make his own voyage to South America on the *Beagle*. There Darwin first gained the insights that led many years later to the landmark publication of *The Origin of Species* (1859). Humboldt had demonstrated how acute and detailed observations of nature in the field could lead to wider patterns of meaning, laying the groundwork not only for Darwin's theory of evolution but also for the science of ecology. Works by Humboldt, Darwin, and their colleagues gave Thoreau a series of contemporary models for brave explorations in his own woods and fields: he would become a scientific seer, walking, recording, measuring, and weaving the details of nature into meaning.[1]

Throughout the years that he was writing and revising *Walden* (1854), Thoreau worked and wedged his way deeper into the details of observed natural fact, further strengthening the foundations for his transcendental flights. Yet this working and wedging was a slow, cumulative process that in itself created new difficulties: Thoreau had no wish to serve science. Rather, he wished to make science serve his own design. Yet how could he appropriate the tools and techniques of natural science without ceding to them the authority of his own self-voiced poetic vision? Science asks nature to speak, to inscribe or write itself, through the transparent agency of the scientist; but Thoreau had to learn how, instead, to be a weaver who caught up the threads of a complex network and braided them into a discourse that would bespeak nature and humanity together. In this process, the delicate shuttle of the journal—once the mere intermediary between experience and text—became itself a work of importance, and *Walden* emerged from it as the consummate product of his weaver's craft, Thoreau's "basket of a delicate texture" (*Walden*, 18).

In the spring of 1850 Thoreau was on the verge of his turn toward a detailed, "scientific" approach to writing nature. Up to that point, his journal had been a combination of workshop and storage shed; by 1851 it had assumed a new scope and seriousness. Undated fragments gave way to daily, dated entries. Rather than cannibalizing and shredding his journal while drafting his finished works, Thoreau began to preserve it intact. It would always be his writer's workshop, but it was also becoming a work in its own right, a self-conscious creation. The time and labor it demanded—days and weeks, eventually years, spent walking and writing about walking—are difficult to imagine; just reading Thoreau's journal in its entirety can mark an epoch in one's life. Why did Thoreau invest so very much time in a work that would have, as he commented wryly in *Walden*, "no very wide circulation" (18)?

One particular passage from this period suggests both the problem Thoreau faced as a writer, and the solution his journal could offer: How to bridge the gap between self and nature? His answer: Throw oneself bodily into the gap and fill it with a machine of one's own making. Sometime in April 1850, in a remarkable passage that has received little critical attention, Thoreau drafted a long and intricate account of a three-way encounter between himself, a meltwater runoff stream in Nut Meadow, and a toy water wheel. His language in this passage is fitful, searching, tentative, and intense, as he wrestles with the meaning of this experience. Ultimately, Thoreau translates his chance discovery of the water wheel, a boy's playful invention, into the beginning of his own adult and necessary invention, his technology of inscription: a journal by which he would braid together self and nature through language, educing nature into discourse.

Thoreau opens this passage with a generalized summary:

> I sometimes discovered a miniature water wheel—a saw or
> grist mill—where the whole volume of water in some tiny rill
> was conducted through a junk bottle in at the open bottom &
> out at the nose—where some county boy whose house was
> not easy to be seen—some arkwright or Rennie was making
> his first essay in mechanics—some little trip hammer in opera-
> tion mimicking the regular din of a factory—

In this timeless, universalized narrative ("I *sometimes* discovered
. . .") the boy, imagined as "some arkwright or Rennie,"[2] is
reenacting the dawn of the Industrial Revolution, an event of the
deep past to which ahistorical nature still connects us: the weeds
and huckleberry bushes overhang the tiny rill "unmolested . . .
as the pines still do at Manchester and Lawrence." The boy is
translated to mythic status: "It was the work of a fabulous,
farmer boy such as I never saw." He then vanishes back into the
primal wilderness: "To come upon such unquestionable traces of
a boy when I doubted if any were lingering still in this vicinity, as
when you discover the trail of an otter" (*Journal*, 3:49)[3]

Following this rehearsal of his major theme—the origin of industry as the dawn of civilization—Thoreau starts over, this time
giving a long narrative of his own highly particularized act of
discovery:

> One Sunday afternoon in march when the earth which had
> once been bared was again covered with a few inches of snow
> rapidly melting in the sun, as I was walking in a retired cross
> road away from the town, at a distance from any farm
> house—I heard suddenly wafted over the meadow a faint tink-
> tink, tink-tink, as of a cow bell amidst the birches & huckle
> berry bushes.

Since the season is too early for cows to be turned out to pasture,
the mystery grows:

> Well still the sound came over the meadow louder & louder as
> I walked on—tink tink tink too regular for a cowbell—and I

conjectured that it was a man drilling a hole in a rock . . .
but it was Sunday & what Concord farmer could be drilling
stone!

Perhaps, Thoreau thinks, the sound is produced by an owl, or
some other bird? But as he advances upon it, it seems to "sink
into the earth," putting him in mind of muskrats, minks, and
otters. Expecting to make a discovery in natural history, he steps

> eagerly over the quaking ground—a peeping hyla & there in a
> little rill not more than a foot wide but as deep as wide swolen
> by the melting snows was a small water mill and at each revo-
> lution the wheel its crank raised a small hammer which as
> often fell on a tongueless cowbell which was nailed down on a
> board—. . . . The little rill itself seemed delighted with the
> din & rushed over the miniature dam & fell on the water
> wheel eagerly as if delighted at & proud of this loud tinkling.
> (*Journal*, 3:50–51)

The incident is only apparently over. The sound continues to
haunt him. One day a fortnight later, after a new snow had fallen,
Thoreau hears it again,

> & what is stranger than all that very evening when I came
> home from a neighbors through the village far in the night—
> to my astonishment I heard from far over the medows toward
> the woods more than a mile off in a direct line the distinct tink
> tink tink of trip hammer—And I called the family to the win-
> dow in the village to hear the sound of the boys trip hammer
> in nut meadow brook—a distant & solitary place which most
> of them had never seen—& they all heard it distinctly even
> some old ears which ordinarily could not hear the birds sing—
> and were greatly astonished—which I had told them of a fort-
> night before as of a thing far away. (*Journal*, 3:51)

Thoreau tries to identify the precise quality of the marvel:
"There was the still spring night—the slumbering village & for
all sound the boy's water wheel," coming to the village from a
"remoteness as of antiquity." Time stretches out before him:

It sounded like a sentence of Herodotus—It was an incident worthy to be recorded by the father of History—away in nut meadow—by Jenny Dugan's—beyond the Jimmy Miles place—as if it were an alto singer among the bitterns. some ardea It was news a wind from Scythia It was the dream or reminiscence of a primitive age coming over the modern life.

He speculates that the flooding of the meadows somehow intensified the sound, or, drawing on Alexander von Humboldt's observations of the Orinoco River, that the night atmosphere somehow helped carry it farther. Science enhanced the myth, suggesting that the boy had the forces of nature on his side: "It seemed," Thoreau comments, "that nature sympathised with his experiments." Yet in the broad daylight of the next day the sound could be heard no more "than the domestic sounds of the early ages You could not hear it—you could not remember it. and yet the fit ear could hear it ever—the ear of the boy who made it." The passage trails off with one final attempt to sound the event's meaning: "& I could not believe that it still agitated with its waves of sound the atmosphere of the village—that it was still echoing thro' the streets" (*Journal*, 3:52–53). And at last Thoreau moves on. He never made use of the incident or this passage in his published writing.

Yet to the reader who knows what will follow, this passage has the premonitory feel of a dawn or originary moment. Before recorded history the stream flows in the meadow, untouched and unremarked. The dawn of historical time is that instant when two distinct human actions coincide with the stream's preexisting flow: first, a fabulous youth emerges from the woods to build a machine, separating human purpose from the nature of otters and muskrat, yet hinging them together through work—work that is play, even artistry, for it intercepts the power of water and translates it into an elemental music. But without record, there is still no event, no history: so the "father of history" himself, Herodotus/Thoreau, strikes out from the town to intercept the power of the event and translate it into language. Only now could others hear the boy's machine, when an astonished Thoreau called them to their windows to listen; and after, none can hear it at all but those who have a "fit ear"—the boy who first made it in nature, the boy-man who remade it in language.

In effect, Thoreau completes a series of articulations. First, the stream speaks in its own voice, articulating itself alone; then, the child interrupts the stream to educe—*educen*, "to direct the flow of"—a second stream of sound, the regular "tink tink tink" that articulates the presence of both the stream and now the boy as well; yet a third is needed, Thoreau the father of history, to interrupt again and educe a third stream of sound, language, writing, the stream of words that will articulate stream and boy and Thoreau, all three: "The world being thus put under the mind for verb and noun, the poet is he who can articulate it," said Emerson (*Collected Works*, 3:12). In the course of weeks the first two streams vanish, but the third flows for another twelve years, setting off myriads of new articulations that still circulate today. For "articulation" both joins and separates: joins or couples the three into an "articulated" structure with jointed, moving parts; and separates each element from the others, dividing them into distinct streams that each nevertheless continue, to those with "fit ears," to articulate, or bespeak, or educe them all—nature, society, discourse.

This kind of articulated structure creates some puzzles that Thoreau solved less easily than the mystery of the source of the "tink tink" call. Was or was not this joining "natural"? Exactly who was entitled to claim authorship here, originary nature or man the interpreter? At first, Thoreau claims himself as sole author in a process wholly natural. As the sound seemed to well up out of the very earth itself, arising from minks or muskrats, Thoreau envisioned his own speech as welling up out of the earth without mediation. In a memorable passage composed some months later, he wrote as if he could actually *be* the stream: "Often I feel that my head stands out too dry—when it should be immersed. A writer a man writing is the scribe of all nature—he is the corn & the grass & the atmosphere writing" (*Journal*, 4:28).

However, such a "scribe" would be not a primal creator but a secondary scrivener, conducting perfect copy from source to destination, nature to society. Thoreau here conceives himself as a transparent or invisible mediary, a hollow channel, or a passive instrument through which nature writes itself: he has neither built nor recorded the water wheel, he *is* the water wheel, through which the stream speaks. Two traditions are evoked here, only apparent opposites. The first is the romantic poet, instrument of the wind like Coleridge's Aeolian Harp, or like Emerson's Poet, who can transcribe the "primal warblings" already written "before time was"; whose "expression, or naming, is not art, but a second nature, grown out of the first, as a leaf out of a tree" (Emerson, *Collected Works*, 3:5-6, 13). Yet Emerson's Poet, who is nature bespeaking itself, is also the classical scientist, who vanishes egoless before nature's truth as it writes itself through him. As a current analyst of science writing recently has said, "The scientist who writes is a person, and the world writes through the person, and the writing is the instrument of the world" (Locke, *Science as Writing*, 134).

Either way, as poet or as scientist, in this ideal the writer transcribes words dictated by a transcendent nature. In Thoreau's day, this literary trope was taking material shape in the nineteenth century's latest scientific technology: the kymograph, invented by the natural philosopher and linguist Sir Thomas Young in 1807, and most famously adapted by the German physiologist Carl Ludwig in 1847 in order to measure blood pressure. Ludwig first attached a column of mercury to a human artery, then placed on it "a rod-like float" attached to a stylus "which registers continuously on the smooth surface over which it glides with the movement of the float. . . . The stylus writes on a sheet of smooth vellum paper, tightly fixed to a copper cylinder which turns with a constant speed by a clock mechanism, pulled by a weight, the speed of which is regulated by a rotating pendulum" (qtd. in Talbott, *Biographical History*, 610). Ludwig's invention transformed the study of physiology by transferring methods used in the physical sciences to the human body (Talbott, *Biographical History*, 610).[4] There seemed no limit to the usefulness of this self-registering measurement device in which a sensitive needle inscribed onto a rotating drum whatever was being measured—temperature, humidity, the quiver of an earthquake, the pulse of a heart, timbre of a voice, electrical activity of the brain. All alike became self-registering through the agency of the machine that coupled quantity and time, producing a stream of inscription translated by the scientist into data, into meaning. Thoreau calibrated his final journal entry to honor this figure: after a violent southeasterly storm, each pebble on the surface of the railroad causeway fronts a northwesterly ridge of sand that it has protected from being washed away,

> . . . and on all sides are these ridges, half an inch apart and perfectly parallel.
> All this is perfectly distinct to an observant eye, and yet could easily pass unnoticed by most. Thus each wind is self-registering. (*Journal*, XIV:346)

Indeed, all things in nature are self-registering, leaving inscriptions in their wake as signs to those few who know how to notice and read them; nature writes herself and the world's body is her text. The inscriptions of Thoreau's pen were the writings of the wind at one remove. The entirety of the journal, which he closed during his final illness with these carefully chosen words, would be the world itself self-registered through his acutely sensitive pen.

It is important to realize that these two figures, the literary writer who disappears into nature and the scientific machine through which nature writes itself, arose together as a complementary pair in scientific and literary culture during the early 1800s. As Simon Schaffer details, it was then no longer credible to claim the self as a privileged site of truth—or more specifically, the gentlemanly self thought capable of rising above partiality or individual bias to universal truth. One cannot conscientiously rise above the very world that one's own mind is in the midst of constructing. Thus the romantic genius is marked not by classical discriminating self-consciousness but, as Coleridge argued in the *Biographia Literaria*, by unself-consciousness—allowing truth, the "divine ventriloquist," to speak through the self (1:164). Truth is arrived at by destroying the personal self, and, as Schaffer says, "the management of nature and of the body would be guaranteed by the *disembodiment* of the intellectual." The new scientific disciplines sought to replace humans with machines: "Self-registration became a key goal for modern instrumental design."

Schaffer concludes: "These two formations, self-registrative technology and disembodied genius, may seem completely antagonistic. Yet they were produced together," suggesting an "intimate relationship between the trust placed in the evidence of self-registering scientific instrumentation and the moral authority of the scientific intellectual" ("Self Evidence," 361–62).

In effect, Thoreau, like Coleridge and Emerson, sought to borrow this structure of invisible authority, which displaces the creative power of the individual mind to the transcendent mind of nature. Yet this figure of the author as silent and transparent mediator conflicts with that other Thoreau, the cranky, voiced, opaque personality who revels in interrupting the smooth flow of narrative discourse to remind us that it is no ventriloquist but *he* who speaks, that the hand and mind inscribing nature are not universal and infinitely translatable, moving indifferently through storm or flesh, but possessions of one man, situated in time and place and proud of it, too. The articulations of nature, society, and discourse are hardly natural: they are the most elaborate of Rube Goldberg inventions, like this one, where a seasonal stream, an anonymous boy, and a peripatetic gentleman from the village are joined into a single improbable contraption. The point about the water wheel was hardly its invisibility or its silence: it was conspicuous and noisy, invasive, a *machine* after all—even the "Ur-Machine" itself, which Thoreau imagined standing at the fountainhead of that other stream of industrial progress.

Thoreau in this period is struggling to invent his own kind of machine, a new technology of inscription—what became, in fact, his journal. Behind those silent words and sketches was a man—a professional maker of pencils, no less—fiddling with the business and clutter of wood and graphite, pencils and notebooks, inkstands and pen nibs, well aware that words were also artifacts that intercepted the light, capable of absorbing or diffracting it but never of vanishing into it. Thoreau may have longed to travel back to invisibility, to be that nameless vanished boy who still belonged to nature like a mink or an otter, and so could unselfconsciously allow nature (including *his* nature) to bespeak itself through him. Yet the only way back is to die quite out of the life so irritatingly cluttered with pencils and papers.

Yet even knowing full well that he cannot leave all paraphernalia of culture behind and still be human, Thoreau nevertheless imagines himself able to do just that:

> Methinks that for a great part of the time—as much as it is possible I walk as one possessing the advantages of human Culture—fresh from society of men—but turned loose into the woods the only man in nature—walking & meditating to a great extent as if man & his customs & institutions was not.— The catbird or the jay is sure of the whole of your ear now— each noise is like a stain on pure glass. (*Journal*, 4:24)

In this passage, written two days before he wished he could be the "scribe of all nature," Thoreau is transparent as a glass window that the opaque world stains with its colors—a lovely image that of course comes to us as white paper stained with black ink. In the familiar dilemma, pure nature cannot interact with pure humanity. When defined as mutually exclusive, they rush away from each other, abandoning Thoreau like a latter-day Adam who wanders the woods "the only man in nature"—our lonely emissary, the sole point of contact where either world can be articulated by and to the other.

Yet the instrument itself belies this fiction. Whether it be the mind that thinks the artifact "glass" or the hand that inscribes graphite marks onto pressed wood pulp with a cedar stick, both mind and hand are irredeemably hybrid, half-bred offspring of the technology that "married" nature and culture. Nor is this marriage seamless: the seam or joint is visible at every point where the human interrupts the natural, creating turbulence in the water to borrow its power, in the air to create a noise. Thoreau connects the noise to knowledge through his act of discovery and publication, for like the self-registering winds of his final journal entry, none of this is significant *until someone makes it so* by observation and translation. That is, to observe is to make something that was *invisible*, *visible*, or significant and meaningful, by assigning it to a system. Rendering visible through observation thus requires an act of turning, educing, or "fashioning" it into a "fact" (from *facere*, to do), which Thoreau can then further

translate into a truth. Even the needle of the self-registering instrument doesn't actually "transcribe" anything: it translates one
kind of movement to another, inscribing marks with pen or pencil that the scientist must, in a demanding series of actions, fashion into an inscription of truth.

Thus for all Thoreau might wish to transmit nature directly,
he has no choice but to refract it into writing, turning nature into
an instrument to his desire. Yet he does still have the choice of
either erasing all the traces left by this local, partial, and arduous
process, letting only the final inscription of truth remain; or of
acknowledging the traces, letting his tracks show. *Walden* does
the former. Its clean and perfected text barricades itself from the
process of inscription rather as Walden Pond is "Walled-in" by
the surrounding topography (*Walden,* 183), speaking in crystal
purity what the bubbling stream of the journal text mutters in
fragments and patches. The journal does the latter. It is messy as
a forest floor, lines crossing and crisscrossing, interfering with
each other, dead-ending, tangling the clarity that truth commands. In effect, his experimental water wheel entry attempts
both approaches, speaking first from on high with the achieved,
eternal, and seamless truth, then backtracking to a specific narrative of that truth's invention, with all its messiness and false
starts. What got Thoreau into all this trouble in the first place
was his desire to close the gap between self and nature, to
"unsee" it, not by transcendence but by throwing himself bodily
into it—ironically entangling him in this network of technology
of discovery and inscription that takes up so much space that it
seems to open the gap all the wider, pushing the two sides farther apart.[5]

One modern way out of this dilemma would be to mystify
the hybrid tangle of woods and man, pencils and hands and
paper, otters and farmer's sons and Herodotus and meadow
brooks and Manchester factories and words and water wheels,
back into the originary dualism of raw Nature and civil Culture;
to whisk the whole clumsy apparatus away such that nature once
again supplies raw matter for the tropes and steam engines that
power the American cultural economy: nature as endless natural
resource to culture's insatiable appetite. In this heroic mode, the

Adamic bareknuckled Thoreau went to the woods to wrestle the raw power of nature into the finished product of textual culture. Yet it was just this modern version of the relationship that Thoreau was seeking to counter when he imagined himself instead as nature's transparent and non-invasive scribe, seducing nature through love rather than wrestling her into submission through force—even if this figure only disguised and deferred the difficulties rather than solving them.

So, for instance, he displaces his unease with the mystified figure of artist-as-scribe into anger at the scientist-as-scribe, for it was in the figure of the scientist that he witnessed the self-effacing invisible author at his most potent: at the very inception of modern science and technology (in a saying endlessly invoked in the nineteenth century), Bacon had proclaimed that "the chain of causes cannot by any force be loosed or broken, nor can nature be commanded except by being obeyed. And so, those twin objects, human Knowledge and human Power, do really meet in one." ("The Great Instauration," 53). The great lesson that the power of command lay through obedience was rehearsed by the farmer boy who learned in play that obedience to the water's flow captured the water's power. Thoreau accuses the egoless, disembodied author of being desiccated, dry and dusty as the highway: "I cannot help suspecting that the life of these learned professors has been almost as inhuman and wooden as *a rain-gauge or self-registering magnetic machine*. They communicate no fact which rises to the temperature of blood-heat" (*Journal,* VI:237; emphasis mine). Curiously, Thoreau is rejecting his own ideal. He wants to be blood-hot, "saturated," "immersed," an embodied lover, not a disembodied analyst. Much of the journal records Thoreau's extended romancing of this dilemma: sometimes aspiring to seamless transparency (though that meant sacrificing bodily passions and blood-heat), sometimes to noisy opacity (dominating the corn, grass, and atmosphere with his own anthropocentric personality).

The contradictions led to something like a settled third alternative position, which is suggested when Thoreau offers to reject both "subjective" and "objective" to locate his interest in their relationship or, as he says, "somewhere between" himself and the object of his interest (*Journal*, VI:236–37; X:164–65). The tripartite figure of author, child, and simple machine also defies simple binary division in the very way that it relates the multiple components by coupling and mutual investment. Does the stream make the sound? Or the bell? Or the child who joined them? Or the child's machine, sounding even in his absence? Or Thoreau, who through the "machine" of his journal couples, or articulates, the whole complex? Take away any one, and the whole complex collapses. The three streams that will in retrospect seem so distinct and separate are, at this juncture, too overlapped and interwound to be clearly distinguishable. It is exactly here that Thoreau, through the practice of the journal, learns to locate himself—or as he says in *Walden*, "to toe that line" (17).

One of his words for this third position is "affinity," as when he wonders, a few lines after wishing himself the scribe of all nature, "What affinity is it brings the goldfinch to the sunflower—both yellow—to pick its seeds" (*Journal*, 4:28). The boundary that clearly distinguishes goldfinch from sunflower is blurred through their "affinity," by which each forms a part of the life of the other (signed by their shared color). This boundary confusion is basic to *Walden*, in which Thoreau as much as the pond becomes "earth's eye" (186), and the pond becomes such a part of the life of Thoreau that the two even today bespeak each other inseparably. Thoreau explores the principle of this boundary confusion at length in the late manuscript "The Dispersion of Seeds," in which he tries to follow the circulation and mutual engagement of each and every element of the Concord forest. For instance, he examines the seeds packed tight in the "strong, prickly, and pitchy chest" of the pitch pine cone, clasped by the thin membrane that will wing them upon their release: "For already some rumor of the wind has penetrated to this cell, and preparation has been made to meet and use it" ("The Dispersion of Seeds," 25). Where is the boundary between wind and seed, when even before opening, one has shaped the other? Another of his words is "anticipation," by which he prepares himself to meet and use the currents of the seasons: "To anticipate, not the sunrise and the dawn merely, but, if possible, Nature herself!" (*Walden*, 17). A third is "intentionality," by which the prepared mind meets the very reality it had envisioned: "The hunter may be said to invent his game, as Jupiter did the horse, and Ceres corn" (*Journal*, XIII:140). In this mode there are no longer any fixed points or positions, only lines of direction that, when ruptured, simply redirect and realign—"the two becomings intertwining and relaying each other in a circulation of intensities that always pushed the deterritorialization further along" (Deleuze and Guattari, *On the Line*, 20).

This "circulation of intensities" aptly describes the odd whirlpool of language that is the water wheel passage. For the coupling begins with an act of interference, the deterritorialization that produces turbulence—in the stream, in the air, in experience—creating sound where before there was but smooth and uninterrupted flow. The coupling thus also produces divisions, blurred enough upstream, but ever clearer the farther downstream one travels. In Thoreau's original encounter with the water wheel, far upstream, it would not have been clear whether it was nature or machine or child or walker or writer who spoke. But by the time the inscription reaches us, Thoreau's writerly voice drowns out all others. Similarly, standing very far upstream from most readers, Thoreau wrote that "the sum of what the writer of whatever class has to report is simply some human experience" (*Journal*, VI:237). His observation was meant to blur the distinction between literary and scientific writing: finally neither could aspire to disembodied transparency, and both had nothing more (or less) to report than some kind of interaction or engagement that twined together author and world— which articulated their relationship. However, we who live downstream are hardly likely to mistake literature for science.

For to make a mark, set pen to paper, or "inscribe" is to interrupt the stream of experience, muddy its clear flow, in order to "cut, separate, sift" it—educe it—into that second flow of language. "The intellect is a cleaver," Thoreau observed; "it discerns and rifts its way into the secret of things" (*Walden*, 98). For help here, I need to recall a second meaning buried in the etymology of "inscribe," which rises from the same root with "scatological" and "scoriae": "to void excrement," cut or separate self from not-self, pure from impure. The effort to cut away the pure involves us inextricably with impurity—noise, excrement, exuviae—or the *"scoriae* of the substantial thoughts of the Creator," as Emerson quoted in *Nature* (*Collected Works*, 1:23). The material world turns out to be not God's true creation but only its waste product—or less delicately, "nothing other than God's *offal*" (Burke, "I, Eye, Ay," 161).

We are thus implicated by our instruments: with every precaution you take against evil, Emerson wrote, "you put yourself into the power of the evil" (*Collected Works*, 2:186). The one thing the scribe *cannot* do is disappear—because writing necessarily involves her with a material, social technology. Every inscription, every word, hopes to lift away from the world some pure thought from the dross of nature; yet every inscription, as a physical mark, lowers thought into the fallen world of matter. The lover immersed in the pure stream of passion must interrupt the stream to inscribe it into language; meanwhile that pure stream of language promised escape from material constraints, but plunges the writer into the nasty business of paper, publishers, genres, audience—as Thoreau knew well from his disappointing experience with *A Week on the Concord and Merrimack Rivers* (1849), and was learning once again as he struggled to see *Walden* through the press.

To use the cleaver of language to cut open the stream of experience is, however, only apparently to separate. Into the gap opened by the division pour new possibilities created by hybridization. In one of *Walden's* best-known passages, Thoreau is inspired by the Sand Bank, where "the deep cut on the railroad" divided past from industrial present and inscribed human purpose on the landscape, to revel in the fantastic proliferation of *"grotesque"* forms that so tightly wedded creation and excrement: "Innumerable little streams overlap and interlace one with another, exhibiting a sort of hybrid product, which obeys half way the law of currents, and half way that of vegetation. As it flows it takes the forms of sappy leaves or vines . . . or you are reminded of coral, of leopards' paws or birds' feet, of brains or lungs or bowels, and excrements of all kinds" (*Walden*, 304–9). All creation begins with making a cut, separating the sameness. As Thoreau says, at that moment one will see the sun glimmering off both surfaces of a fact "as if it were a cimeter, and feel its sweet edge dividing you through the heart and marrow, and so you will happily conclude your mortal career" (*Walden*, 98).

Why muddy—or bloody—one's hands at all? Why take that romantic turn, making art "organic" by projecting the ideal through the real? Why aspire to be "the corn & the grass & the atmosphere writing" when one could be a *person* writing? The organic theory of art renders nature organic, or instrumental, to the purpose of the creator, who thereby takes on the originating power of God, or becomes, in Emerson's words, the "second nature, grown out of the first." Imagining himself at the dawn of the machine age, Thoreau observes a water wheel capturing the power of nature, converting divine power, the spring runoff, to human use, be it sounding a bell, grinding corn, powering factories, or empowering an aspiring writer: nature as the "fountain" of divine power, be it material, artistic, or spiritual. Out of this structure arose two interlapped technologies, one of machines, a utilitarian technology for our physical use, and one of metaphors, a symbolic technology for our spiritual use; both use nature to go beyond nature.

Where articulation distributes and weakens individual agency, romantic power concentrates and strengthens it—but at great cost. Literary culture in Thoreau's day distinguished itself by cutting itself away from science and technology, which are seen as that which separates us from, rather than connecting us to, nature. Writing ("écriture") becomes a fall from "presence" into "absence." To assert that Thoreau devised a technology of inscription seems to insult Thoreau the artist, as if he had built a machine to do his writing for him. The British essayist and journalist Thomas De Quincey famously scorned the "literature of knowledge" in favor of the "literature of power," representing the first by a "cookery-book" and the second by *Paradise Lost*. "What do you learn from 'Paradise Lost'? Nothing at all. What do you learn from a cookery-book? Something new . . . in every paragraph. But would you therefore put the wretched cookery-book on a higher level of estimation than the divine poem?" (De Quincey, "Poetry of Pope," 55–56). The stricture extends to all science and technology and helps to demarcate literature as the realm of transcendent truth by washing it clean of mere knowledge—though De Quincey chooses to overlook the role cookery-books might in fact have played in creating the realm of *"humid* light . . . human passions, desires, and genial motions" through which the literature of power must operate to reach its high aim (55). As Thoreau found, technology can be the way to articulate those very passions, even build a life around them.

I have suggested that Thoreau found a third position between disappearing into nature and letting nature disappear into him, and I want to suggest that redefining technology can help us understand how. Let us define technology not as the menial or utilitarian machine or the alienating monster, but as "a range of heterogeneous actors aligned into a network." The technological artifact itself is only one element constituting this alignment, one link in a long chain of actors that "can be interpreted and rearranged from the position of any actor" (Zehr, "Demolition Derbies," 482). If the boy had ever recognized himself in the story told by Thoreau, he might have amused his audience with a quite different account; rearrange the machine so that it grinds corn rather than ringing a bell, and the moral collapses; remove the late snow that gave rise to the meltwater runoff, and Thoreau, cruising the fields with notebook in hand, is writing about something else altogether. The three key technologies that intersect here create the story. The first is industrial technology, which was aligning so many actors into such an enormous network that people spoke in terms of revolution: the water wheel was overturning the old ways of life. The second is literary technology, which aligns an equally vast number of actors. Thoreau himself was involved in its perfection, both by his successful redesign of the common American pencil (which made gathering field notes much easier) and his invention of a machine to produce superior graphite (or "plumbago") dust for the new reproductive technology of electrotyping (Petroski, "H. D. Thoreau," 12–14). The third is symbolic technology. Metaphors themselves work to *"grid* our perceptions and influence our actions" (McDonald, "Te(K)nowledge," 543, emphasis his), creating relationships where none existed before, structuring our most basic assumptions about the organization of the world.

Thus, Thoreau's desire to throw himself bodily into the gap between man and nature plunged him into a widening array of cultural practices: he needed to invent for himself a way of living and of writing, to create the entire network of the journal—of which only the material artifact itself now survives, a kind of archaeological remnant. All this would seem to have created more problems for Thoreau than it deserved, but for Thoreau the journal solved the one problem that counted: it redistributed the enormous gap between the word and the world into a multitude of smaller gaps, which it was now possible, even easy, to traverse. As a man alone in nature he faced emptiness, but, armed with a technology of inscription, every day, every walk, became full of incident; his journal grew and grew. One day's walk entailed the next, one year's work entailed the year following, for as strong as the multiplying connections were, to interrupt the flow, to break the chain of continued articulations even once, would have been to lose everything (Latour, *Pandora's Hope,* 78).

For instead of a futile desire to merge with nature, he now could act on a productive desire to articulate nature, borrowing its will rather as the boy borrowed the will of the stream, and delegating his will to nature, rather as the boy delegated the stream to speak for him even in his absence. Not only does the journal speak in Thoreau's absence, for many readers the whole of nature—or at least New England nature—will always "speak" Thoreau. The gulf is filled because the very act that opened it— invention of the water wheel, of the railroad, of the journal, of "Walden," of writing, of self-consciousness—is what fills it in a proliferation of possibilities, of connections.

The kind of writerly technology Thoreau developed and deployed through the 1850s is usually associated with science, for it demanded conscientious and repeated observation, careful measurement, and painstaking identification of natural objects and phenomena by their scientific names. The nature of Thoreau's desire pulled him into the alignments and patterns that constituted the network of science, not because he wanted to be a scientist, but because he wanted to reach what he called the rock-solid granitic truth that lay beneath the accumulations of discourse and society. Thoreau found the methods and tools—the technologies—of science useful because his goals converged with the goal of science: toward finding "truth," associated in both cases with the "facts" of nature.

More precisely, science offered a way to construct long, delicate, but robust chains of significations, by which Thoreau could load his writing with the real. To understand this requires following the field naturalist in his work, as Bruno Latour followed a soil scientist in the Amazon, tracing with specificity and detail the way in which the ground of the local is made into a globally circulating scientific article. The scientist begins by drawing a transept across the surface of the ground, digs at measured intervals to take soil samples from measured depths, transfers the dirt to a box, and places the box into a grid of boxes, named a "pedocomparator." At what point does the thing become a sign? At *every* point: the sequence of actions creates "an unbroken series of well-nested elements, each of which plays the role of sign for the previous one and of thing for the succeeding one" (56). The soil scientist physically transfers soil from his hand to soil in a sample box: "We should never take our eyes off the material weight of this action. The earthly dimension of Platonism is revealed in this image"—the movement is not from soil to the idea of soil, but from earth-in-the-ground to earth-in-coded-geometrical-cube:

> And yet René does not *impose* predetermined categories on a shapeless horizon; he *loads* his pedocomparator with the meaning of the piece of earth—he educes it, he articulates it. . . . Only the movement of substitution by which the real soil becomes the soil known to pedology counts. The immense abyss separating things and words can be found everywhere, distributed to many smaller gaps between the clods of earth and the cubes-cases-codes of the pedocomparator. (49–51)

—or between the flash of a living bird and the drawers of a zoological museum, the leaves in the breeze and the pages of an herbarium, the green earth and a journal notebook, a vision in the eye and a rude sketch by the hand. Thoreau's project was to learn how to distribute the "immense abyss" into many smaller gaps. Digging to that granitic truth would mean getting his hands dirty—and learning in the process that reality may be less a solid core of "hard bottom and rocks in place" subtending "the mud and slush of opinion, and prejudice, and tradition, and delusion, and appearance, that alluvion which covers the globe" (*Walden* 97), than a quality that "circulates . . . like electricity through a wire, so long as this circuit is not interrupted" (Latour, *Pandora's Hope*, 69). Learning to speak the language of nature meant learning to speak the language of naturalists, for it was they who gave him the tools to educe the meaning he sought.

By such means did the method and language of science give Thoreau a way to grid his own perceptions, to make the world visible in all its plenitude. To inscribe, to mark, literally makes nature "remarkable," not as an undifferentiated mass but along a grid of particulars. So for instance, botany makes plants visible— even down to lichen dust and grasses and individual varieties of wild apple. Weather makes time visible, down to specific seasons not found on any calendar, even down to the microclimatic uniqueness of each moment in every location. Daily walks become transepts, lines of direction like the sampling techniques used by field ecologists, during which Thoreau records (or "remarks" upon) all that alters identifiably, from day to day. Every stage can be infinitely subdivided, infinitely multiplied—in fact, this technique made so much visible that Thoreau periodically went through crises of visibility. "As soon as we go into the field or turn on an instrument," notes Latour, "we find ourselves drowning in a sea of data" (*Pandora's Hope,* 39). Thoreau simply saw too much to comprehend, impressing upon him the complementary usefulness of focus, or what he called "intentionality of the eye," which cuts away some objects to bring others back into view.

The usual trope of visibility in the nineteenth century was panoptic, whereby inscribing something would bring it, not the author of the inscription, into visibility. For—going back to the scientific investment in disembodied observers and self-registering instruments—the inscription is not authored by any human agent; nature writes itself through the instrumentality merely arranged by the scientist. However, in a theory of articulation, there is no retreat, nothing is "self-evident." No one can fade into invisibility as unmoved mover, or universal, unmarked, and unseen knower: the object made visible, the means of visibility, and the author of visibility are all made evident. One of the most remarkable examples of this is *Walden's* map (see, p. 253) of Walden Pond, drawn by Thoreau himself from a survey he took during his first winter as a resident of its shores. As I have said, in "Where I Lived and What I Lived For," Thoreau had declared his goal to "settle ourselves, and work and wedge our feet downward through the mud and slush of opinion . . . till we come to a hard bottom and rocks in place, which we can call *reality*, and say, This is, and no mistake" (97–98). In "The Pond in Winter," Thoreau literalizes his ambition, using the methods of science to cut through the slush of superstition:

> As I was desirous to recover the long lost bottom of Walden Pond, I surveyed it carefully, before the ice broke up, early in '46, with compass and chain and sounding line. There have been many stories told about the bottom, or rather no bottom, of this pond, which certainly had no foundation for themselves. It is remarkable how long men will believe in the bottomlessness of a pond without taking the trouble to sound it. (285)

The map that follows details the precise shape of "God's drop," including the cut made by the Fitchburg Railroad and the location of his house, and displays the sample measurements of the pond's depth along transepts inscribed across the ice. As if to emphasize the solidity of the pond's bottom, Thoreau even gives us "profiles" of Walden's vertical length and breadth. The reader who turns the page and finds this map is abruptly disconnected from the stream of language that has so far rendered the pond transparent to inner vision; instead, a tangle of transepts juts across the once-clean page, and a clutter of numbers connects us less to the pond's "depth" than to its surface, across which we must now imagine *Walden's* author tramping with compass and measuring chains, stooping at regular intervals to drill the ice, lower his sounding line, and haul it back up again, counting off foot by foot and inscribing with a pencil into a notebook the seemingly endless chains of numbers. If we follow the process through, we must then recall the author painstakingly transferring the readings to a fair copy map, and then to a "Reduced Plan," which a professional lithographer must then transfer to a printing plate for final publication.[6]

To repeat the procedure in our mind's eye is to be implicitly invited to duplicate it in our own experience. Observation, to be scientific, must be capable of independent confirmation, and indeed in 1942 Edward S. Deevey, Jr., confirmed the accuracy of Thoreau's survey ("Re-Examination," 2–3; Stowell, *Thoreau Gazetter,* 9). Furthermore, Thoreau himself claimed to have verified his most significant discovery by repeating his procedure at White Pond. The upshot was his observation "that the line of greatest length intersected the line of greatest breadth *exactly* at the point of greatest depth" (289), which led him to a moral lesson: "draw lines through the length and breadth of the aggregate of a man's particular daily behaviors and waves of life into his coves and inlets, and where they intersect will be the height or depth of his character" (291). What is the relationship of moral to map? The moral expresses a relation not just among three dimensions of measurement, but between the object being measured and the subject rendering both calculation and judgment. Similarly, the map that interrupts our reading reconnects us to the busy-ness of the author who has worked so hard to bring reader and pond into relationship with each other, a relationship embodied in the map that concatenates the hard reality of physical nature, the tedious procedures of observational science, the moral truth carried by the natural law that relates them both, and the "somatic poetry" (New, "Beyond the Romance Theory," 402) that makes this complex visible in a fallen world, where nature might be self-registering—but humanity is dependent on its instruments. Thus the tools of inscription implicate everyone who touches them, from object, to artist, to viewer or reader, in a complex network of dependencies.

Articulation interrupts the dominant structure of panoptic vision, deflecting it back on itself. Thus it can serve to neutralize the romantic dilemma for a practitioner like Thoreau. It has often been remarked that Thoreau preferred the older science of natural history to the new science of biology; however, the latter sought not to make forms visible but to make them "invisible" such that their formative laws would shine through—the laws of transcendental anatomy, of physiological process. Thoreau saw this most immediately in the work of Louis Agassiz, a protegé of Humboldt and one of Emerson's friends, who had arrived at Harvard from Switzerland in 1846 and swiftly risen to dominate American natural history. For Agassiz, to read the "great book" of nature correctly was to see in the "facts" of nature not the workings of a material agency but the thoughts of the Creator bodied forth in matter, thoughts legible to the scientist by virtue of his own "affinity with the Divine Mind" (*Essay on Classification*, 9). Agassiz labored heroically to modernize and professionalize science in America, becoming in the process America's own Humboldt, the latest symbol of modern science. This achievement was accompanied by his virulent and highly public opposition to Darwin, as Agassiz supported his own dogmatic certainty in multiple special creations of nature according to a static, permanent, and unchanging plan against Darwin's vision of a nature materially interconnected and in constant flux, evolving under the contingencies of chance variation against the pressures of natural selection. Darwin's staunchest American ally was the Harvard botanist Asa Gray, whose work Thoreau had had in hand ever since he first started to collect and identify plants. Thoreau's reading in the naturalists Humboldt, Darwin, and Gray, his immediate enthusiasm for Darwin's theory of evolution, and his own careful work on the knotty and central problems of plant geography and seed dispersion all mark him as attentive to an understanding of science where categories are neither reflections of Divine Mind nor crude human impositions on nature's ineffable mysteries, but rather educed from nature by an exacting process of substitutions, from things to signs—so exacting that it is reversible, allowing the reader to track from signs back to things, from a published article back to the forest outside the town of Boa Vista in the Amazon, from Thoreau's most distilled, polished, and omnipresent language back to messy, complex, material, local nature.

A theory of articulations can also provide a useful methodology for critique, by bringing forward all the actors into the light, even those who would prefer to hide in the shadows of the stage they have created and manage, concealing their technologies even from themselves. They would stand then, not unmasked—for as Emerson said, we are all implicated by our tools—as merely, once again, visible. Thus might vision be reclaimed, as Donna Haraway hopes, for "a possible politics of articulation rather than representation." In her words, "Theory here is exceedingly corporeal, and the body is a collective; it is an historical artifact constituted by human as well as organic and technological unhuman actors. Actors are entities which do things, have effects, build worlds in concatenation with other *unlike* actors" ("Promises of Monsters," 311). In this view, nature cannot be reduced to a mere resource for the commanding will, for not all the "actors" will cooperate—some will offer resistance, and some will offer surprises. Thoreau followed his own theory of civil resistance from the social to the natural sphere, commemorating moments when nature defied or disappointed his own designs. And he was ever alert to the moments of surprise—as when "far in the night" the sound of the water wheel leaped across a fortnight in time and more than mile in distance to astonish the "slumbering village" of Concord.

In sum, Thoreau's problem in April 1850 was to construct a technology that would channel the power of nature through him, toying like the boy's "first essay in mechanics" to find a technology of inscription that would lie level with the stream of experience and translate it into language. He approached the problem in the Emersonian fashion, hoping to bespeak himself through the amplifying power of nature, but the technology itself intervened, forcing him to "inscribe," to make the cut that would both divide and connect. The technology—not as a single artifact, but as a range of interconnected actors—drew him into a lingering entanglement where every inscription, every cut, only spawned more complications, and every divide became a fertile interface. The journal that was to heal the division between man and nature instead proliferated in articulations. The moment that stands so far upstream, April 1850 in Nut Meadow, articulates the joints that connect and divide stream, boy, and man, or wilderness, machine, and poet; thus braiding together nature, culture, and discourse. Farther downstream, *Walden* both joins and separates a glacial pond, a culture both detached from and deeply invested in nature, and a literary tradition unalterably marked by Thoreau's peculiar technology of inscription.

NOTES

1. I have explored this lineage in more depth in Laura Dassow Walls, *Seeing New Worlds: Henry David Thoreau and Nineteenth-Century Natural Science* (Madison: University of Wisconsin Press, 1995).

2. Sir Richard Arkwright (1732–1792) invented the water frame spinning machine in 1769; his invention captured the power of water for use in the huge textile mills that helped begin the Industrial Revolution in England and New England. John Rennie (1761–1821) was a British civil engineer best known for designing bridges, most famously the London Bridge, built by his son, Sir John Rennie, and completed in 1831.

3. Volumes in the ongoing but incomplete Princeton edition of Thoreau's *Journal* will be cited using Arabic numerals, and volumes in the 1906 Houghton Mifflin edition will be cited using Roman numerals.

4. See also Reiser, *Medicine and the Reign of Technology*, 100–101.

5. As Frederick Garber shows, Thoreau's "fable of inscribing" not only places him in the "gap" between words and actuality but also gives him the means to turn that gap into a habitation, a home in the world (*Thoreau's Fable of Inscribing*, 71). "These tracings"—the traces of mind in the world, from cellar holes to footpaths, arrowheads to (presumably) abandoned toy waterwheels—"are modes of working in the world that are ultimately modes of being in the world. To put it most precisely, they are modes of being in the world whose purpose is to inscribe being into the world" (96). "Inscription" is more than text; it is a mode of action, action that becomes, as here, *inter*action.

6. The sequence of three maps described here is reproduced, with an instructive commentary, by Robert F. Stowell in *A Thoreau Gazetteer*, 5–9.

WORKS CITED

Agassiz, Louis. *Essay on Classification*. 1857. Reprint, edited by Edward Lurie, Cambridge: Harvard University Press, 1962.

Bacon, Francis. "The Great Instauration." 1620. In *The Works of Francis Bacon*, vol. 8, edited by James Spedding, Robert Leslie Ellis, and Douglas Denon Heath, 15-54. New York: Hurd and Houghton; Cambridge, England: Riverside Press, 1870.

Burke, Kenneth. "I, Eye, Ay—Concerning Emerson's Early Essay on 'Nature' and the Machinery of Transcendence." In *Language as Symbolic Action*, 186–200.Berkeley: University of California Press, 1966.

Coleridge, Samuel Taylor. *Biographia Literaria*. In *Collected Works*, vol. 7, edited by James Engell and W. Jackson Bate. Princeton: Princeton University Press, 1983.

Deevey, Edward S., Jr. "A Re-Examination of Thoreau's *Walden*." *Quarterly Review of Biology* 17 (March 1942): 1–11.

Deleuze, Gilles, and Felix Guattari. *On the Line*. New York: Semiotext[e], 1983.

De Quincey, Thomas. "The Poetry of Pope." 1848. In *The Collected Writings of Thomas De Quincey*, vol. 11, edited by David Masson, 51–97. London: Adam and Charles Black, 1896–1897.

Emerson, Ralph Waldo. *The Collected Works of Ralph Waldo Emerson*. 5 vols. to date. Edited by Alfred R. Ferguson et al. Cambridge: Harvard University Press, 1971–.

Garber, Frederick. *Thoreau's Fable of Inscribing*. Princeton: Princeton University Press, 1991.

Haraway, Donna. "The Promises of Monsters: A Regenerative Politics for Inappropriate/d Others." In *Cultural Studies*, edited by Lawrence Grossberg, Cary Nelson, and Paula Treichler. 295–337. New York: Routledge, 1992..

Latour, Bruno. "Circulating Reference: Sampling the Soil in the Amazon Forest." In *Pandora's Hope: Essays on the Reality of Science Studies*, 24–79. Cambridge: Harvard University Press, 1999.

————. *We Have Never Been Modern.* Cambridge: Harvard University Press, 1993.

Locke, David. *Science as Writing.* New Haven: Yale University Press, 1992.

McDonald, James H. "Te(k)nowledge: Technology, Education, and the New Student/Subject." *Science as Culture* 4, no. 4 (1995): 535–64.

New, Elisa. "Beyond the Romance Theory of American Vision: Beauty and the Qualified Will in Edwards, Jefferson, and Audubon." *American Literary History* 7, no. 3 (Fall 1995): 381–414.

Petroski, Henry. "H. D. Thoreau, Engineer." *American Heritage of Invention and Technology* 5, no. 2 (Fall 1989): 7–16.

Reiser, Stanley Joel. *Medicine and the Reign of Technology.* Cambridge: Cambridge University Press, 1978.

Schaffer, Simon. "Self Evidence." *Critical Inquiry* 18 (Winter 1992): 327–62.

Smith, David G., ed. *The Cambridge Encyclopedia of the Earth Sciences.* New York: Cambridge University Press, 1981.

Stowell, Robert F. *A Thoreau Gazetteer.* Edited by William L. Howarth. Princeton: Princeton University Press, 1970.

Talbott, John H. *A Biographical History of Medicine.* New York: Grune and Stratton, 1970.

Thoreau, Henry David. "The Dispersion of Seeds." In *Faith in a Seed: "The Dispertion of Seeds" and Other Late Natural History Writings.* Edited by Bradley P. Dean, 23–173. Washington D.C.: Island Press, 1993.

————. *Journal, Volume 3: 1848–1851.* Edited by Robert Sattelmeyer, Mark R. Patterson, and William Rossi. Princeton: Princeton University Press, 1990.

————. *Journal, Volume 4: 1851–1852.* Edited by Leonard N. Neufeldt and Nancy Craig Simmons. Princeton: Princeton University Press, 1992.

————. *The Journal of Henry David Thoreau.* Edited by Bradford Torrey and Francis H. Allen. Boston: Houghton Mifflin, 1906.

————. "Natural History of Massachusetts." In *The Natural History Essays,* edited by Robert Sattelmeyer, 1–29. Salt Lake City: Peregrine Smith, 1980.

―――. *Walden*. 1854. Reprint, edited by J. Lyndon Shanley, Princeton: Princeton University Press, 1971.

Wood, Alexander, and Frank Oldham. *Thomas Young, Natural Philosopher, 1773–1829*. Cambridge: Cambridge University Press, 1954.

Zehr, Stephen C. "Demolition Derbies: The Ritualistic Destruction of Technology." *Science as Culture* 4, no. 4 (1995): 481–501.

The Theory, Practice, and Influence of Thoreau's Civil Disobedience

Lawrence A. Rosenwald

"I, on my side, require of every writer, first or last, a simple and sincere account of his own life, and not merely what he has heard of other men's lives." This is an excellent principle of Thoreau's, and I shall begin this chapter by giving at least an account of the viewpoint from which I have written it.

I myself have been a war tax resister for twelve years, and I became one partly through reading Thoreau's essay and feeling its pressure.[1] What matters to me about the essay, therefore, is chiefly the complex relation between text and action. The essay emerges from Thoreau's action, interprets that action, is read, and then turned back into action again by its readers. I say this from my own experience; but I would not be saying it so emphatically if Thoreau's essay had not mattered so much to the action of so many of its readers. The list of them is astonishing. It famously includes Tolstoy,[2] Gandhi, and Martin Luther King, Jr. It also includes the anarchist Emma Goldman, the English educator Henry Salt, the German-Jewish philosopher and activist Martin Buber, the American peace activist Ammon Hennacy, a deliberately anonymous fighter in the Danish resistance, the World Fellowship Center director Willard Uphaus, the African National Congress founder Trevor N. W. Bush, the Freedom Rider William Mahoney, and such notable contemporary tax resisters as Errol Hess and Randy Kehler.

There is a paradox here, in the fact of the essay's influence. Thoreau seems on the face of it a man unlikely to have influenced the people he demonstrably did influence. The essay is individualist, secular, anarchist, elitist, and antidemocratic; but it has influenced persons of great religious devotion, leaders of collective campaigns, and members of resistance movements. How could this have happened?

The following analysis focuses chiefly on the background of Thoreau's essay, and in that context on the argument the essay makes. Both of these accounts, however, have been shaped to respond to the question of the essay's influence on action. And it has turned out, for me at any rate, that the question of its influence is best answered precisely by an investigation of its history and argument.

The Nature of Thoreau's Action

The bare facts of Thoreau's tax resistance are these.

1839: Thoreau's name is added to the Concord tax rolls.

1840: Thoreau's name is added to the First Parish Church tax rolls; Thoreau is assessed the church tax, refuses to pay it, is threatened with jail; someone else pays the tax; Thoreau requests that his name be removed from the church tax rolls, and his request is granted.[3]

1842: Thoreau stops paying the poll tax.[4]

1846: On July 24th or 25th Sam Staples arrests Thoreau and puts him in jail; someone, probably Maria Thoreau, pays the tax, and Thoreau is released the next day.

But what do these actions mean? Thoreau himself explains why he refused to pay the church tax:

> I did not see why the schoolmaster should be taxed to support the priest, and not the priest the schoolmaster. . . . I did not see why the lyceum should not present its tax-bill, and have the State to back its demand, as well as the church.[5]

Thoreau does not object to any particular church policy or practice; he is not saying, "Change this policy and I will pay." He suggests that the schoolmaster and the lyceum have as much right to tax as the church does, and that if all institutions could present their tax bills, then he would feel at ease in paying them; but again, what matters is not a particular policy but the underlying structure.

Similar reasoning evidently underlies the nearest precedent for Thoreau's 1842 refusal to pay the poll tax, namely, Bronson Alcott's refusal to pay the same tax in 1840.[6] Alcott was arrested on January 17, 1843; he was brought to the town jail in which Thoreau later spent the night, was held there for two hours, then was released when Samuel Hoar paid the tax for him. Ten days later, in a letter to William Lloyd Garrison's *The Liberator*, Alcott's friend Charles Lane gave a rationale for Alcott's action:

> This act of non-resistance, you will perceive, does not rest on the plea of poverty. . . . Neither is it wholly based on the iniquitous purposes to which the money when collected is applied. But it is founded on the moral instinct which forbids every moral being to be a party, either actively or permissively, to the destructive principles of power and might over peace and love.[7]

In a subsequent letter, published on March 3, 1843, Lane elaborated:

> Because this citizen as a man, as a Christian, has conscientious scruples in doing aught in support of a government which spends the people's money in prisons, gunpowder, halters, and the like civilized gear, that very government lays violent hands upon him, and imprisons him for a term, only shortened by its good will and pleasure.[8]

To make sense of this, we have first to know what Lane meant by calling Alcott's tax refusal an "act of non-resistance." "Non-resistance" was then a resonant and precise term; it referred to William Lloyd Garrison's New England Non-Resistance Society, founded in 1838, and to that society's doctrines. Like modern pacifism, non-resistance forbade both individual violence and state violence, even state violence intended for self-defense. But Garrison and his colleagues were more systematic than most modern pacifists, and non-resistance as they articulate it forbids not only all violence but all cooperation with violence, e.g., holding office in a state that maintains a standing army, standing police force, or jail. It even forbids voting, as Adin Ballou proclaims in *Christian Non-Resistance*: "I will hold office on no such conditions. I will not be a voter on such conditions. I will join no church or state, who hold such a creed or prescribe such a covenant for the subscription of their members."[9]

All of this is called non-resistance because, for thinkers like Garrison and Ballou, the central moral question is, how are we to respond to injury and evil? The "almost universal opinion and practice of mankind," writes Ballou, "has been on the side of resistance of injury *with* injury" (34). And it is this answer that non-resistants reject, claiming instead that:

> by adhering to the law of love under all provocations, and scrupulously suffering wrong, rather than inflicting it, they shall gloriously "overcome evil with good," and exterminate all their enemies by turning them into faithful friends. (35)

To call Alcott's tax refusal "an act of non-resistance," then, means that by it Alcott refuses to cooperate with a potentially violent state, one that spends money on "prisons, gunpowder, [and] halters." Alcott's grounds for refusing to pay the poll tax are thus a little more specific than Thoreau's for refusing to pay the church tax, but only a little. Thoreau objects in principle to the church's having the right to tax, not to any church practice. Alcott does object to particular state practices: "prisons, gunpowder, [and] halters." But prisons and gunpowder and halters, and "the destructive principles of power and might," are the practices and principles of nearly every state; in practice, objecting to them is objecting to the state in general.

At its beginning, it seems that Thoreau's tax refusal meant pretty much what Alcott's meant. Alcott defended Thoreau's tax refusal "on the grounds of a dignified non-compliance with the injunction of civil powers."[10] Thoreau himself, in describing Alcott's arrest, associated himself with Lane and lays emphasis on "the State" rather than on state policies. And as late as January

26, 1848, in a Lyceum lecture on "The Rights and Duties of the Individual in Relation to Government," Thoreau was still presenting his and Alcott's actions as alike. Alcott describes the event as follows:

> Heard Thoreau's lecture before the Lyceum on the relation of the individual to the State—an admirable statement of the rights of the individual to self-government, and an attentive audience.
>
> His allusions to . . . his own imprisonment in Concord Jail for refusal to pay his tax, to Mr. Hoar's payment of mine when taken to prison for a similar refusal, were all pertinent, well considered, and reasoned. I took great pleasure in this deed of Thoreau's. (201)

The First Title of Thoreau's essay

By May 1849, however, when his revised lecture comes out in Elizabeth Peabody's *Aesthetic Papers*, Thoreau has changed its title to "Resistance to Civil Government" and dropped all reference to Alcott. And these changes suggest that Thoreau has rejected much of what his tax refusal must originally have stood for.

The title as a whole is strikingly at odds with the non-resistant position on citizenly conduct. The chief documents of non-resistance forbid not only government based on violence but also almost all forceful resistance to it. "We advocate no jacobinical doctrines," Garrison writes:

> the spirit of jacobinism is the spirit of retaliation, violence and murder. . . . If we abide by our principles, it is impossible for us to be disorderly, or plot treason, or participate in any evil work: we shall submit to every ordinance of man, for the Lord's sake.[11]

Garrison does provide an escape clause, with potentially wide-reaching implications: "We shall . . . obey all the requirements of government, except such as we deem contrary to the commands of the gospel" (16). But the text emphasizes the rule rather than the exception, and does not specify the cases in which the rule would not apply.

Thoreau's title, then, implicitly rejects Garrison's non-resistance. But it also evokes the existing positive meanings of "resistance" and thereby associates Thoreau with Garrison's colleague and antagonist Frederick Douglass. (Thoreau knew who Douglass was, refers to him in a March 1845 letter to *The Liberator*, and had probably read Douglass's 1845 *Narrative* by the time he wrote the essay.) Consider a notable passage from the *Narrative* on Douglass's "resistance" to the slavebreaker Covey:

> Mr. Covey seemed now to think he had me, and could do what he pleased; but at this moment—from whence came the spirit I don't know—I resolved to fight; and, suiting my action to the resolution, I seized Covey hard by the throat; and as I did so, I rose. He held on to me, and I to him. My *resistance* was so entirely unexpected that Covey seemed taken all aback. . . . He asked me if I meant to persist in my *resistance*. I told him I did, come what might; that he had used me like a brute for six months, and that I was determined to be used so no longer. . . . Covey at length let me go, puffing and blowing at a great rate, saying that if I had *resisted*, he would not have whipped me half so much. The truth was, that he had not whipped me at all. (Emphasis added.)[12]

Douglass' "resistance" means self-defense, a refusal to cooperate with Covey's attempts to beat and subdue him. It does not mean leading a rebellion like Nat Turner's, or a raid like John Brown's; but it does mean, in Ballou's phrase, "resistance of injury *with* injury." Thoreau's new title associates him with resistance in that sense.

Transformation of the Action in the Essay

After the confrontatory title, the first two paragraphs of the essay are disappointing. In them, Thoreau argues derisively and predictably against government in general. He subscribes to the motto, "'That government is best which governs not at all," and claims that "when men are prepared for it, that will be the kind of government they will have" (62). He does address one particular governmental policy, namely the Mexican War, but only abstractly, treating it not as an act of wickedness but as a violation of procedure: "witness the present Mexican War, the work of comparatively few individuals using the standing government as their tool" (62). His objections to government are as general as Lane's or Garrison's but less fervent; he portrays government as something comically weak, "a sort of wooden gun to the people themselves" (62), an obstacle to enterprise and trade and commerce. Everything in these paragraphs could be agreed to by a modern-day Republican.

But then Thoreau changes ground:

> To speak practically and as a citizen, unlike those who call themselves no-government men, I ask for, not at once no government, but *at once* a better government. Let every man make known what kind of government would command his respect, and that will be one step towards obtaining it. (64)

By "no-government men" Thoreau means non-resistants, and here he turns earnestly away from them. He is now a citizen, not an outlier. He acknowledges the possibility of a government that would command his respect; and he asks that citizens like himself specify what that sort of government would be, and how the existing government falls short of it.

There are more changes, too. In the next paragraph, Thoreau makes clear that citizens' demands on their government must be based, not on the opposition between government and enterprise or between government and character, but on the opposition between government and conscience. And he casts himself and other witnesses of conscience not as no-government men but as super-government men:

> The mass of men serve the State . . . not as men mainly, but as machines, with their bodies. . . . A very few, as heroes, patriots, martyrs, reformers in the great sense, and *men*, serve

the State with their consciences also, and so necessarily resist it for the most part; and they are commonly treated by it as enemies. . . .

He who gives himself entirely to his fellow-men appears to them useless and selfish; but he who gives himself partially to them is pronounced a benefactor and philanthropist. (66–67)

Then, finishing the turn, he specifies how the existing government falls short of his ideal:

When a sixth of the population of a nation which has undertaken to be the refuge of liberty are slaves, and a whole country is unjustly overrun and conquered by a foreign army, and subjected to military law, I think that it is not too soon for honest men to rebel and revolutionize. (67)

When a government supports slavery and wages unjust wars in its support, it is time for "honest men to rebel and revolutionize"; when that government does away with slavery, it will command Thoreau's respect.

Thoreau maintains this position untill the end of the first section of the essay. That is why it makes sense for him to cut all reference to Alcott. His resistance in this part of the essay is local rather than global, contingent rather than absolute. He is not saying, "I separate myself from a state I do not recognize, and shall therefore pay it no tax"; instead, he is saying, "I join myself as a citizen to a state I wish to improve, and shall therefore pay it no tax until, wishing to conciliate me, it does away with slavery and stops waging unjust wars."

Thoreau's radical change of position has large consequences. Associating himself with "resistance" puts him, as noted, at a distance from the "no-government men" and from the Christian pacifism out of which non-resistance grows; associating his resistance with particular evils puts him nearer to more combative traditions. Barbara Andrews, whose 1974 Goddard College thesis remains the most comprehensive and illuminating account of war tax resistance in the United States, associates Thoreau with the tradition of "selective tax resistance" focused on particular social change; she thereby links him to the Algonquin Indians who refused to pay taxes to the Dutch for strengthening Fort Amsterdam, and to the American Revolutionists who refused to pay the Stamp Tax to the British in the 1760s. Staughton Lynd and Alice Lynd make a similar linkage, describing Thoreau's essay as:

> a subtle and ambiguous synthesis of the previously disparate Quaker and Lockean traditions. Thoreau . . . affirms the peril of coercion in spiritual matters; he refused to pay a tax for the support of the established church several years before his more celebrated refusal of the Massachusetts poll tax. At the same time Thoreau breaks with Garrison's disavowal of jacobinism, and flatly declares that "all men recognize the right of revolution" and that "it is not too soon for honest men to rebel and revolutionize."[13]

To link the Christian pacifism associated with the Quakers to the political liberalism and support for revolution associated with John Locke is indeed a "subtle and ambiguous synthesis"; but it is this synthesis that makes Thoreau's argument useful. It, not the nonresistant rejection of government or coercion generally, is what has mattered to the activist leaders whom Thoreau has influenced. Take two celebrated examples. Martin Luther King took comfort in Thoreau's essay on the eve of the Montgomery bus boycott:

> I remembered how, as a college student, I had been moved when I first read this work. I became convinced that what we were preparing to do in Montgomery was related to what Thoreau had expressed. We were simply saying to the white community, "We can no longer lend our cooperation to an evil system."[14]

In speaking of "an evil system," King, like Thoreau, is thinking locally rather than globally; what makes the system evil is not the nature of a system of transportation but the particular injustices practiced on the Montgomery buses. Hence the goals the bus

boycotters agreed on: "(1) courteous treatment by the bus operators; . . . (2) passengers . . . seated on a first-come, first-
served basis . . . (3) Negro bus operators . . . employed on
predominantly Negro routes" (436). Thoreau's stated goals are
grander than these, but they are equally particular.

Mohandas Gandhi's first important encounter with Thoreau's
essay came in 1906, in South Africa; he was then fighting the
"Black Act," which required Asians to register with the government and have their fingerprints recorded, as if they were crimi-
nals. What Gandhi got from Thoreau is clear from what he
printed in *Indian Opinion*, the newspaper in which he conducted
part of his political and spiritual campaign; the passages he selected present Thoreau's local protest, not his global one. Consider, for example, "under a government which imprisons any
unjustly, the true place for a just man is also a prison" (76). For
non-resistants, anyone imprisoned is unjustly imprisoned;[15] for
Thoreau and Gandhi, the crucial distinction is precisely that between just imprisonment and unjust. And the actual campaign
against the "Black Act" showed Gandhi making the same sort of
local distinction; he was imprisoned for refusing to register, left
prison when the government agreed to make registration for Indians voluntary, and returned to prison for burning registration cer-
tificates when the government failed to abide by its agreement.

But there is a problem here: Thoreau's "subtle and ambiguous
synthesis" is founded on a fiction. His account of his tax resistance in the essay revises his tax resistance in the world, in his
community of Concord. In the essay, Thoreau cites the Mexican
War as a reason for refusing to pay the poll tax. In the world,
Thoreau's action predated the war by four years. In the essay,
Thoreau refuses the tax because, as he writes, "I cannot for an instant recognize that political organization as *my* government
which is the *slave's* government also" (67). In the world, he apparently began refusing taxes out of an unwillingness to recognize
any political organization whatsoever.

And this revision undermines the essay's argument. If government in general is the problem, then it does not matter which
government one refuses to pay taxes to, or what those taxes
are funding. If the Mexican War and slavery are the problem,

though, then the taxes one refuses have to be funding those things in particular. And that was, in a strict sense, not the case. The poll tax Thoreau refused to pay was a composite tax; it could include state tax, county tax, and town tax. It was not a federal tax. (The federal government was not collecting direct taxes; the Mexican War was financed by customs duties, sales of public land, and loans.) Only once in the decade, in 1845—three years after Thoreau started refusing the tax—was it even a state tax; and Massachusetts had in any case passed a personal liberty law, forbidding the use of state resources for executing the laws regarding fugitive slaves. Most of the time, then, Thoreau was refusing to pay tax to Middlesex County and the town of Concord, neither of which could plausibly be called the slave's government. Thoreau boldly writes, "I do not care to trace the course of my dollar, if I could, till it buys a man, or a musket to shoot one with" (84). The problem is, though, that it would be hard to trace the course of Thoreau's dollar to either point. What men was Concord buying?

It is important to acknowledge this problem, but important also to assess it justly. In linking the slave's government and the poll tax, Thoreau was strictly wrong but broadly and prophetically right. There was no easy separation between levels of government, no firewall between Washington and Concord, and one thing that made that clear was what happened whenever a fugitive slave was apprehended in Massachusetts. Consider the 1851 case of Thomas Sims. Sims was apprehended in April by federal deputy marshal Asa Butman and held in the U.S. courthouse because he could not, by the personal liberty law, be held in a state jail. But the guards stationed around the court house were Boston policemen, and State Supreme Court justice Lemuel Shaw, who was appealed to for a writ of *habeas corpus*, denied jurisdiction. When Boston policemen defend a fugitive seized by a federal marshal, and a Massachusetts justice defers to the federal government's jurisdiction over that slave, how feasible is it to separate town and state from country? Thoreau prophetically intuited their interdependence in 1849.

As for Thoreau's belated rewriting of his 1842 motives to make them accord with his 1849 concerns—the fact is that sometimes responses to particular issues and events supersede principles, or rather become principles. That is what Simone Weil means when she writes that our ideas of injustice have to start from the moment when someone says *on me fait du mal* ('they're hurting me'); it is also what happened to many leftist intellectuals in the 1990s, when they came to believe that the need to stop genocide in Bosnia outweighed, indeed substituted for, their skeptical systemic analysis of American military intervention. And probably that is what happened to Thoreau between 1842 and 1849. In 1842 it seemed right to refuse taxes as a means of separating oneself from government, in response to the nature of government generally. In 1849, after the annexation of Texas and the Mexican War—after a clear demonstration of the expansive power of the slave interests—it still seemed right to refuse taxes, but now as a means of engaging with government, to combat those interests. Thoreau foregrounded his later motives rather than his earlier ones, even at the cost of inconsistency, because, at the later moment, they made better sense.

Meanings of the Action in the Essay

Thoreau's essay gives his original action numerous new meanings.

(1) We might summarize some of these meanings by saying that once he has turned away from the "no-government" men, Thoreau turns away from Emerson—not from Emerson in particular or by name, that is, but rather from all those who share Thoreau's beliefs on slavery and the war, and on the sovereignty of conscience, without taking a similar course of action. One meaning of his action, then, is precisely that it is action, and not something else. Thoreau first opposes action to opinion:

> There are thousands who are *in opinion* opposed to slavery and to the war, who yet in effect do nothing to put an end to them. (69)

Then he opposes action to voting and electoral politics in general:

> Even voting *for the right* is *doing* nothing for it. . . . The re-
> spectable man, so called, . . . forthwith adopts one of the
> [presidential candidates selected at the Baltimore convention]
> as the only *available* one, thus proving that he is himself *avail-
> able* for any purposes of the demagogue. (69–70)

And he might have gone on to oppose action to words. Emerson's words about resistance, in "The American Scholar" and
more specifically in "Politics," are more vivid than holding an
opinion and more resonant than casting a vote; indeed, Emerson's emphasis on putting forth "[our] total strength in fit actions"[16] is, in words, a precise account of Thoreau's program.
But an account is all that it is; the familiar notion that Thoreau
did what Emerson talked about doing is on the mark here. As
Staughton Lynd writes, "What was central for Thoreau was neither nonviolence nor civil disobedience but direct action: the
absolute demand that one practice—right now, and all alone if
necessary—what one preaches."[17]

(2) But why, among all the direct actions one might do, does
Thoreau single out tax resistance? The implicit answer says a lot
about the nature of civil disobedience:

> It is not a man's duty, as a matter of course, to devote himself
> to the eradication of any, even the most enormous wrong; he
> may still properly have other concerns to engage him; but it is
> his duty, at least, to wash his hands of it,[18] and, if he gives it
> no thought longer, not to give it practically his support. If I
> devote myself to other pursuits and contemplations, I must
> first see, at least, that I do not pursue them sitting upon an-
> other man's shoulders. (71)

Like Emerson, Thoreau disliked doing politics. John Jay Chapman's remark, that "Emerson represents a protest against the
tyranny of democracy,"[19] says something about why; Emerson
and Thoreau saw in the politics of a democracy a force likely
to absorb and decenter them. That is why Emerson in "Self-
Reliance" tells the philanthropist—who may perfectly well be an
abolitionist—to go away and stop bothering him. Thoreau was

no fonder of philanthropists than Emerson was, and in working out a rationale for his own action he posits a life in which political action is a limited obligation, and a person may "properly have other concerns."

But Thoreau also sees what Emerson does not, namely, that with regard to paying taxes, it is impossible not to act, in one way or another. One can pay the tax and support the state, or refuse the tax and defy the state. Thoreau's civil disobedience is the choice he makes when he has no choice but to act; it is not only action, but necessary action, unwilling action, action that is thrust upon the actor. The tax collector comes to the door, and Thoreau has to choose whether to pay. What he does has much in common with what Rosa Parks did in 1955, when she refused to give up her seat to a white bus rider in Montgomery, Alabama. It has less in common with other modes of civil disobedience. Consider, for example, the occupation of an army recruiting station in Boston at the start of the Gulf War, in January 1991. I myself was a support person in this action and approved of it; but Thoreau might not have. The people who occupied the station went out of their way to get there, coming from their various homes to the station expressly to occupy it and to be arrested for their action. Rosa Parks, on the other hand, committed civil disobedience without going a single step out of her way; in fact, she committed it precisely by trying to proceed along her way, seeking not to be arrested but simply to go home.

(3) Thoreau's action is also male action. I say this not because of such explicitly misogynist remarks as that the state is as "timid as a lone woman with her silver spoons" (80), but rather because Thoreau emphatically associates acting from conscience with being a man:

> Oh for a man who is a *man*, and, as my neighbor says, has a bone in his back which you cannot pass your hand through! . . . How many *men* are there to a square thousand miles in this country? Hardly one. Does not America offer any inducement for men to settle here? (70)

This association between conscience and manhood is pervasive and uncontradicted. At crucial passages in the essay, "man" is the crucial word—e.g., "if ten men whom I could name,—if ten *honest* men only,—aye, if one HONEST man" (75). Like Emerson, Thoreau imagined resistance in relation to maleness; both of them depicted the pressures of democracy on the individual as threats to manhood. Others did too; one of the most vivid accounts of that position is in fact given by Alexis de Tocqueville, in a notable passage on the tyranny of the majority that Thoreau might have subscribed to:

> In that immense crowd which throngs the avenues to power in the United States, I found very few men who displayed that manly candor and masculine independence of opinion which frequently distinguished the Americans in former times.[20]

It is no accident that Thoreau's essay has influenced so few women. Women like Rosa Parks can act in Thoreau's spirit; but few women activists make much of Thoreau's essay.[21]

(4) Thoreau spent the night in prison by accident, at least according to local history; a veiled woman brought the money to pay his tax the evening of his arrest, but the jailer had already taken his boots off and said that he wasn't going to put them back on. Thoreau in the essay, though, makes his imprisonment a moral necessity, and probably no sentence of the work has been quoted more than the one in which he does so: "Under a government which imprisons any unjustly, the true place for a just man is also a prison" (76).

It would be going too far afield here to describe Thoreau's role in the history of the meaning of imprisonment, though certainly he contributed to our sense of the prison as a place of vision, from which it is possible to see social truths ordinarily hidden. Thoreau in the essay links his imprisonment to his voluntary poverty:

> I have contemplated the imprisonment of the offender, rather than the seizure of his goods,—though both will serve the same purpose,—because they who assert the purest right, and consequently are most dangerous to a corrupt State, commonly have not spent much time in accumulating property. (77)

And that link is important. Tax resisters in the historic peace churches did not practice voluntary poverty; they often sought only to pay money into non-military funds, and sometimes when the government denied their petition to do this, it punished them only by fining them, its goal after all being chiefly to raise money. Thoreau contributes to a different image of the dissident: not the revolutionary but the ascetic, or rather the revolutionary as ascetic, whose political action is in accord with, is almost a consequence of, what we would now call his or her lifestyle.

(5) Finally, Thoreau's action is resistance. I have discussed this term earlier, in reference to the public meanings given it by Garrison and Douglass. In the essay, though, Thoreau gives the term a more idiosyncratic meaning, in relation to the symbol of machinery.

Leo Marx, in *The Machine and the Garden*, has famously demonstrated the power of this symbol, and its association with strong American self-images. He has also demonstrated the complexity of Thoreau's relation to it, though chiefly with reference to passages in *Walden*. "Resistance to Civil Government" dramatizes an equally complex relation. In it, Thoreau is asking two questions. First, in the large symbol of the machine as government, what sub-symbols represent injustice, in particular slavery and unjust wars? And then, what sub-symbols represent resistance? It seems at first that the answer to the first question is "necessary friction" (73) or at most some particular submachine, "a spring . . . exclusively for itself" (73)—in other words, something construable as part of the normal functioning of the metaphorical machine.

But then Thoreau stands back, as if to say, no—the scale of this comparison is wrong. Slavery is not construable as necessary friction, as the unavoidable imperfection that keeps every mechanical device from being a perpetual motion machine. Slavery is something bigger and more perverse, an impediment to efficient action deliberately built into the machine; it is something that implies a lack of respect for the basic mechanical principles that Thoreau the pencil-maker knew and cherished, something that leads Thoreau to break his own metaphor: "But when the friction comes to have its own machine, . . . I say, let us not have such a machine any longer" (67). Machines have friction, but friction cannot metaphorically describe slavery; to describe slavery, Thoreau needs the paradoxical image of friction having a machine.[22]

Then, having ascertained that slavery is not friction but the machine itself, Thoreau takes over friction to describe the right mode of dissenting action: "Let your life be a counter friction to stop the machine" (73—74). If slavery is the machine, then the individual's job is to stop it; and Thoreau's respect for good mechanical design becomes a resistance to mechanism.

"Resistance," pun intended. Among the positive meanings of the word are some that make it a synonym of "friction." Friction means, among other things, "the resistance which any body meets in moving over another body" (*Oxford English Dictionary* [OED]). An 1840 OED citation speaks of "the friction and resistances of the engine." "Resistance" thus offers a vivid mechanical image of what political opposition should be: a clog on the action of the machinery of government, when that machinery has been taken over for a counter-mechanical purpose. Thoreau devised an ingenious machine for grinding fine graphite; it must have cost him something to imagine political action as a means of making a machine grind to a halt.

(6) Finally, I should note what specific meanings Thoreau does not give his action, what meanings he leaves open. He does not associate it either with a secular or a religious perspective; though he alludes to the New Testament as a document of political use, he draws authority not from it but from "conscience." Not, though, from individual, arbitrary conscience, from Emersonian whim. Let Emerson act on whim, let Garrison and company fulminate as intensely against the Sabbath as against slavery; like King and Gandhi, Thoreau presents his action in relation to practices condemned by a broad consensus: slavery, the Mexican War, the Jim Crow Laws, the South African Black Act. That is why one reproach made against Thoreau's program, namely that it gives too much liberty to the individual conscience, is invalid; Thoreau might in theory give the conscience too much liberty, but the action he describes is directed against things condemned not only by his conscience but also by his community.

Most important, Thoreau does not associate his action with a position on violence. Tolstoy, Gandhi, and King have of course associated Thoreau's essay with a rejection of violence. An anonymous member of the Danish resistance learned a different lesson from it:

> Thoreau's "Civil Disobedience" stood for me, and for my first leader in the resistance movement, as a shining light with which we could examine the policy of complete passivity which our government had ordered for the whole Danish population. . . . I lent Thoreau's books to friends, told them about him, and our circle grew. Railroads, bridges, and factories that worked for the Germans were blown up.[23]

And though they contradict each other, both readings of Thoreau are right.

Thoreau speaks of a "peaceable revolution" (76) and brilliantly describes an action that has a long history of association with nonviolence. Moreover, his need to economize on action, to leave room in his life for "other concerns," attracts him to certain nonviolent actions on the ground of their simplicity. But nonviolence is not a first principle for him; it is at most a practical preference. The essay takes almost no position on the matter. (That, too, distinguishes it from nonresistant writing, which is always deriving particular positions from an axiom of nonviolence.) Thoreau criticizes the Mexican War not as a war but as an unjust war; he criticizes not prisons, but unjust imprisonments. He says that if we are cheated "out of a single dollar by [our] neighbor . . . [we] take effectual steps at once to obtain the full amount, and see that [we] are never cheated again" (72), and he does not stipulate that the effectual steps be nonresistant ones. In the one passage that considers that matter explicitly, he accepts the possibility of violence with equanimity:

> But even suppose blood should flow. Is there not a sort of blood shed when the conscience is wounded? . . . I see this blood flowing now. (77)

This is somewhat evasive—Thoreau does not make clear, though he could have, whether the blood that might flow belongs to resisters or slaveholders. What is clear is that Thoreau is willing to have someone's real blood flow, because, in his view, metaphorical blood is flowing already.

It is thus almost an accident that the essay depicts a nonviolent action. Between 1842 and 1849, the direct action that Thoreau found himself called to do was a nonviolent one. But as Thoreau himself wrote, that was only his "position at present":

> One cannot be too much on his guard in such a case, lest his action be biassed by obstinacy, or an undue regard for the opinions of men. Let him see that he does only what belongs to himself and to the hour. (84)

Later, after the passage of the Fugitive Slave Law in 1850, and still more after John Brown's raid, Thoreau defends violent actions on the same grounds as those on which he has defended nonviolent action—because, by that time, what belonged to the hour had changed, and the actions he found himself called to defend were violent. Consider this passage from "A Plea for Captain John Brown":

> It was [Brown's] peculiar doctrine that a man has a perfect right to interfere by force with the slaveholder, in order to rescue the slave. I agree with him. . . . I do not wish to kill nor to be killed, but I can foresee circumstances in which both these things would be by me unavoidable.[24]

Both the earlier and later essays explain and defend the direct action that Thoreau found appropriate to the moment. And that pragmatic focus on a particular action makes Thoreau's essay legitimately available to sharply opposed readers; both King and Gandhi, on the one hand, and the anonymous fighter in the Danish resistance on the other, are reading Thoreau rightly.[25]

On the Second Title

"Civil Disobedience," the name given Thoreau's essay for its posthumous publication in 1866, may or may not have been

Thoreau's title; the evidence leaves both possibilities open.[26] But whoever devised the title had an influence on the afterlife of the essay.

Most people take "civil" in "civil disobedience" to mean "citizenly" rather than "courteous." The standard French translation is "Désobéir aux lois" (disobeying the laws). That takes "civil" as referring to the object of disobedience; "civil" disobedience means disobeying the laws governing citizens. A German translation, "Über die Pflicht zum Ungehorsam gegen den Staat" ("On the Duty of Disobedience to the State"), emphasizes the same meaning (Timpe, *Thoreau Abroad*, 89). Martin Buber refers to Thoreau's "Traktat über den 'bürgerlichen Ungehorsam'" (19) ("Tractate on 'civic/bourgeois disobedience'"), adding a connotation of "middle-class," though still removing the suggestion of "civility."[27] And certainly most accounts of Thoreau's essay push "civil" towards "civic," in accord with Thoreau's own claim that he is speaking "practically, as a citizen" (64).

But when the phrase was new—and it seems to have been used for the first time as the 1866 title[28]—"citizenly" and "courteous" might have had equal claim, and almost all actions that American protestors call "civil disobedience" are nonviolent actions, though in theory a citizen's disobedience could be as violent as the Boston Tea Party or John Brown's raid. In one famous case, moreover, we can watch the "civility" sense having an effect. This is Gandhi's comment in *Young India* for March 23, 1921:

> Civil Disobedience is civil breach of unmoral statutory enactments. The expression was, so far as I am aware, coined by Thoreau to signify his own resistance to the laws of a slave state. . . . But Thoreau was not perhaps an out and out champion of non-violence. Probably, also, Thoreau limited his breach of statutory laws to the revenue law, i.e. payment of taxes. Whereas the term Civil Disobedience as practised in 1919 covered a breach of any statutory and unmoral law. It signified the resister's outlawry in a civil, i.e., non-violent manner. . . . Until I read that essay I never found a suitable English translation for my Indian word, *Satyagraha*.[29]

It was then the "civility" sense that made it possible for Gandhi to name his movement after Thoreau's term. No doubt Thoreau's work would have affected Gandhi even under a different title; but the particular words mattered. If they were not Thoreau's, then it seems that that accident, too, has helped to give Thoreau's essay its influence.

Conclusion

Emerson wrote of "the severity of [Thoreau's] ideal"[30] and suggested that "it was easy to trace to the inexorable demand on all for perfect truth that austerity which made this willing hermit more solitary even than he wished." This is a common reproach, though not usually so well formulated. But looking closely at Thoreau's most inexorably demanding essay hints at another truth as well: that Thoreau undogmatically sorted through all of the traditions available to him, rejecting what he could not use and holding fast what was good. The non-resistance of Garrison, Ballou, and Alcott, the revolutionary action of 1775, the Transcendentalist emphasis on conscience, the large historical events and small personal accidents of Thoreau's own time, his mechanical expertise, and his masculine insecurity are all sifted for use in the essay. What has made the essay capable of exerting so great an influence is not only the severity of its ideal but also its concreteness and unsystematic pragmatism.

NOTES

My very great thanks to Bill Cain, Lewis Hyde, and Taylor Stoehr, for exhilarating and edifying conversation about the matters treated in this essay.

1. I have discussed this in "On Wartax Resistance."

2. Tolstoy is actually a questionable case; Clarence Manning's "Thoreau and Tolstoy" sets out the differences between the two men rather than their similarities. Jerzy Krzyzanowski's "Thoreau in Russia" sets out the basic facts: in 1894, Tolstoy read an article on Thoreau by John Trevor in *Labour Prophet*; this led to his ordering a

copy of "Civil Disobedience," then arranging for its translation in 1898, for publication in the journal *Free Word*. Passages from Thoreau, like passages from Emerson, turn up in Tolstoy's *A Circle of Reading*, and Tolstoy sometimes refers to Thoreau, but almost always as part of a formulaic list including Adin Ballou, Emerson, William Lloyd Garrison, and Theodore Parker.

3. Robert Gross, in a personal communication (2/8/99), points out that it may be a mistake to "accept at face value Thoreau's account of his first act of tax resistance, his refusal to pay the 1840 First Parish Tax." He suggests, convincingly, that "Thoreau's claim that he was told to pay the tax or go to jail is questionable. On January 1, 1834, church and state were formally disestablished in Massachusetts. Thereafter, nobody was required by law to pay a tax in support of a local church. To be sure, for a decade or so, many towns continued to collect parish taxes, and if a person did not want to pay, he had to give formal notice that he was "signing off" the parish. That is what Thoreau did in 1840 and what more than half the tax-payers in Concord had already done by that date. (See John Sweet's essay on the Concord church in *Massachusetts Historical Society Proceedings* 104 [1992]: 73–109.) This was the routine procedure, known to one and all. Jail for non-payment, as I understand it, no longer existed as a legal sanction.

So, why did Thoreau represent the episode the way he did? Maybe he was misinformed, though that seems unlikely. His aunts had signed off the First Parish in order to join the Trinitarian Church, and his mother had first left, then returned to the First Parish. These acts had taken place before formal disestablishment, but they do indicate a familiarity with the legal procedures in the Thoreau family. A likelier reason is Thoreau's desire to dramatize himself. Had he noted that he was just another one of many score who had been signing off the First Parish rolls, he would have undercut the persona he assumed in the text. The 'state' would have dwindled in its force, and he would have appeared less heroic. And that reduction of the first act of tax resistance might have affected his account of the subsequent ones."

This seems to me exact and convincing, and I thank Professor Gross for his erudition and generosity.

4. On the nature of this tax, see John Broderick's excellent "Thoreau, Alcott, and the Poll Tax."

5. Thoreau, "Resistance to Civil Government," in *Reform Papers*, 79. Page numbers for subsequent quotations will be given parenthetically in the text.

6. Barbara Andrews, in "Tax Resistance in American History," sets out the wider background of tax resistance, focusing on resistance in the historical peace churches; but it does not seem from Thoreau's account that this wider background was relevant to his action.

7. Charles Lane, "State Slavery," *The Liberator*, 16.

8. Lane, "Voluntary Political Government," *The Liberator*, 36.

9. Adin Ballou, "Christian Non-Resistance," 52; page numbers for subsequent quotations will be given parenthetically in the text.

10. Alcott, *Journals*, 184. Page numbers for subsequent quotations will be given parenthetically in the text.

11. William Lloyd Garrison, "Declaration of Sentiments, 1838," in Staughton and Alice Lynd, *Nonviolence in America*," p. 16; page numbers for subsequent quotations will be given parenthetically in the text. Note that Garrison's choice of the term "jacobinism" tendentiously associates resistance with the French Revolution and the Reign of Terror, and thereby discredits it.

12. Frederick Douglass, "Narrative of the Life," in *The Narrative and Selected Writings*, 80–81.

13. Staughton Lynd and Alice Lynd, "Introduction," to *Nonviolence in America*, xix.

14. Martin Luther King, "Stride toward Freedom," in *A Testament of Hope*, 429. Page numbers for subsequent quotations will be given parenthetically in the text.

15. However improbable this seems, it is true; Garrison writes, "to extort money from enemies, or set them upon a pillory, *or cast them into prison,* or hang them upon a gallows, is obviously not to forgive, but to take retribution" ("Declaration of Sentiments," 28; emphasis added).

16. Emerson, "The American Scholar," in *Selections from Ralph Waldo Emerson*, 71.

17. Staughton Lynd, "Henry Thoreau: The Admirable Radical," quoted in Michael Meyer, *Several More Lives to Live*, 165.

18. As if in half-conscious self-criticism, Thoreau links himself by this phrase to Pontius Pilate, who, refusing to resist the multitude's call to crucify Jesus, "washed his hands before the multitude, saying,

I am innocent of the blood of this just person: see ye to it" (King James Bible, Matt. 27:24).

19. John Jay Chapman, "Emerson," in *The Shock of Recognition*, 601.

20. Alexis de Tocqueville, *Democracy in America*, vol. 1, 266.

21. On all this see also the excellent essay by Dana Nelson in this volume.

22. My thanks to my mathematician neighbor and friend, Louis Piscitelle, and to my chemist colleague and friend, William Coleman, for illuminating conversations on this point.

Lewis Hyde pointed out to me that in a strict sense there is nothing paradoxical about a friction having its own machine—Thoreau's own graphite grinding machine, to say nothing of any coffee grinder, is a friction that has its machine. But Thoreau's phrasing suggests that he wants the image to be understood as a paradox nonetheless.

23. Anonymous, "Thoreau and the Danish Resistance," in *Thoreau in Our Season*, 20.

24. Thoreau, "A Plea for Captain John Brown," in *Reform Papers*, 132–33.

25. Gandhi knew all this, I think; at one point he writes with dry irony, "Thoreau was not perhaps an out and out champion of nonviolence" (Gandhi, *Non-Violent Resistance (Satyagraha)*, 3).

26. Wendell Glick, "Textual Introduction," in *Reform Papers*, 320.

27. Martin Buber, "Man's Duty as Man," in *Thoreau in Our Season*, 19.

28. Glick, 320.

29. Gandhi, *Nonviolent Resistance*, 3–4 and 14.

30. Emerson, "Thoreau," in *Selections*, 392. The subsequent quotation from the essay is drawn from the same page.

REFERENCES

Adams, Raymond. "Thoreau's Sources for 'Resistance to Civil Government.'" *Studies in Philology* 42 (1945) : 640–53.

Andrews, Barbara. "Tax Resistance in American History." Undergraduate thesis, Goddard College, 1976.

Alcott, Amos Bronson. *Journals.* Edited by Odell Shepard. Boston: Little, Brown, 1938.

Ballou, Adin. "Christian Non-Resistance." In *Nonviolence in America: A Documentary History,* edited by Staughton Lynd, 31–57. Indianapolis: Bobbs-Merrill, 1966.

Broderick, John C. "Thoreau, Alcott, and the Poll Tax." *Studies in Philology* 53 (1956) : 612–26.

Buber, Martin. "Man's Duty as Man." In *Thoreau in Our Season,* edited by John H. Hicks, 19. Amherst: University of Massachusetts Press, 1966.

Chapman, John Jay. "Emerson." In *The Shock of Recognition,* edited by Edmund Wilson, 600–58. New York: Grosset and Dunlap, 1953.

Douglass, Frederick. *The Narrative and Selected Writings.* Edited by Michael Meyer. New York: Modern Library, 1984.

Drinnon, Richard. "Thoreau's Politics of the Upright Man." In Walden *and "Resistance to Civil Government,"* 2d ed., edited by William Rossi, 366–77. New York: Norton, 1992.

Emerson, Raldo Waldo. *Selections from Ralph Waldo Emerson: An Organic Anthology.* Edited by Stephen E. Whicher. Boston: Houghton Mifflin, 1957.

Gandhi, M. K. *Non-Violent Resistance (Satyagraha).* Edited by Bharatan Kumarappa. New York: Schocken, 1961.

Garrison, William Lloyd. "Declaration of Sentiments, 1838." In *Nonviolence in America: A Documentary History,* rev. ed., edited by Staughton Lynd and Alice Lynd, 13–17. Maryknoll: Orbis, 1995.

Glick, Wendell. "Thoreau and Radical Abolitionism: A Study of the Native Background of Thoreau's Social Philosophy." Ph.D. diss., Northwestern University, 1950.

Harding, Walter. *The Days of Henry Thoreau: A Biography.* New York: Dover, 1982.

Hedemann, Ed, ed. *Guide to War Tax Resistance.* 3d ed. New York: War Resisters League, 1986.

Hendrick, George. "The Influence of Thoreau's 'Civil Disobedience' on Gandhi's *Satyagraha.*" *New England Quarterly* 29 (1956): 462–71.

———. "Thoreau and Gandhi: A Study of 'Civil Disobedience' and *Satyagraha.*" Ph.D. diss., University of Texas, 1954.

Hicks, John H., ed. *Thoreau in Our Season.* Amherst: University of Massachusetts Press, 1966.

Hyde, Lewis. "A Tall White Pine: Thinking about Prophecy." In *From the Island's Edge,* edited by Carolyn Servid, 262–71. St. Paul, Minn.: Greywolf Press, 1995.

Hyman, Stanley Edgar. "Henry Thoreau in Our Time." *Atlantic Monthly* 178 (November 1946): 137–46.

King, Martin Luther, Jr. *A Testament of Hope: The Essential Writings of Martin Luther King, Jr.* Edited by James Melvin Washington. San Francisco: Harper & Row, 1986.

Krzyzanowski, Jerzy R. "Thoreau in Russia." In *Thoreau Abroad: Twelve Bibliographical Essay,* edited by Eugene F. Timpe, 131–40. Hamden, Conn.: Archon, 1971.

Lane, Charles. "State Slavery—Imprisonment of A. Bronson Alcott—Dawn of Liberty." *The Liberator,* 27 January 1843, 16.

———. "Voluntary Political Government." *The Liberator,* 3 March 1843, 36.

Lynd, Staughton, ed. *Nonviolence in America: A Documentary History.* Indianapolis: Bobbs-Merrill, 1966.

Lynd, Staughton, and Alice Lynd, eds. *Nonviolence in America: A Documentary History.* Rev. ed. Maryknoll: Orbis, 1995

Manning, Clarence A. "Thoreau and Tolstoy." *New England Quarterly* 16 (June 1943): 234–43.

Marx, Leo. *The Machine in the Garden.* New York: Oxford University Press, 1964.

Meyer, Michael. *Several More Lives to Live: Thoreau's Political Reputation in America.* Westport, Conn.: Greenwood, 1977.

Rosenwald, Lawrence. "On Wartax Resistance." *Agni* 35 (1992): 27–36.

Rossi, William, ed. Walden *and "Resistance to Civil Government."* 2d ed. New York: Norton, 1992.

Salt, Henry S. *Life of Henry David Thoreau.* 1890, rev. 1908. Reprint, edited by George Hendrick, Willene Hendrick, and Fritz Oehlschlaeger. Urbana: University of Illinois Press, 1993.

Stoehr, Taylor. *Nay-Saying in Concord: Emerson, Alcott, and Thoreau.* Hamden, Conn.: Archon, 1979.

"Thoreau and the Danish Resistance." In *Thoreau in Our Season,* edited by John H. Hicks, 20–21. Amherst: University of Massachusetts Press, 1966.

Thoreau, Henry David. *Reform Papers.* Edited by Wendell Glick. Princeton: Princeton University Press, 1973.

Timpe, Eugene F., ed. *Thoreau Abroad: Twelve Bibliographical Essays.* Hamden, Conn.: Archon, 1971.

Tocqueville, Alexis de. *Democracy in America.* 2 vols. Translated by Henry Reeve. Rev. Francis Bowen. Further rev. Phillips Bradley. New York: Vintage, 1990.

Wood, Barry. "Thoreau's Narrative Art in 'Civil Disobedience.'" In Walden *and "Resistance to Civil Government,"* 2d. ed., edited by William Rossi, 421–28. New York: Norton, 1992.

"That Terrible Thoreau"

Concord and Its Hermit

Robert A. Gross

Henry David Thoreau was not an easy man to like. Blunt, outspoken, even combative in conversation, he uttered the truth as he saw it, no matter what others thought or felt. But he tightly guarded the solid wall he erected around himself. From his earliest days, he seemed peculiar. As a schoolboy, he earned the contempt of his peers by refusing to join their play; "he seemed to have no fun in him," one recalled. At college, he was no more successful. His Harvard classmates found him "cold and unimpressible" and made him the "butt for jokes." Not that Thoreau made an effort to win anyone over. In Concord, he would pass neighbors on the street or in the woods without ever pausing to say hello. When an old chum walked seven miles to see him at Walden Pond, Thoreau announced "he had no time for friendship." Even his defenders conceded he was "brusque." Elizabeth Hoar said, "One would as soon think of taking the arm of an elm-tree as Henry's." "I love Henry," she added, "but I can never like him."[1]

If Thoreau's personality alienated some, his public antics infuriated many more. He seemed to go out of his way to offend. One Sunday morning, returning from the woods with a pine tree he had dug up for transplanting, he passed right in front of the meetinghouse as the worshipers were coming out. Did he duck down an alley or hide behind a bush to avoid notice? Not at all. He flaunted his Sabbath-breaking: Transcendentalist and tree paraded down the street, "leaving the church-goers gaping and horrified." Rebuked by his aunt, Thoreau was unapologetic. "Aunt Louisa, I have been worshiping in my way and I don't trouble you in your way." In *Walden*, he was not so tolerant. That account surveyed the ways of the neighbors "in this town" and reached a damning judgment. "Every where, in shops, and offices, and fields, the inhabitants have appeared to me to be doing penance in a thousand remarkable ways." It was "young men, my townsmen," who were burying their manhood in the soil, pushing barns and farms before them as they crept "down the road of life." Based on his travels in Concord, Thoreau sadly concluded that "the mass of men lead lives of quiet desperation." Resolved to wake them up, he sounded his dissent as loudly as chanticleer in the morning. "The greatest part of what my neighbors call good I believe in my soul to be bad."[2]

The neighbors repaid him in the same coin. A Harvard graduate without a regular job, Thoreau appeared idle and irresponsible. Right after college, he had been hired to teach in Concord, at the very school he had attended as a boy, and at a time when such posts were scarce. Within two weeks, he had thrown away the opportunity. Urged by a member of the school committee, who visited his class and found it too noisy, to flog the children, lest "the school spoil," the new master sullenly did as he was told. He picked out a few students at random and hit them with the ferule, then quit in a pique. Such wayward conduct came to typify Thoreau in the common view. He had the gall to change the name he was given at birth. "His name ain't no more Henry D. Thoreau than my name is Henry D. Thoreau," one man said in disgust. "And everybody knows it, and he knows it. His name's Da-a-vid Henry and it ain't never been nothing but Da-a-vid Henry. And he knows it!" Whatever his name, he wasted his time in the woods; worse, in an act of "sheer carelessness," he accidentally set fire to some 300 acres and, after sounding the alarm, sat on a rock and contemplated the blaze, while others struggled to put it out. "Damned rascal," he was called behind his back.

Nor did his sojourn at Walden earn him much respect. He

was derided as "the Hermit of Walden Woods," his vaunted independence dismissed. Rumor had it that he survived his experiment in deliberate living only with help from home. "We have good authority for believing that his closet was often replenished from his mother's larders," a newcomer to Concord, Harriet Hanson Robinson, recorded in her diary. Far from being original, Thoreau looked merely willful. In many eyes, he was a bad copy of Emerson, the Concord Sage. "He is considered to resemble Mr. Emerson," Robinson noted, "but I do not think he does. Mr. E. is a god by the side of him."[3]

Not everybody disliked Thoreau, but even the well disposed were at a loss to comprehend him. "Thoreau was an enigma to all of us," recalled Joseph Hosmer, who had grown up with him. "No one could place him." He baffled Horace Hosmer, too. The younger brother of Joseph, Horace briefly attended the academy kept by John and Henry Thoreau and boarded in the Thoreau household. "I did not pretend to understand Henry D.," he remembered. "I looked upon him as a growing man." Hosmer considered himself an exception: to most people, Thoreau was "an aimless and impracticable dreamer."[4]

Perhaps so, but farmers hired him for odd jobs, landowners employed him as a surveyor, and lovers of nature traded information with him about local flora and fauna. Others were eager to enlist him as an escort for parties of ladies and gentlemen on the river and in the woods. Thoreau would have nothing to do with such schemes. He preferred the company of ne'er-do-well hunters and fishermen, who eked out a living on the margins of the town, to that of the village elite. For the lack of hospitality, he was resented as "rude and unaccommodating." The Transcendentalist Bronson Alcott could celebrate him as "a sort of resident Surveyor-General of the town's farms, farmers, animals, and everything else it contains" and, in his role as superintendent of schools in 1861, propose that the town commission Thoreau to produce an "illustrated Atlas of Concord" for the use of children and citizens alike. Not surprisingly, nobody took the hint. After his death, Concord proved no more willing to honor its native son. Though Thoreau boasted his association with the town—"I have never got over my surprise that I should have been born in the most estimable place in all the world," he wrote in 1856—the town did not return the compliment. Guidebooks for tourists played up Emerson and Hawthorne as the great writers of Concord; Thoreau appeared as a minor figure. And when the locals visited Walden Pond, they went for recreation, not on a pilgrimage to a sacred site.[5]

It is common to blame Ralph Waldo Emerson for fostering the unflattering image of his onetime protégé and friend. When Thoreau died in May 1862, Emerson delivered the eulogy at the memorial service, and that discourse set the terms for Thoreau's posthumous reputation. The Concord Sage paid tribute to a profound student of "Nature's secret and genius." Devoting "his genius with such entire love to the fields, hills and waters of his native town," Thoreau gained a rare intimacy with nature. The very birds and fishes had become, "as it were, townsmen and fellow creatures." Emerson admired his friend's keen "power of observation" and praised still more the spiritual end it served. To Thoreau, as to his biographer, nature was a symbol of the soul, its sights and sounds laden with higher meaning. "He was equally interested in every natural fact. The depth of his perception found likeness of law throughout Nature, and I know not any genius who so swiftly inferred universal law from the single fact." To realize such "spiritual perception" was the Transcendental mission Emerson had defined for "the true philosopher and the true poet" decades before in *Nature*. Henry David Thoreau had heeded that call and kept the master's faith.

But at how large a price! So pure was his purpose, so constant his quest for nature's truths, that Thoreau cut himself off from his fellow men. His was truly the life of "a hermit and stoic," rich only in renunciations. "The severity of his ideal interfered to deprive him of a healthy sufficiency of human society." Unsparing of himself, Thoreau could not allow for the compromises and faults of others. "That terrible Thoreau," his friends called him, in a double-edged tribute to the "dangerous frankness" of his relations with them. Who could forget his "accusing silences" and "searching and irresistible speeches, battering down all defenses"? Isolated in austerity, Thoreau had forfeited the leadership to which he seemed destined. "I cannot help counting it a fault in him that he had no ambition," Emerson concluded and then, in an unforgettable turn of phrase, branded him a failure. "Wanting this, instead of engineering for all America, he was the captain of a huckleberry party."[6]

"It is difficult to imagine a eulogy by a close friend more damaging to a writer's reputation than Emerson's," writes Robert Sattelmeyer. Limned as a "bachelor of thought and nature," Thoreau was trapped in Emerson's gaze, exactly as he had been at the start of his career. In *A Fable for Critics* (1849), the poet James Russell Lowell had mocked Thoreau as an Emerson wanna-be, stealing the apples from his neighbor's orchard. In the wake of Thoreau's death, Lowell renewed the charge. Thoreau's writings were now "strawberries from [Emerson's] own garden," but hardly as sweet. To be sure, Thoreau could write "sentences . . . as perfect as anything in the language," but his work expressed an unhealthy spirit. Thoreau was all ego, with no "faculty of generalizing from outside of himself." This judgment by "the most widely respected American critic of his time" stuck. Thoreau's image was fixed as the Hermit of Walden, indulging misanthropy in what the *New York Times* in 1865 called "a cold and selfish isolation from human cares and interests."[7]

These jibes drive Thoreau's defenders to distraction. He was not all sharp edges, they insist. He had a devoted band of friends. Children loved him. A warm heart beat beneath that cold exterior. He had courted Ellen Sewall and lost; nobody could ever take her place. He was a loyal brother and a sensitive son. If he did occasionally thunder against human "stupidity," greed, meanness, and other follies, that was a measure of his high hopes for humanity, not a sign of cynicism. Thoreau's art and thought are not, in any event, reducible to personality. The retreat at Walden expressed a serious social critique. His studies of nature explored the interdependence of all living things. Far from being secluded in the woods, he was attuned to his town and to his times.[8]

Yet, this campaign to humanize Thoreau misses the mark. Whatever the distortions of Emerson and Lowell, their assessments were not unique. Contemporary critics of *Walden* had also seized upon the hermit image to characterize the author and dismiss his work. In other formulations, he was portrayed as Robinson Crusoe in New England and a "Yankee Diogenes." Were the reviewers misguided, too? Actually, the critics were repeating what the neighbors had been saying for years. The antisocial strain in Thoreau irritated many in Concord. They indicted his individualism as selfishness, deemed him unneighborly, and spurned his radicalism. Were they all wrong? That is one response, and it is invoked to account for the townspeople's displeasure. A herd of conformists, who did lead lives of "quiet desperation," the neighbors could not abide a nay-sayer like Thoreau, and they naturally resented the mirror he held up to the town. "For generations," Horace Hosmer maintained, "the Concord people had been raised from the cradle to the grave to fear God and the Hoar family, to be respectable, to vote a straight ticket . . . & to pay their taxes without question or murmur." But this position merely rehearses Thoreau's quarrel with the community. And it begs a central issue: how did Thoreau, the only native of Concord in the Transcendentalist circle, a man who spent nearly all of his life in the town and proclaimed that "I carry Concord ground in my boots and in my hat," turn out so differently from the neighbors? Was it an accident of personality, compounded by philosophy? Or was he subtly bound to them, as he occasionally conceded, by "a thousand imperceptible ties"?[9]

At first glance, Thoreau's life in Concord appears, like his ideal home, "as open and manifest as a bird's nest." Compared to the neighbors, even those his own age, Thoreau was strange. He carried individualism to an extreme. When he set down in Walden Woods, "a mile from any neighbor," the townspeople were concerned; just about the first questions they asked were "if I did not feel lonesome; if I was not afraid; and the like." With good reason. Hardly anybody in Concord lived alone. In 1850, just three years after Thoreau's sojourn at Walden, the census-taker found only thirteen individuals, in a town of 2,249, keeping house on their own, apart from family and friends. Nearly all were women: old, poor widows and spinsters, without anybody to care for them. Their isolation constituted a cruel necessity, not a philosophical choice. "Who could live alone and independent?" Concord's minister Ezra Ripley once asked the congregation.

"Who but some disgusted hermit or half crazy enthusiast will say to society, I have no need of thee; I am under no obligation to my fellow-men?" Only the "willing hermit" of Walden delighted in solitude.[10]

Thoreau also shunned the rituals of civic life. In an era of popular democracy, he did not vote, nor did he join his neighbors in town meeting. He was a notorious tax resister. He "signed off" the parish in 1840 and avoided public worship. "Know all men by these presents," he dramatically declared, "that I, Henry Thoreau, do not wish to be regarded as a member of any incorporated society which I have not joined." Hardly any attracted him. While his neighbors were forming dozens of voluntary associations—libraries, lyceums, charitable and missionary groups, masonic lodges, antislavery and temperance societies, among others—to promote the common good, Thoreau became a member of just one, the Concord Lyceum. It gave him the opportunity to lecture the town.[11]

Thoreau boasted his independence and outpaced his neighbors in dissent. Even so, others marched to the same music he heard. Neither church nor state commanded universal allegiance. For two centuries, Massachusetts had sustained the Puritan ideal of religious order. It required the inhabitants of every town to found a church and fund it through taxes. Concord, settled in 1635, readily complied. Then in 1834 came disestablishment. Bowing to demands from spiritual minorities, Massachusetts separated church and state. No longer was support for religion a civic duty. It became a matter of voluntary choice. Thoreau's neighbors seized their new freedom. They deserted the town church in droves; by 1840, when the 22-year-old Thoreau signed off, two-thirds of the taxpayers had done the same. Far from being a bold voice of conscience, Thoreau followed the crowd. Nor was he alone in his abstention from voting. On election day, a good many townsmen stayed away from the polls. Even the raucous campaign of 1840, when Whigs stole the Democrats' populist thunder and rallied for "Tippecanoe and Tyler too," failed to stir three out of ten eligible voters. During the Mexican War half boycotted the ballot, perhaps out of the same alienation that led Thoreau to civil disobedience. Amid the din of politics in the Jacksonian age could be heard murmurs of disgust.[12]

"To act collectively is according to the spirit of our institutions," Thoreau acknowledged in *Walden*, and he was prepared to act upon that truth, but only upon his own terms. In the late 1830s, antislavery activists in New England began petitioning Congress to stop the expansion of the peculiar institution. Just out of Harvard, "D. H. Thoreau," as he still styled himself, joined that effort, signing statements against the annexation of Texas, the admission of new slave states to the Union, and the practice of slavery in the District of Columbia. Though this campaign drew only a minority in Concord, at best a third of the town, it was a family affair for the Thoreaus. The new graduate lined up alongside his father and mother, older brother, and aunts in the abolitionist cause. He did so for a couple more years, then abruptly dropped out.[13] Even as the Mexican War swelled the antislavery ranks, Thoreau determined to go it alone, in dramatic gestures of protest. "It is not my business to be petitioning the governor or legislature," he explained, "any more than it is theirs to petition me." While others expressed their opinions on paper, he went to jail for a night. Less publicly, he aided the flight of fugitive slaves to safety in Canada. Thoreau was flexible on the subject of petitions. He could not stay aloof when a black man in Boston was unfairly convicted of murder and sentenced to die; lest silence imply consent to the state's "crime," he added his name to a protest signed by some 400 neighbors. On another occasion, Thoreau started a drive to raise money for an Irish laborer who had won a spading contest at the county cattle fair, only to be cheated out of the $4 prize by his mean-spirited employer. The initiative suited Thoreau's militant temperament; if something had to be done, he did not wait for others. After John Brown was captured, tried, and sentenced to hang for his abortive bid to spark a slave rebellion in western Virginia, Thoreau was shocked to find that nobody, not even William Lloyd Garrison, was willing to rise in his defense. So, he took on the task himself, announcing that he would address his fellow citizens in Town Hall. That plan upset local abolitionists and Republicans; fearful of a popular backlash against antislavery, they urged

Thoreau to cancel the speech. "I did not send to you for advice," he replied, "but to announce that I am to speak." Like his hero John Brown, Thoreau set his own course, independent of others, and strode steadfastly toward his goal. Against a world of greed, hypocrisy, and moral timidity, he cast himself as a lone man of principle, sincerely enacting "the purpose of a life."[14]

For all his extravagance, Thoreau expressed an impulse to individualism felt by many contemporaries and formed in response to fundamental changes in New England. Theirs was an "age of Revolution," in Emerson's words, which took the small, ordered society founded by Puritans and defended by Minutemen and unsettled it through the expansive forces of capitalism and democracy. That transformation remade the rural economy, as farm families gradually abandoned efforts to supply their own needs and deepened their dependence on the market. Throwing off old constraints, they loosened ties to neighbors, rationalized their work, and bound their fortunes to the larger world. So, in turn, did artisans alter their sights. No longer confined to custom jobs for a narrow clientele, many pursued profits from general sales; others sought places in the mills springing up throughout the countryside and in the growing cities. A society of owners and operatives loomed. The spread of markets brought fresh diversity and fluidity to the region. Lively central villages took shape in country towns, demarcated by banks, stores, shops, printing and post offices, courthouses and lawyers, and inns, all geared to the quickening movement of goods, money, and people. Through these outposts of urbanity circulated the latest ideas in the Western world, thanks to an abundance of books, magazines, and newspapers in the literary marketplace and to the vigorous activities of academies, libraries, lyceums, Sunday schools, and other innovative institutions. Exposed to cosmopolitan currents of thought, endowed with unparalleled choices, New Englanders questioned established ways and strove to reconcile old and new.[15]

These relentless changes reshaped the contours of everyday life. With dazzling opportunities came disturbing uncertainties. "The question of the times," as Emerson put it, "resolved itself into a practical question. . . . How shall I live?" For farmers, the calculations were demanding: cling to tradition and risk decline; gamble the future on new crops, markets, and methods; start over on the frontier or in the expanding cities. Similar decisions beset artisans, merchants, and professionals. Such choices put pressures on family life. Parents were challenged to prepare children for a world in flux. As the passage of farms and trades from fathers to sons faltered, so did the practices of raising the young. Patriarchal authority, under fire since the Revolution, lost hold. The rising generation struggled to steer its course through uncharted terrain. What calling should a young man pursue? Where should he settle? When would he marry and start a household? No more fixed were the futures of women, who struck out for new roles within and beyond the home. Under these circumstances, where ancient precepts collided with contemporary imperatives, Emerson discerned deep-seated discontent. Was it any wonder that young men "find themselves not in the state of mind of their fathers, and regret the coming state as untried, as a boy dreads the water before he has learned to swim?" Characteristically, Thoreau embraced that message and dove off the deep end. "What old people say you cannot do you try and find you can. . . . I have lived some thirty years on this planet," he declared in *Walden*, "and I have yet to hear the first syllable of valuable or even earnest advice from my seniors."[16]

The dilemmas of change bore with special force on Thoreau's generation. Where Emerson, born in 1803, grew up in Boston during the waning years of the old order, Thoreau came of age in Concord with the new. At his birth in 1817, Concord was a small country town of some 1,740 inhabitants, not much bigger than it had been in 1800, when his grandfather John Thoreau moved there from Boston, sixteen miles east on the coast, and started a store on the common. (He died the next year.) Long a trading center for Middlesex County and a seat of courts, Concord bustled with business at the century's start. Its merchants advertised "the largest assortment of *English Goods*, ever offered in any Country Town" at prices "cheaper in Concord than at Boston!" The village supported a collection of clockmakers employing a modern division of labor to produce timepieces "by the dozen" for sale in "any part of the country." From the town's farms flowed cartloads of barreled beef and pork, destined for West Indian plantations, and surpluses of wood, rye, and hay to build and feed the expanding ports. These enterprises were buoyed by the surge in American commerce during the wars of the French Revolution. But the boom ended abruptly, with a trade embargo in 1807 and then war with Britain in 1812. Henry Thoreau's father John was one victim of the crash. After finishing his clerkship as a merchant in 1808, he launched a store in Concord center; it folded within two years. For a decade, he cast about for ways to support a growing family, trying and failing with stores in Chelmsford and Boston, teaching school, farming, and turning ultimately and successfully to pencil-making. His protracted search for a living reflected New England and Concord's painful adjustment to hard times.[17]

Henry Thoreau's youth coincided with a long wave of growth, extending from the 1820s through the 1850s, during which Concord rode the tide with the rest of New England into Industrial Revolution. For a time, expansion benefited small towns and big cities alike, even as it integrated them into a single economic region. Concord enjoyed a modest rise in numbers, its population reaching 2,000 in 1830 and cresting at 2,249 two decades later. The change was most visible in the central village, where capitalist enterprise thrived. In 1830 an optimistic citizen drew up a commercial directory for the town, in anticipation of an urban future. It listed some nine stores, forty shops, four hotels and taverns, four doctors and lawyers, and a variety of county associations, nearly all in the center. Thoreau grumbled that he could not walk the streets without being accosted by signs "hung out on all sides to allure him" into the shops. "The vitals of the village," he reckoned, "were the grocery, the barroom, the post-office, and the bank." A crucial source of money and credit, the bank was key to the new economic order. As its notes circulated in trade, they became the chief currency of exchange. Merchants who had once welcomed farm goods in payment of bills now favored cash as "the one thing needful." Business assumed a more impersonal air with the cash nexus. Instead of haggling over prices, storekeepers preferred to post single charges, take it or leave it. Access to credit could determine suc-

cess or failure for a struggling firm. After entering pencil-making
on his own in 1824, John Thoreau borrowed constantly to finance
the business. By 1843 a sizable share of his inventory, some $800
worth of pencils, sat idle in the Concord Bank, hostage to an un-
paid loan. There is no record that it was ever released.[18]

Outside the village, Concord retained a traditional look, with
some 200 farms, about sixty acres each, dotting the landscape, as
in the colonial era. These enterprises sustained a familiar agricultural economy, based on cereals, grasses, and cattle, down to
1840. But the continuity was superficial. Within its framework,
farmers steadily devoted more and more attention to urban markets. They concentrated on oats and hay to feed the burgeoning
population of horses that pulled the teams and omnibuses of
Boston and Lowell. Large tracts of wetland were drained and
pastures plowed for the production of "English hay," the cultivated grass that Thoreau scorned as the very emblem of a cash
crop, its every aspect exploited for profit—"carefully weighed,
the moisture calculated, the silicates and the potash." So, too,
were Concord's woodlands stripped to meet a remorseless demand for lumber and fuel; by 1850 only one acre in ten stood in
forest. These commodities supplanted the staples of old-time
farming. Once the Erie Canal brought cheap wheat flour from
the Genessee country to the local bakeshop, farmers stopped
growing rye and corn for homemade bread, in a departure from
"simplicity and independence" that Thoreau could not fathom.
And with cheap cotton textiles from New England's factories on
sale at the dry goods store, there was no point to raising flax and
wool for homespun. These changes paved the way for more stunning shifts after the coming of the railroad in 1844. With Boston
less than an hour away, farmers jettisoned the old husbandry
altogether and found a new livelihood in milk, vegetables,
and fruits, including a native variety of grape, developed by a
goldsmith-turned-gardener named Ephraim Bull, to which the
town gave its name.[19]

As farmers adapted to shifting markets, they altered basic conditions of their work. In the preindustrial countryside, neighbors
regularly aided one another to accomplish seasonal tasks. Individuals "changed works," helping out in plowing, for example, in

exchange for assistance in reaping, and they came together in larger "bees" for heavy or tedious labors, such as raising a roof or husking corn. These cooperative efforts were indispensable in a world where many lacked enough labor or tools to get by. Combining work and leisure, they knit separate households into a dense web of interdependence. But the market revolution sundered those ties. Agricultural reformers condemned bees as wasteful frolics, given over to heavy drinking and coarse entertainment. As for "changing works," farmers should be sparing; too often it led to "lounging and idleness, and neglect of business." Efficiency mattered more than sociability. When modern men needed work done, they hired help or did it themselves. Increasingly, that meant relying upon strangers rather than kin. As land became scarce in old towns like Concord, the frontier beckoned to the young, whose "wagons," Emerson noted, "have rattled down the remote western hills." Taking the place of sons and daughters was a new class of hired hands: transient laborers who signed on for a few seasons and were soon gone or Irish immigrants, who by 1855 made up nearly a fifth of Concord. Whatever their origins, they were paid the going wage. As in the store, so on the farm, social relations grew more impersonal. The claims of cash eroded the chain of community.[20]

Concord registered the change in widening distances among its citizens. Never an egalitarian place, the town experienced a deepening divide between rich and poor. The commercial elite—the top fifth of taxpayers—captured the lion's share of the expanding wealth. In 1801 it controlled well over half the town's assets; twenty-five years later, two-thirds; by 1850 the figure was 82 percent. At the same time, the ranks of the propertyless swelled. In 1826 some 250 men—more than half the adult males—owned no land at all; by 1850 the landless numbered 419, or seven out of every ten. When Thoreau embarked on his experiment in independent living, he was lucky to find a sponsor in Emerson, who offered land, rent free, at Walden Pond. Typical of the town's young males, the 28-year-old Harvard graduate had nothing taxable to his name, except his self. Though he claimed "letters as his profession," he appeared on the tax lists as merely one among many landless laborers, obliged to others for their daily bread. In the shops and farms, workers came and went with hardly a trace. A factory village rose up in west Concord, centered around a cotton and woolen mill; though the owner, Edward Damon, quickly entered the elite, the sixty operatives, recruited from elsewhere, remained an anonymous mass, unseen and unremarked. No more stable was the native population. In July 1841 the editor of the *Concord Republican,* William S. Robinson, came across the record book of the Young Men's Debating Society, to which he had belonged a mere decade or so before. Lasting only a few years, from 1827 to 1831, the club had enrolled fifty-one members. As Robinson scanned the list, he was amazed to discover that the aspiring Ciceros of Concord had dispersed far and wide:

> How is the little circle scattered! Four fifths of those who joined so freely in the debates, and gesticulated so eloquently in the dialogues and "single pieces" in the old School House, have departed from the scene of their boyhood. Some are trading in the far South, and in the new States and Territories; some have gone onto the Ocean; some are engaged in professions and trades in our large cities; some are preaching the Gospel; some are teaching youth; some are mechanics and farmers, settled in their own and neighboring States.

Five months later, Robinson joined the exodus.[21]

In this fluid setting, society fractured into diverse and competing interests. A small core of families, rooted on the land or vested with power, presided over a churning scene. Townspeople were divided not only by class and residence but also by religion, politics, and culture. Since 1635 Concord had sustained the Puritan ideal of one town, one church; then in 1826, reacting against the liberal bent of the First Church, a group of orthodox Calvinists seceded from Ezra Ripley's Congregationalist parish and formed a Trinitarian alternative; the dissidents included Thoreau's aunts and, briefly, his mother. Not long after, the Standing Order of Massachusetts came toppling down. Free to choose their own faith, Concord's inhabitants cast their lots among Trinitarians and Unitarians, Methodists, Universalists, and other sects. Some preferred to be "Nothingarians" and support no denomination at all. Not so the Irish, who planted a Catholic church on the common in 1865. Politically, Concord was no more unified. In the first decades of the republic, the townsmen had enlisted in the bitter fight between Federalists and Republicans but seldom carried partisan passions into local affairs. From the 1830s on, politics accentuated social strains. Anti-Masons launched a populist uprising against the Masonic lodge, which they denounced, with some exaggeration, as a citadel of the local elite and seized control of the town. Though that crusade soon waned, Jacksonian Democrats picked up the cause, waging rhetorical battle against the local "aristocrats" of the Whig party for the next two decades. Singled out for special abuse was the Social Circle, a select, self-perpetuating society of the town's leading men, who got together for regular dinners and conversation in one another's homes. In their company was Ralph Waldo Emerson, who deemed the club "the solidest of men, who yield the solidest of gossip." To suspicious outsiders, it looked more like a conspiracy to control town meetings—"nothing more or less, than a volcano of smothered Masonic spirit bursting out in another place."

Such rancor struck the Reverend Ezra Ripley, the town patriarch for some sixty years and a leading Mason, as a symptom of a community in decay. Neighbors used to know one another, share mutual interests, respect others' views, he told the town in 1837. But no more. "With more than a few, it has been too much the practice of neighbors and fellow citizens to live like strangers, and to cherish little or no sympathy for one another. One class of citizens hold themselves at a distance from another class,—one individual from another." With so little in common, they inflated "differences in opinion, on religion and politics" and polarized the community. The octogenarian parson yearned for a consensus that never was. But he intuited the social dynamics of pluralism in a democratic age. Embracing the principle of voluntarism, the townspeople forged an array of affiliations, according to their diverse interests and opinions. Concord could not supply a single identity for them all. To be sure, everybody, even Thoreau, took pride in the town's central role at the start of the American Revolution, when on April 19, 1775, invading Redcoats were routed by local Minutemen in "the first forcible resistance to British aggression." Even so, neither history nor common residence could contain the conflicts driving local politics down to the Civil War.[22]

Henry Thoreau liked to position himself on Concord's margins, a bemused observer of his neighbors' foibles, with more serious business to pursue than making money. That was a literary pose. He was, in fact, a product of the central village, where he spent most of his life, either in his parents' or in Emerson's home, and he was deeply implicated with his family in the economic transformation of his native town. On his mother's side, he was descended from the Loyalist elite of Weston, Massachusetts, the prominent Jones clan, whose estate was confiscated in the Revolutionary War; his maternal grandmother married Asa Dunbar, a minister-turned-lawyer in Keene, New Hampshire, and after his death wed a landed gentleman in Concord. Both husbands had sympathized with the British cause. By contrast, John Thoreau, his grandfather, represented new money. Immigrating to Boston from the Jersey Islands just before the war, he got his start in privateering aboard Patriot ships; with his stake, he went into trade and prospered. At his death in 1801, he bequeathed an estate of $25,000, making his widow Rebecca the third-richest taxpayer in Concord. Status and wealth were thus family heritage.[23]

Unfortunately, the legacy was mismanaged. Year by year, Rebecca Thoreau slipped into genteel poverty, while her son John, at age twenty-one, rashly mortgaged his share to open the short-lived store on Concord common. Despite his difficulties, he married Cynthia Dunbar in 1812 and embarked on a peripatetic quest to recoup his fortunes. The solution appeared, quite by accident, in pencil-making, when his feckless brother-in-law stumbled onto a graphite deposit in rural New Hampshire. Incapable of turning that claim, on his own, into a successful business, he recruited John Thoreau for the task and was soon gone. Thoreau entered a field that had been opened up in Concord by William Munroe, an ambitious cabinetmaker determined to find an alternative to clock- and furniture-making during the troubled times surrounding the War of 1812. The pioneer did not welcome competition. When Thoreau's pencils outsold his own, Munroe put pressure on a nearby miller to stop grinding his rival's graphite into powdered lead. The gambit backfired; the furious miller cut off Munroe instead. But would-be monopolists were not Thoreau's only challenge. Technologically, he labored long and hard to produce a clean, reliable pencil. Luckily, his versatile son Henry was available to work on the problem. Thanks to his ingenuity, the firm turned out fine pencils "for the nicest uses of the Drawing Master, Surveyor, Engineer, Architect, and Artists Generally," writing instruments "without peer in the country." To finance their production, John Thoreau was in constant need of capital, for which he turned, not always successfully, to local lenders. He was obliged to do his own advertising and marketing over a wide territory. Henry Thoreau accompanied him on sales trips to New York. The family packed boxes and shipped orders. To cut transportation costs and improve access to the Boston market, John Thoreau participated in a statewide petition campaign in 1835 for the elimination of all tolls on bridges into the capital. Energetic entrepreneurs, the pencil-makers "John Thoreau & Son" were as fully engaged in the market revolution as any other business in Concord.[24]

Surveying the commercial prospects of Concord at its bicentennial in 1835, local historian Lemuel Shattuck confidently predicted an expansive future. "The manufacturing and mechanical business of the town is increasing, and promises to be a great source of wealth." Shattuck had good reason for optimism. That year marked the peak of Concord's development as a hub of crafts and trade. The heyday of the central village soon passed, as larger forces eclipsed the small towns of New England. First, the Panic of 1837 and subsequent depression temporarily set back regional growth; then, with the coming of the railroad and steam power, industry relocated in big cities, with vast supplies of cheap labor. Having lost comparative advantage, the small shops of towns like Concord were forced to find a specialized niche or die. The Thoreaus survived this natural selection. In fact, they gained handsomely from the process. It turned out that the ground lead used for their pencils was ideal for electrotyping, a new invention of the 1840s that enabled printers to duplicate standing type and hence to cut the costs of composition. By this means, publishers could furnish a continuous supply of cheap books to the public, in tune with changing demand. When a company in Boston proposed to take all the black powder he could supply, John Thoreau snapped up the deal. Pencil-making was quickly dropped. By 1854, when *Walden* was published, the family was shipping its product by rail to printers in Boston, New York, Philadelphia, and even cities in the West. As a shareholder in the Fitchburg Railroad, the carrier through Concord to the wider world, John Thoreau profited doubly from the increasing traffic. His son Henry harbored misgivings. The Iron Horse invaded his retreat at Walden with its piercing cry. It despoiled the "pastoral life" of the countryside for the sake of profit. It heightened the demand for fuel that denuded the land of trees, even as it raised the value of real estate and kept Thoreau busy surveying woodlots for local farmers. Perhaps most unsettling was the function of the family graphite, which greased the machinery of a mass publishing industry pouring out "little reading" for the masses. Thoreau inveighed against these developments in all of his writings. Yet, in his family's interest, he made himself a willing agent of the very industrial capitalism that was shattering the rural independence he cherished.[25]

Those efforts paid off. The Thoreau family was hard-pressed for money throughout Henry's boyhood. Unable to afford a house of their own, John and Cynthia Thoreau shuttled with their four children from one rental quarter to another in the central village. To make ends meet, Cynthia Thoreau took in boarders and stretched the food budget by eliminating coffee, tea, and sugar from the diet. Not until 1844 was the family secure enough to acquire its own home, and that was built by Henry and his father in an unfashionable area just opening up behind the railroad tracks. Even so, the parents, especially Cynthia Thoreau, retained the genteel expectations with which they were raised. The savings on food were invested in pianos for the girls, Helen and Sophia, and in education for all the children. Everybody pitched in to pay Henry's Harvard tuition. Despite their modest means, the Thoreaus moved in the best village circles. John and Cynthia Thoreau sat in a good pew at the First Church, entertained elite friends in their home, and contributed to local charities. So refined was the Thoreau family that young Horace Hosmer, the son of a farm laborer, was astonished at the contrast it presented to the grim rural scene he had previously known. After boarding in that household, he concluded that "John Thoreau and his wife," with their pure living and high aspirations, "were superior to the common run of human animals around them, that they loved truly and begot children *after their kind*." Eventually, with the profits from black lead, the minister's daughter and merchant's son returned to the village in style. Purchasing a substantial home on Main Street, which they managed with the aid of two Irish servants, they enjoyed the last decade of their marriage on the fringe of the economic elite. John Thoreau even became a landlord, renting the humble property he had built behind the train depot to such tenants as Harriet Hanson Robinson, whose editor husband was back in town and who took such a dim view of "Henry D." [26]

While the Thoreau family steadily climbed back up the social ladder, son Henry strayed ever farther from the conventional path to success in antebellum New England. Deemed "more scholarly" than older brother John, he went off to Harvard College in August 1833 carrying the social ambitions of his parents. Then as now, higher education was expensive, and it took considerable sacrifice for the Thoreaus to pay the tuition and board. But the ancient college in Cambridge was the traditional gateway to the learned professions and the ticket into the Boston-area elite. Year after year, Concord sent its sons to the seat of learning along the Charles, from which they emerged to assume careers as doctors, lawyers, ministers, and teachers. Whatever the calling, they were gentlemen all, groomed to be a distinctive class, set apart by culture, manners, and wealth from the great mass of New Englanders. Thoreau acquired the knowledge and the refinement but passed up the material trappings.[27] Upon graduation, he took up the post of schoolmaster, first at the Concord school from which he abruptly resigned, then in tandem with brother John at the town's private academy. Teaching was a common stopgap for Harvard men before deciding on a life's work. For Thoreau, it offered a way station on an uncertain journey to adult independence. During the nearly three years of the academy (1838–1841), the young man showed every sign of fitting into the social scene. The school flourished, drawing pupils from prominent local families and from as far away as Cuba. Thoreau enjoyed the company of his peers; he threw melon parties, went on group outings to local ponds, wooed Ellen Sewall, and, when she turned him down, tried to interest another young woman. He was active in civic affairs, signing petitions against slavery and serving as curator of the lyceum, before which he took part in public debates. Then in 1842, following the closing of the school and the death of brother John, Thoreau, at age twenty-five, got off the conventional track. Marriage was no longer an option. At the very moment his contemporaries were starting to wed, Thoreau assumed the stance of a confirmed bachelor. Migration was not on the agenda. Though he had once flirted with an invitation to teach in Kentucky, he never labored beyond the vicinity of Concord, except for a spell on Staten Island, New York, where he tutored the children of Judge William Emerson, Waldo's brother, only to fall desperately homesick and hurry back to his native town. Apart from brief vacations and a few business trips, he stayed close to home, subject to the severe scrutiny of neighbors who had known him all his life. "When a man remains where he was reared," observed one guidebook of the day, "his neighbors and especially his relatives, will see nothing but the little tricks of boyhood and the mistakes of early manhood. Locate among strangers." Ignoring that advice, Thoreau felt its harsh truth. To some townspeople, he would be forever "David Henry."[28]

However wayward Thoreau's course, it was set on a career just taking form around the time he graduated from college: professional writer. That ambition crystallized when Thoreau came under Emerson's wing in the late 1830s. Fourteen years the senior, Emerson was then at his most visionary, a radical seer summoning "the young men of fairest promise" in New England to cast off tradition, look within themselves, and fulfill their genius. From such self-reliance, he prophesied, would arise a culture as sublime as American nature. Emerson's words inspired Thoreau, as did his personal example; the onetime minister had forsaken a fixed career in the pulpit for the vagaries of freelance lecturing and writing. Could Thoreau do the same? Emerson certainly thought so and encouraged his literary aspirations. But there was a hitch. Traditionally, a man of letters was a gentleman of means, employing his leisure to pen essays for a coterie of peers. Lacking such status, an aspiring writer needed a sinecure from church or state or the backing of a patron. Sponsorship carried costs. So long as he was beholden to others for support, the "American scholar" had to satisfy their expectations along with his own. In Emerson's opinion, he floundered for a strong, manly voice. Instead of pursuing greatness as "Man Thinking," the typical writer deferred to common prejudice and courted approval in countinghouse and parlor. The literary marketplace promised an alternative to such dependence. Just as farmers were abandoning older forms of production, so, increasingly, were writers. Rather than cater to personal patrons, many preferred to address a general public, in hopes of gaining greater freedom of expression. Access to that audience was brokered by a new class of entrepreneurs, the editors and publishers of Boston, New York, and Philadelphia. Through their commercial aegis, a profession of authorship—writing for strangers, in exchange for cash—was taking shape. Unfortunately, it developed at an erratic pace. Sales of magazines and books, though growing, could not assure steady income, especially for would-be writers from middling families. Emerson was lucky. Thanks to an annuity from his first wife's estate, he could escape the financial bind and risk an uncertain market for his wares. Thoreau could not.

So, the genial Emerson turned patron himself and made Thoreau *his* project. He provided a sort of residential fellowship in his home: in exchange for services as handyman and editorial assistant, Thoreau gained access to Emerson and his library and the free time to pursue a literary life. The Concord Sage introduced him to leading Boston thinkers, passed along various ventures, such as an anthology of English poets that had languished on Emerson's desk, and commissioned his writings for *The Dial*. He arranged for the tutoring job on Staten Island, so that Thoreau could cultivate contacts in the publishing capital of Manhattan, a short ferry ride away. He helped secure an imprint for his protégé's first book, *A Week on the Concord and Merrimack*

Rivers. At Emerson's urging, Thoreau unwisely pledged to pay the costs of production. When the book failed miserably, selling a mere 200 of the 1,000 copies in print, the distressed author was stuck with a huge debt. To finance the payment, he turned, like his father, to the Concord Bank and secured a loan of $200, due in six months; Emerson guaranteed the note. By then, the canny Transcendentalist was worth $50,000, qualifying for a contemporary list of *The Rich Men of Massachusetts*. That work praised him as "a benevolent man" and rightly so. Without his support at the start of Thoreau's literary career, there would have been no *Walden*.[29]

In his enthusiasm for "*the* man of Concord," Emerson forgot his reservations about literary patronage. He slipped into a proprietary attitude toward his disciple. Time and again, in private and public, he predicted greatness for "my Henry Thoreau." But eventually, the patron became exasperated with the client. Thoreau fell short of his promise. His writings disappointed; his dislike of society proved tiresome. As Emerson gained wealth and renown, he could not fathom why Thoreau buried himself in the woods. "My dear Henry," began a mock-letter he composed in his journal, "A frog was made to live in a swamp, but a man was not made to live in a swamp." Though that letter went unsent, the sentiment was conveyed even before Thoreau suffered the embarrassing fiasco of *A Week*. The result was a rupture in the friendship that deepened over the years. Yet, had the two remained kindred spirits, the connection would still have burdened Thoreau. Subtle forms of hierarchy and dependence bound the two men in ways that neither could acknowledge directly. As the protégé, Thoreau was the junior partner, recipient of his benefactor's good will. Gathered into Emerson's circle, he was perceived as a satellite of the great man, reflecting his sun. Subordination bred resentment. "Friendship is . . . a relation of perfect equality," Thoreau affirmed in *A Week*. "It cannot well spare any outward sign of equal obligation and advantage. The nobleman can never have a Friend among his retainers, nor the king among his subjects." [30]

Thoreau was thus driven to seek professional independence in the literary marketplace. He honed his talents at nature and travel writing, genres with great appeal for middle-class readers, and placed pieces in such popular magazines as *Graham's*, *Putnam's*, and *Atlantic Monthly*. He lectured on the lyceum circuit. His major achievement was negotiating a contract for *Walden* with the Boston firm of Ticknor & Fields, soon to be "the most successful and prestigious publisher in New England." Despite these successes, Thoreau chafed at the compromises required to sell his work. He was easily enraged at tampering with his words. In 1853 editor George William Curtis, a onetime friend in Concord, accepted "An Excursion to Canada" for the new *Putnam's Monthly Magazine*. The essay was set to appear in five installments, but after Curtis excised a few critical remarks about the Catholic church without his permission Thoreau pulled it from the magazine midway. His reaction was the same when *Atlantic Monthly* editor James Russell Lowell, his old nemesis, cut an irreverent line from Thoreau's prose that might have offended orthodox Christians. "I do not ask anybody to adopt my opinions," Thoreau declared, "but I do expect that when they ask for them to print, they will print them, or obtain my consent to their alteration or omission."[31]

The free market, the hallmark of nineteenth-century capitalism, was as constraining for Thoreau as the older system of patrons and clients. In "Life without Principle," a lecture delivered not long after *Walden* was published, he lashed out at both. On the one hand, the writer was degraded by dependence on the market: "If you would get money as a writer or lecturer, you must be popular, which is to go down perpendicularly. . . . You are paid for being something less than a man." On the other hand, public patronage could be just as demeaning. It enlisted writers in the service of power by appealing to low appetites. "Even the poet-laureate would rather not have to celebrate the accidents of royalty. He must be bribed with a pipe of wine; and perhaps another poet is called away from his muse to gauge that very pipe." Rejecting all such dependence, public or private, Thoreau determined to weave his "basket of delicate texture" as he saw fit and "avoid the necessity of selling it." Following the failure of *A Week*, he earned his living in diverse ways—day labor, surveying, the pencil business—and spent it on simple needs.

Spared the need to write for pay, he set his own intellectual agenda and, for the last decade or so of his life, devoted himself to those solitary studies of nature Emerson never appreciated. For the sake of independence, Thoreau spurned respectability and set himself apart from the neighbors, a seeming "loafer" in a world of "work, work, work." His favorite direction for a walk led west, away from Concord village.[32]

Within the town, there were contemporaries who put a high premium on independence, but not at the price paid by the local "hermit." Amidst the social transformation of New England, they wrestled with the same issues as did Thoreau: vocational choice; marriage and family; the claims of community and tradition; the opportunities and pressures of the marketplace; the desire for money, status, and power; the moral dilemmas posed by inequality and slavery. In Thoreau's judgment, too many of his neighbors succumbed to the onslaught of change, in weary "resignation" to an implacable fate in which "there is no choice left." Perhaps so, but we will never know. If Thoreau was right, they went down to defeat in "quiet desperation," leaving no trace of their thoughts. The documents that do survive tell a different story. In the diaries, letters, and memoirs preserved at the Concord Free Public Library and in other Boston-area depositories lies the record of active men and women, engaged in deliberate efforts to make their own lives in an unsettling era they struggled to comprehend. Like Thoreau, they were restless spirits, straining against a past they still revered, drawn to a future about which they felt ambivalent. Coming of age in the period between the War of 1812 and the Mexican War, they yearned for the heroism of the Revolutionary fathers, even as they challenged the dictates of parents and the authority of ministers and magistrates. They stirred with an intensity that was often missing at church. They idealized the small town of their birth but were bent on reforming its way of life. They turned to nature for relief from the material changes they wrought on the landscape. They expressed nostalgia for a history they were leaving behind. These acts marked a generational declaration of independence, a value they embraced as fervently as Thoreau. In occasional moments, the Transcendentalist acknowledged that affinity. Though he spoke "mainly to the mass of men

who are discontented," Thoreau conceded in *Walden* that there
were many "who found encouragement and inspiration in precisely the present condition of things . . . —and, to some extent, I reckon myself in this number." [33]

Consider the life choices made by several male contemporaries of Thoreau: the physician and medical reformer Edward
Jarvis; the lawyer and politician John Shepard Keyes; the antislavery editor William S. Robinson; the workingman and sometime
pencil-maker Horace Hosmer. Concord natives all, the four men
span the formative decades of Thoreau's youth. The eldest,
Jarvis, born in 1803, was coeval with Emerson and old enough to
be Thoreau's master at the center school in 1826. Robinson was
born in 1818, a year after Thoreau; Keyes three years later. Both
were his classmates. The youngest, Hosmer, was a "lonely" ten-
year-old, fresh off the farm, when he boarded in the Thoreau
household in 1840 and attended the Thoreau brothers' academy.
Reared and educated in the same town, the four nonetheless
grew up under different circumstances and followed divergent
paths. Only one was a child of privilege: scion of Concord's most
powerful politician in the 1820s and 1830s, Keyes inherited his father's law practice and advanced to even higher offices. Jarvis enjoyed comfortable origins; his father started out with a bakeshop,
expanded into general storekeeping (once hiring John Thoreau
as his manager), and through land speculation and commercial investments retired to a substantial farm. Both Jarvis and
Keyes attended Harvard, the latter arriving at Cambridge just as
Thoreau was leaving (he stayed for a few nights in his townsman's dormitory room). By contrast, Robinson went to neither
academy nor college, despite excelling as a student—Jarvis
placed him "at the head of the class"—and showing a fondness
for books; his shoemaker father, unable to pay the tuition, apprenticed him to a printer. Hosmer, the son of a farm laborer,
was the poorest of all; apart from his brief instruction by the
Thoreau brothers, he got what learning he could from the district schools. These disparities persisted through adulthood.
Keyes grew rich, thanks to the lucrative opportunities that came
the way of men in power; Jarvis acquired stature in his profession
and a handsome estate. But Robinson forfeited financial security

rather than compromise principle; though he rose to minor prominence in Boston-area journalism, he was constantly battling with employers and changing jobs. Hosmer tried a variety of trades—mechanic, salesman, farmer—but never escaped the working class. Rooted in Concord and the environs of Boston, the four resisted the lure of the West and cast their lot with the region of their birth. Together with Thoreau, they bore the impress of antebellum New England, with its intellectual awakening, its ferment of reform, its quest to perpetuate old virtues in a new order. In later years, having lived through Civil War and Reconstruction and into the machine age, the four men looked back on the days of their youth and assayed the changes they had seen. In this backward glance, the figure of Henry Thoreau stood out among their contemporaries, a pole-star of independence by which they could measure their own progress through life. Well after he had gone to his rest, "chanticleer" retained the power to stir up the neighbors.[34]

It was at the center school on Concord common that Edward Jarvis, the new master, first encountered Thoreau, a boy of eleven, in September 1826. Only four days before, Jarvis had graduated from Harvard and at age twenty-three had come home to keep school before deciding upon his life's work. It was an act of duty, undertaken to comfort a "very lonely" father, following the deaths of Jarvis's mother and older brother earlier that year. But the decision was charged with conflicted feelings. The faithful son sought both to live up to the expectations of family and friends and to break free for a life on his own. That tension produced a vocational crisis, lasting well over a decade, similar to the dilemmas his pupil Henry Thoreau would eventually face. It had been a struggle just for Jarvis to obtain a college education. As a boy with a relish for reading, he had made plain his distaste for the family bakeshop and his ambition for a "literary profession." Unfortunately, Deacon Jarvis already had one son at Harvard and, ever careful about money, thought he could not afford two. So, without consultation, the father apprenticed Edward, at age fifteen, to a nearby woolen mill for training as a manufacturer. Outwardly compliant, the youth seethed with resentment, notwithstanding a long fascination with machines.

Away from home for the first time in his life, he felt desperately
lonely and clashed with his employer—"My mistress was a vi-
rago. My master a tyrant and conceited squire"—and fellow
workers. The only solution was to remove the boy from the mill
and ship him to Harvard, whatever the cost. There he acquired
classical learning and genteel polish, but no career. Unsuited to
his first choice, the ministry, owing to a speech defect, Jarvis was
still considering his options when he entered the classroom in
1826 and found Henry Thoreau and nine-year-old "Willy" Robinson in the midst.[35]

Concord greeted the graduate with misgivings. Could a
young man rule over a school where he had only recently been a
pupil? Deacon Jarvis had pushed the appointment of his son
through the school committee over such doubts, but the objections persisted, to the new master's dismay. "Many went to the
committee telling them the money would be lost, the time worse
than lost, the school had better be shut up for I could not keep
the school. I could not govern the children as they would not
obey one with whom they had been familiar." As it turned out,
Jarvis easily won the day, establishing "the reputation of being a
very exact disciplinarian without severity" and earning his students' respect. He was not only offered renewal in the post but
recruited to run the local academy for three years, both opportunities he declined in favor of studying medicine. Even so, the
brief controversy exposed the obstacles to independence con-
fronting Jarvis, like Thoreau, in his native town.[36]

Everywhere the young man turned in the 1820s he felt con-
strained. At Harvard, Jarvis had picked up, along with genteel
manners, an elitist disdain for the vernacular culture of rural
New England. Old customs that had once bound neighbors together in friendly feeling now appeared intolerable. When his
mother died, Jarvis insisted that the family abandon the practice
of supplying the pallbearers with liquor. No matter that this was
a traditional gesture of hospitality; to the censorious Jarvis, it dis-
tracted from the solemn business of mourning. He was no more
respectful of other canons of community. As a schoolmaster in
the neighboring town of Acton during one college vacation, he
offended his employers by declining to pay the usual visits to the

students' homes. "I was thought proud, aristocratic, indeed I was." He provoked the same condemnation by his conduct as master of ceremonies at the wedding of a kinsman. By his command, the time- honored procession to the home of the betrothed was banned, lest it draw the "the gaze of boys, young women, and gossips." His boldest challenge to tradition came when he and several young women proposed to join the First Church, on condition that it drop the public ceremony for admitting new members. Claiming to be too "diffident" to "make so public a demonstration of their act," the applicants petitioned the Reverend Ezra Ripley for a private induction "before the church alone." In an aggressive colloquy with the venerable pastor, the 25-year-old Jarvis belittled the ritual of admission as "a pompous show of the increase of the church." That corporate body, once a prop of Puritan order, failed to evoke the young man's awe. To his mind, religion was a personal affair, best left to the private conscience. Every Christian should be allowed to join in public worship, no questions asked. This was too much for the liberal Ripley, who cautioned that "too many innovations may disgust & offend the tender." But the parson accommodated the conscientious objectors part way. They would not have to stand in the broad aisle of the meetinghouse, exposed to full view, when they accepted the covenant of the church. Instead, they were allowed to rise in their high wooden pews, shielded from the stares of strangers. In the name of privacy, Jarvis added to the rents in the familiar fabric of community. Henry Thoreau would flee from the prying eyes of neighbors in his wake.[37]

Much as Jarvis desired independence, that goal eluded his grasp. Anxious for adulthood, he raced into an engagement with Almira Hunt, over his father's protest, only to wait nearly seven years before he was well-enough established to wed. The delay reflected the difficulties in starting a medical practice. After learning his profession in Boston and Concord, the young doctor cast about for an attractive place. The Unitarians in Concord, New Hampshire, were eager for a physician of their denomination; the Whigs of Hallowell, Maine, alienated by the Jacksonian sentiments of their current doctor, were looking for someone more politically correct. To the idealistic Jarvis, such criteria were outrageous; he wanted to be judged on his merits, on his character and knowledge alone. But in a society where business was still conducted along the lines of kinship, religion, and even party, it was difficult to escape the politics of patronage. Even when he did land a practice in the Connecticut Valley town of Northfield, Jarvis was appalled to find himself under fire from jealous rivals, who told lies to steal away his patients. Instead of enjoying independence in his profession, as he had anticipated, he was forced to compete for trade. "Tis not he who knows the most, but he that makes the widest pretensions & most accommodates himself & his science to the ignorance & preconceptions of the world," the disillusioned doctor grumbled, "that prospers most among feeble mortality." Like Henry Thoreau, Jarvis refused to tailor his truths to popular whims.[38]

Jarvis hoped for a release from these cares when a chance to start over again in Concord opened up in 1832. But the frustrations only grew worse. Leading members of the Trinitarian church tried to impede his settlement, in hopes of recruiting a physician of their own faith. Jarvis won that skirmish. Far more difficult to surmount was the barrier of public opinion. He had been warned that "a man should never attempt to get business in the town where he was born" and had ignored the advice. Surely he would not be branded forever with "the follies [and] the weaknesses of my youth." Yet hard as he tried, Jarvis could not overcome the neighbors' preference for his mentor Josiah Bartlett, the premier physician in town. After five years in Concord, the young doctor and his bride were no better off financially than when they started. True, there were compensations. "Personally, socially, mentally," he believed, "he could hardly desire a better place or a better people to live with." The young couple lived close by family and friends; Jarvis had been welcomed into civic leadership and even admitted into the Social Circle. Earnest for local improvements, the doctor crusaded for temperance, pushed school reform, supported the library, lyceum, and Sunday school, promoted the commemoration of Concord's history, and joined in the Ornamental Tree Society's campaign to beautify the central village. By such means, he endeavored to remake the rural community according to the voluntarist norms of a new middle-class culture.

But public progress could not make up for private disappointment. By 1836 Jarvis foresaw only a long, depressing future in Bartlett's shadow. Rejecting that fate, he seized upon reports that the rising city of Louisville, Kentucky, was looking for a Yankee doctor and headed West in search of "some more energy, more stimulus of life." For all his love of Concord, he longed to be out on his own, in a community where he could make his own way, untrammeled by the past, free from narrow prejudices and selfish alliances, and achieve his full potential. In a word, Edward Jarvis aspired to be a self-made man.[39]

Not for long. Though he was initially enthusiastic about his new home, even encouraging Thoreau to take a teaching job in Louisville, Jarvis soon pined for the old neighborhood. The Yankee doctor was simply not cut out to be a pioneer in Henry Clay country, with its unbridled liberty for whites and harsh slavery for blacks. Set against that disorderly scene, the "rigid social influence of New England," binding people together through the force of "pervading public opinions," regained its appeal. By 1842 Jarvis was back in Massachusetts for good, settling in the Boston-area town of Dorchester, where he established himself as a specialist in the treatment of the insane and as an expert in the emerging field of social statistics. He was close enough to Concord for regular visits, far enough away for personal independence. As his private practice thrived, the doctor reconciled himself to the free market, which had brought prosperity and enhanced freedom in his life, and he highlighted these benefits of the market revolution in the historical works he composed in the late 1870s after retiring from medicine. In *Traditions and Reminiscences of Concord, Massachusetts,* Jarvis offered "A Contribution to the Social and Economic History" of the community he had never left in spirit. Conjuring up the vernacular world of his boyhood, the doctor reconstructed the homely details of a lost way of life: what rural folk ate and drank, the clothes they wore, the books they read, the furniture in homes, the tools in field and shop, the open hospitality and cooperative practices by which they aided one another. This was, of course, the rural scene he had found stifling in youth and had set out to reform as a civic-minded professional. The passage of decades had softened his description but not altered his judgment. Jarvis's account is a tally of material and moral progress from the colonial era to the Gilded Age. Through specialized production for regional and national markets, the people of Concord reaped the advantages of a diversified, modern civilization. The standard of living climbed to ever-higher levels; the books and ideas of the wider world expanded minds. Manners became refined. Thanks to the advance of trade, neighbors were freed from customary duties and could join together in voluntary association for mutual benefit. Community was stronger than ever.

> It is better that each should do his own work, with his own hands, or by such aid as he can compensate in the ordinary way. Those burdens that in past years required the cooperation of friends and neighbors are now but ordinary affairs and are met by the ordinary means and their own exertions. . . . people both individually and socially are as happy and more prosperous and are loving, generous and ready to aid in distress, poverty and sickness, whenever they shall present themselves in any family or neighborhood.

Jarvis's reform program had triumphed.[40]

This optimistic narrative of progress suited a Gilded Age middle class shedding old doubts about economic change and indulging in material abundance. But Jarvis was not an apostle of industrial capitalism. His text took its themes from antebellum debates about commerce and culture and, whether by design or not, set itself in opposition to Concord's best-known work on the subject. For what was *Traditions and Reminiscences* but a massive refutation of *Walden*'s jeremiad on the division of labor and the dehumanization of men? In Jarvis's telling, the people of Concord led lives not of "quiet desperation" but of satisfying labor, intellectual improvement, and social utility. Yet no mention of Thoreau appears in his pages. Jarvis reserved comments on his onetime pupil for another manuscript written three years later, in which he recalled the "Houses and People in Concord, Massachusetts, 1810 to 1820." Among those residences was the white frame structure on the common once occupied by the immigrant John Thoreau. The storekeeper received a brief notice, as did his son John, the trader turned pencil-maker. But the bulk of the entry concentrated on the famous Thoreau, who had spent but a single year of infancy in Concord during the decade under study. Not that he had done anything much for the town in later life. As Jarvis portrayed him, Thoreau was a loner, "absorbed in matters within himself." A "good scholar" with a bent for writing literature and natural history, the Harvard graduate had never realized his promise. He "studied no profession," though he was an excellent surveyor. He distrusted "domestic and family life," as seen in his solitary retreat at Walden. No "public man," he took no interest in schools, "affairs of general improvement," or charity. "Absolutely honest and conscientious," he frowned on the "business habits" and "system of trade and finance prevalent in the world." Nature was his realm, where he spent time by himself "in the fields and woods of Concord and on the river"; occasionally, he took a trip "by foot" away from Concord "but not remotely in this country nor abroad." Little came of his nature studies. Thoreau never produced the "natural history of Concord" expected of him. Lacking "the mental discipline" required for such work, he was content with "a high reputation among a limited class." His life was, in short, a study in negation, in striking contrast to Jarvis's unceasing efforts to do good. The two men had shared an impulse in youth to challenge authority and resist coercion. In separate ways, each had staked claims for individual privacy and for a society founded on voluntary consent. But in his former schoolmaster's judgment, Thoreau had flunked the test of social usefulness. Off on his own project of "self-culture," he had gotten lost in the woods. "He had a distrust of general society. His ideal of the social relation was very different from that generally entertained." As a result, he ended up not "*the* man of Concord," but merely a curious character in local history, whose cabin at Walden would never deserve mention in any future tribute to the houses and people of the town.[41]

That was pretty much the view of John Shepard Keyes, who regarded Thoreau as "wholly a Concordian," an "odd stick" with small standing among the neighbors. "Those who knew Thoreau personally," he remarked in 1896, "have found nothing so surprising as the cult which has grown up about him or so difficult of a rational explanation." Keyes was then seventy-five years old, a longtime judge and politician in Concord, whose experience of life had definitely not been circumscribed by his native town. During the antebellum era, the ambitious lawyer advanced from selectman to state senator, served six years as Middlesex County sheriff, and wielded considerable power in statewide politics. An "Old Whig," he bolted his party for the anti-Catholic Know-Nothings in the mid-1850s before moving reluctantly into the Republican camp a few years later. A lukewarm opponent of slavery, Keyes represented the conservative bloc in the new party and, as a delegate to the 1860 Republican convention in Chicago, was the lone man from Massachusetts to vote against Abraham Lincoln's nomination for president. Surprisingly, that dissent did not hurt him. With solid credentials in law enforcement and in military affairs (he was a colonel in the county militia), he was commissioned to guard the incoming president at the inauguration, when threats from angry southerners swirled through Washington, and for his successful performance was rewarded with the position of federal marshal for Massachusetts during the Civil War. At the close of the conflict, Keyes returned to his base in Concord, assumed a local judgeship, and devoted himself to the town, its history, and its natural beauty. Putting Henry Thoreau in his place was evidently part of that job.[42]

Actually, Keyes never cared much for his "very odd" neighbor. As a boy, he trailed a few years behind Thoreau in the village school and the academy and enjoyed a casual acquaintance with the entire Thoreau family throughout youth. He went to "sociables" and "melon sprees" in their home, took strolls with the younger daughter Sophia, and spent his first nights at Harvard in Henry's dormitory room. On one occasion, he borrowed "the Musketaquid," the boat the Thoreau brothers built for their trip up the Concord and Merrimack Rivers, and irritated Henry by failing to return it to the proper place. The two youths competed for the attention of the same girls, with Thoreau sometimes winning out. Keyes participated in the lyceum and listened disdainfully to his townsman's performances. He deemed a public discussion of non-resistance by Bronson Alcott and Thoreau "the most foolish as well as amusing that I ever heard, it amounted to plain common nonsense and awfully highflown into the bargain." In later years he read *A Week on the Concord and Merrimack Rivers* and *Walden* as soon they came out and was a little more impressed, if not by the philosophy, which he skipped, then by the "accurate and delightful" descriptions of nature. Outwardly, the two men maintained "pleasant" relations, yet at bottom they were temperamental opposites. Where the one was shy and thoughtful, the other was outgoing and light-hearted. Thoreau kept a journal for serious reflection; Keyes filled up his diary with "adventures . . . without the thoughts." In college, he thrived not in the classroom, but in the camaraderie of undergraduate life. He partied, danced, drank, swore, gossiped, flirted with girls, and ignored his books with all the gusto of fraternity boys today and with the similar results of low grades and parental disapproval. Though he sobered up somewhat after graduation, he was avid for the wealth and power the Transcendentalist shunned. No egalitarian, he took pride in the company of the Concord "elite" and rightly considered himself part of "the bon ton upper crust." On his twentieth birthday, he found on his desk an unexpected gift from his father: a bank book in his name, recording $250 in deposits and interest. At the death of the Honorable John Keyes in 1844, the son was bequeathed, with his widowed mother and brothers, an estate valued at $40,000, the largest probated in Concord up till then. A few years later the lawyer bought a new home in the village, close by the courthouse, and spent some $3,500 on renovations, including two piazzas and the first bay window in town, all of which he lovingly recounted in his autobiography. By contrast, Thoreau's simple cabin at Walden, composed of recycled boards from an Irishman's shanty, cost its proud builder a mere 28.22\frac{1}{2}$.[43]

Despite all of these privileges, or perhaps because of them, Keyes went through a vocational crisis as intense in its way as what Jarvis and Thoreau experienced, though far more short-lived. As a boy, he absorbed stirring tales of military glory from grizzled veterans of the Revolution and delighted in militia trainings on the common. With a vision of himself as "a dashing cavalry officer . . . displaying a bright uniform [and] mounted on a black horse," he had his heart set on a military career. Without telling his father, he sent off to Washington for an application to West Point. When the response arrived on official stationery from the adjutant general of the army addressed to the youth, it caught the attention of Concord's postmaster, none other than the Honorable John Keyes. The father sat the son down for a serious talk about the future. The army was out of the question, though the senior Keyes did have the political clout to swing a nomination to West Point; it offered a one-way ticket to nowhere, "there being only frontier Indian wars on hand." The son would go to Cambridge, after which he was expected to study law and enter the father's practice. Young Keyes complied "unwillingly" but acted out his anger in numerous escapades. Where Thoreau turned inward in dissent from the prescribed course and Jarvis was torn between a drive for independence and a need for his elders' approval, Keyes indulged in disobedience and drink. Back home from college, he came and went as he pleased, without bothering to tell his parents, and more than once stumbled home from a late night "spree" to encounter a red-faced father and get "a tremendous scolding about Temperance . . . equal in fury to my last Sunday's one on Extravagance. Then however it was my 'foolish abominable INFERNAL habits' which were blasted and why? Because I drank a mug of flip at the ball here. I shall drink when and what I please while I can get it. Hon. John Keyes," he vowed in his diary, "for all your blasting.—Sir, Shut up."[44]

Independence was the goal of this youthful rebellion, a term Keyes invokes in his diary as frequently as Thoreau in *Walden*. He marked the Fourth of July 1841 "in a very curious manner by showing myself independent of frowns and warning looks" from his father "and doing just as I pleased." Accompanying the family to church, he spent the time not in prayer but in ogling young women. A week later, back in Cambridge, the graduating senior skipped services for sailing on Fresh Pond. With classes over, "we were independent of 'church & state,'" and relished "this feeling of Independence at being beyond the reach of college laws." Commencement opened a "grand era" in his existence: "Henceforth I am to be a man. . . . Henceforth I must live for myself alone." This sentiment rested on a solid material foundation.

With the surprise gift of money in the bank, Keyes rightly felt "more independent"; it "gives me the wherewithal to seek my fortune with." The trouble was that the young man lacked direction. He thrashed around in gestures of protest, without any rationale for his discontent. Interestingly, he was attracted to high-minded young women in Emerson's circle and consulted the great man's essay on "Love" "by moonlight to find out if I was influenced by the malady." But he had no sympathy for Transcendentalism or any other brand of reform. Though he claimed to prefer "a long solitary ramble in the woods" to dreary hours "sitting in the house of God," he was just as likely to carouse in "Nature's temple" with rowdy friends, in all-night binges of fishing and drinking. When he did go to Sunday meeting and pay attention, he applauded sermons against "the prevailing humbugs of the day such as Abolitionism, Emersonianism &c." What, then, was he to do? Chained to his father's law office, anxious for real independence, the young man fumbled for a way out. He toyed with the idea of taking a job as a tutor on a Virginia plantation, then weighed more seriously a proposal from Edward Jarvis, still in Louisville, to become a schoolmaster in the western city. It was a chance to free himself from the burdens of family, to escape to a place where he could truly be his own man. But no more than Thoreau could Keyes abandon Concord. "I that is my Father have decided not to go to Louisville this fall," he reported on November 30, 1841, "and I won't go in the spring after getting through all the dull stupid winter & summer coming on in all its glory. No I shant go at all now." Keyes was, in the end, a young fogy, too attached to wealth and privilege ever to put his fantasies of independence into practice.[45]

As it turned out, Keyes got his wish without ever leaving home. In August 1844 the Honorable John Keyes suddenly died, at age fifty-eight, and overnight his son and namesake found himself, three years out of college, the head of a household and the heir to a substantial estate, law practice, and political dynasty. Inheritance secured independence. Marrying the serious, intellectual Martha Prescott, the daughter of his father's onetime law partner and later political enemy, he settled down and assumed his duties to family and community. "I think I was older that year than I have ever been since," he recalled in middle age, "the cares and responsibilities of life coming so rapidly on me at four and twenty." While Thoreau was squatting at Walden, in simplicity and independence, his younger classmate was acquiring the complex responsibilities of civic leadership. From his post in the bean field, a mile from the town center, Thoreau heard the distant echoes of cannon at a militia muster and expressed mock pride "that the liberties of Massachusetts and of our fatherland were in such safe keeping." Lieutenant Keyes of the Concord Company was undoubtedly on the training field that day, in a quick march to the top echelons of power. At age twenty-five, he was admitted to the select Social Circle. Twice he ran for town representative to the General Court and lost, then moved straight up to the state senate. And he took on his father's mantle of holding the ground against abolitionism. In 1845 antislavery activists called on the lyceum to invite Wendell Phillips, the radical abolitionist celebrated for his eloquence, to speak. As one of the curators of the lyceum, responsible for arranging the seasonal series, Keyes fought the proposal, in the conviction that controversial topics like abolition were inappropriate to a "literary society." When the membership approved the invitation, Keyes and another curator quit their offices in protest. They were replaced by Emerson and Thoreau. Keyes got even a few years later when he stopped cold another attempt to bring Phillips to Concord. Even as he moved into the Republican ranks and developed sympathy for challenges to the South and its peculiar institution, he continued to be nettled by the outspoken radicalism of Thoreau. At the town ceremony to mourn the hanging of John Brown in 1859, which Keyes helped to organize, it was agreed that all of the speakers would read aloud passages from appropriate literary works, lest they be carried away by passion and utter "treasonable" thoughts. Everything went according to plan, Emerson quoting from Milton, Alcott from "some heathen philosopher," until it was Thoreau's turn to mount the stage. As Keyes recounted the event decades later, he was still nonplused. "D. H. Thoreau with his usual egotism broke the agreement and said some rambling incoherent sentences, that might have been unfortunate if they had not been unintelligible."[46]

Keyes exacted his revenge on Thoreau's posthumous reputation. In the late nineteenth century, as critics looked back at the renaissance of letters in antebellum New England and sought to create a canon of its writers, the worldly judge played a little-known hand in influencing what was said about Thoreau. In 1886 Francis Underwood, a founder and editor of the *Atlantic Monthly*, sought out Keyes's view of his Concord classmate for a collection of biographical sketches of the "builders of American literature." Keyes readily complied with a negative portrait. "You may think my view of him 'Philistine,' for I confess to something of that in me—," Keyes prefaced his remarks, "but as you have the other side in the 'life' and 'cult' of him, your picture may be truer for the shadows." That salvo was repeated a decade later when George W. Cooke prepared an essay on "The Two Thoreaus" for the *Independent* magazine. Noting that Thoreau evoked passionate but polarized responses from readers, Cooke talked to two people who had known him personally, one a detractor, the other an enthusiast. Both informants remained anonymous. The detractor was clearly Keyes, who conceded that "his way of regarding Thoreau was that of the Philistine." Nonetheless, insisted the man at the center of the local establishment, his perspective was "that of the people in Concord who knew Thoreau intimately."[47] And what they had seen up close they had never liked. Keyes rehearsed all the old slurs and added new ones to the mix. Thoreau came of undistinguished origins, his father "a poor dull inefficient man, always in debt," the mother "a proud ambitious woman" intent on "having Henry Educated." Ordinary at school, unremarkable and unpopular in college, something of a joke as a teacher, ludicrous as a lecturer, he was altogether a social failure. Rejected by his peers, the "shy and silent" youth tried to remake himself by imitating Emerson, "whose tones, manner, accent and expression as well as ideals and opinions" he took on "till all who knew both were amused and exasperated." Once he retreated to Walden, Thoreau turned still more solitary and eccentric, as evidenced, Keyes thought, by his cold demeanor, careless dress "always suggesting . . . something of the hermit," and resistance to civic obligations like paying taxes. Forgotten in this account were the melon parties and social outings Keyes had enjoyed in Thoreau's company. In a stab at being fair, the self-appointed spokesman for Concord acknowledged a few positive traits in his subject—"an agreeable voice," "a dry wit," "some tenderness in his eyes," "a warm smile" for those he liked—and noted that Thoreau had not always been so unsocial. What changed him? Recalling his competition with Thoreau for the affections of Ellen Sewall and Mary Russell—courtships in which Keyes fared worse than his rival—he attributed the Transcendentalist's reclusiveness to a broken heart. "He was not a mere intellectual machine but in his young manhood had a love affair . . . [that] amounted to nothing, except that not being reciprocated . . . perhaps tended to make him more recluse and unsociable." Whatever the cause, it was a shriveled soul Keyes discerned in everyday life, not the healthy, vigorous spirit, in tune with nature, who springs forth from the pages of *Walden*.

This version of Thoreau recalls Keyes's own youthful obsessions: flirtations with girls in one romantic dalliance after another; pursuit of popularity among his chums; indifference to ideas; hostility to reform. It would thus be easy to write off Keyes as the "Philistine" he mockingly called himself. But there was a deeper level to his critique. The solid citizen with a taste for intellectual women, whose own daughter had married the son of Ralph Waldo Emerson, had not, it turns out, skipped all the philosophy in Thoreau's writings; he had, in fact, developed a perceptive reading of the works:

> His philosophy of life was that of an educated Indian: to read Plato in his wigwam, visit the college library when not hunting and fishing, and have all the learning and civilization of the past ages, ready at hand when he cared to seek them, to pay no taxes, walk where he chose without regard to fences or paths, but carefully survey and accurately measure each man's land who would pay him for it, attend no church or school, but preach himself when invited and secured listeners.

"An educated Indian" is an apt way to capture Thoreau's announced project of leading a wilderness life in the midst of a settled civilization. For Keyes, the problem lay in the writer's translation of literature into life. When it came down to it, Thoreau was all ego. His communication with others was invariably one way. With "an unbounded faith in himself" but no ambition, he did what he wanted, "independent of all political and social considerations." Others might gather up the world's wisdom in libraries. Thoreau borrowed the books, with no thanks to those who had stocked the shelves. Having sacrificed his own dream of independence to a combination of patriarchal will and materialistic desire, Keyes had no tolerance for the social vision in *Walden*. Nor could a civic leader who had spent a lifetime in public service feel any respect for an idler who gave nothing back to the community. Like Jarvis, Keyes had somehow absorbed on Sabbath mornings, for all his seeming inattention, the basic message Ezra Ripley preached from the pulpit: nobody lives alone. To ignore that lesson was to end up a selfish hypocrite like Thoreau, isolated and unloved.

Nobody lives alone. Horace Hosmer and William S. Robinson, both of whom heard the Reverend Dr. Ripley preach in the Concord meetinghouse during their childhood, took that message to heart and applied it in unconventional ways. So, in their opinion, did Thoreau, an independent man of principle, speaking his conscience freely and fearlessly, whatever the economic or social cost. On that model Robinson conducted a contentious career for three decades in Boston-area journalism and Hosmer, a jack-of-all-trades, turned his back on "calm stupid propriety loving Concord" for the invigorating air of the unfashionable hill town of Acton next door. As Robinson saw it, "the real meaning and duty of life . . . was not to live for ourselves alone, or for those we love, but to forget ourselves, to aim at a higher life, and to do some one thing to make the world better, wiser, and happier for one having lived in it." That was the creed Hosmer learned from long association with the Thoreau family, first as a boy in their home and later as an employee in the pencil business. "It is the crime of this age that men and women *do not aspire to live purer, higher, better lives.*" Admiring Thoreau for embodying ideals they shared, the two men give us a different slant on the Concord writer from Jarvis and Keyes. Theirs is a view from outside the village elite. Raised in workingmen's families, educated largely in public schools, and seldom secure financially despite constant work, they belonged to that vast laboring class in New England—clerks, mechanics, and farmers—whom Thoreau addressed in *Walden*, "the mass of men who are discontented, and idly complaining of the hardness of their lot or of the times, when they might improve them." In their grass-roots Transcendentalism, Robinson and Hosmer took the ideal of independence and self-reliance, adapted it to their circumstances, and thereby revealed the cultural power and social reach of Thoreauvian values for ordinary individuals in Victorian America.[48]

Freedom of expression forms the major motif of Robinson's movement through the turbulent worlds of politics and journalism. Born and reared in Concord village, where his family had lived since just before the Revolution, "Willy" was the sixth and youngest child in a journeyman hatter's family constantly on the edge of poverty. The Robinsons, like the Thoreaus, had once seen better days. Lieutenant Emerson Cogswell, the maternal grandfather, had been a founding member of the Social Circle, only to fade from prominence when his hat-making business failed and his property was seized for debt. The father's line, comprising five generations of shoemakers, tanners, and hatters, included prominent Revolutionary patriots. By 1818, when the future newspaperman was born, "the wheel of the family fortune had reached the lowest point in its descent." William Robinson, Sr., was a heavy drinker, whose long-suffering wife bore the burden of instilling "good habits" in the children. Her favorite was Willy, a bookish boy who shined in the local schools, where he became friendly with John and Henry Thoreau. Though the family was too poor to send him to the "Catermy," the popular nickname for the private academy, the youth excelled at Latin under "Master" Jarvis and attracted the interest of a local gentleman, who offered to sponsor him at Harvard. The promising lad could pay the cost, it was suggested, by doing some work for the college, such as cleaning rooms and tending fires. No thanks, replied his father, who had pride, if not money. "He shall never take a broom there: if he can't get a living without rubbing against that college, he may beg." Whatever resentment the boy felt at this decision was expressed obliquely. "You ask whether I am going to college?" he wrote an older brother at age fourteen. "I think not. A college-life appears to me to be a great deal harder than any other. If I expected to be Governor of Massachusetts . . . or a 'Daniel Webster,' I should go to college; but a person may be President of the United States, and yet not go to college. Henry Clay never went to college, and Benjamin Franklin, neither. I don't expect to be any of these great characters. I think I shall learn a trade ."[49]

Robinson found a different route into the world of books and reading. Apprenticed to a Concord printer at age seventeen, he took to the press with alacrity and soon was not only setting type but also writing squibs for the *Yeoman's Gazette*. The printing office was his college and pulpit, as it had been for Franklin a century before. An enthusiastic Whig, the fiery youth threw himself into the partisan war against Jacksonian Democrats and was rewarded with the chance, at age twenty-one, to run his own paper, the *Concord Republican*, with financial support from a consortium of prominent men, including the Honorable John Keyes. At the same time, Robinson caught the spirit of reform from Emerson. The Transcendentalist's manifesto that "faith makes us, and not we it and faith makes its own forms," issued at the Harvard Divinity School in 1838, was a revelation to "the thoughtful youth." It was "impossible to estimate the incalculable effect" of that pronouncement "upon the minds" of young men, he later recalled. Robinson lost interest in Ripley's sermons and in the Universalist doctrines favored by his dissenter-father and became "a reverent follower of the new teacher." The young editor was soon "a constant reader" of *The Dial*, the organ of the new intellectual movement, and he interspersed poems by Emerson and others amidst the political columns of the *Republican*.[50]

The encounter with Transcendentalism was fateful for his journalistic career. Inspired by a dynamic vision of individual freedom, Robinson infused his politics with an abolitionist fervor that propelled him into conflict with his backers time and again over the next two decades. In the partisan world of antebellum newspapers, editors without means were as dependent on patrons as were impecunious writers. Political parties provided the pay, in exchange for which journalists promoted the cause. That was the case whether a printer ran his own press or worked for wages. Unable to generate enough support among local Whigs, Robinson had to sell the *Republican* in 1841 to an ambitious politician who moved it to Lowell, the textile manufacturing city on the Merrimack River that was quickly overshadowing Concord as a political center in Middlesex County. Robinson went along with the paper, embarking on a peripatetic life that would shuttle him through editorial offices in Boston, Concord, Lowell, and Worcester. But not New York. Recruited by Horace Greeley's *Tribune*, he took a trip to Manhattan to scout out the city and was appalled by the sight of a "large brick institution" where his children would be herded into school. "Not at all like the Concord schoolhouse," he fumed. New York City was no place to raise a family. Robinson hurried back to Massachusetts, where he endured a constant struggle to survive as an independent-minded journalist. Like Thoreau, Robinson was too much the Yankee ever to give up criticizing his New England neighbors.[51]

At the heart of the journalist's troubles was his refusal ever to sacrifice antislavery principle on the altar of political expediency. By 1848 the thirty-year-old Robinson had built the *Lowell Courier* into a prosperous paper, widely read in Whig circles, and was preparing to settle down in the thriving "City of Spindles" with his fiancée Harriet Hanson, the one-time Lowell mill girl and poet and later women's rights activist whose biography of her husband would become the principal memorial and source on his life. Then the Whigs nominated the slaveholding General Zachary Taylor for president. Declining to abandon "the freedom of the slave," Robinson insisted on exposing the candidate in the *Courier* as "neither antislavery nor Whig." That was anathema to the "lords of the loom" in Lowell, who pressured the paper's owner to silence the crusading editor. Robinson quit, rather than subordinate conscience to cotton. The move made him a hero in Free Soil circles and secured support for an independent paper of his own, the *Lowell American*, as the voice of "FREE DEMOCRACY." Liberated from partisan dictates, heedless of advertisers, the editor enjoyed the freedom for the first time to run a paper as he saw fit. "To do the thing he thought right, to say the words he knew ought to be said—this, for him, was to live," Harriet Hanson Robinson would later write. Unfortunately, such fearless journalism won admirers but not enough money. Preserving independence required the same strategy followed by Thoreau. The Robinsons supplied as much of their own needs as they could: the editor set the type, produced the copy, and enlisted his wife to read proof; she cared for the house without help and cut expenses to the bone. Indifferent to fashion, Robinson cared little about appearances, but his wife still remembered, three decades later, how she was reduced to an "allowance" of "two calico dresses a year." Even that was not enough to save the paper. Robinson left Lowell for the vagabond lot of a journeyman editor and freelance writer. There were bright spots, such as the nearly three years (1854–1857) the family spent in Concord, from which the journalist commuted by train to a job in Boston on *The Commonwealth*. The prodigal son was delighted to be back in "the best town in the world" and to renew acquaintance with the Thoreau family, from whom they rented a house. His wife was glad for the unwonted prosperity but disliked her landlord's son and hated the town, partly because William was blackballed for admission to the Social Circle, but even more because Concord seemed a boring suburb after Lowell and Boston:

> Concord is a very nice place [Robinson recorded in her diary],
> ever honored for being my darling's birthplace, to say nothing
> about its being there that the "first forcible resistance was
> made" &c. But it is a dull old place, it is a narrow old place, it is a
> set old place. It is a snobbish old place, it is an old place full of
> Antediluvian people and manners. It is a sleepy old place. . . .
> It is full of graveyards, and the winters are endless. The women
> never go out, and the streets are full of stagnation. It was so still
> that walking up and down the street filled me with horror. . . .
> A good place to be born and buried, but a terrible wearying
> place for one to live who was blessed with energy and life.

To Harriet's satisfaction, the Robinsons moved on, but under bleak circumstances. Once more falling out with editors over politics, William could get work mainly as a freelance columnist.

As the witty "Warrington," a *nom de plume* taken from the sharp, jovial newspaper editor in William Makepeace Thackeray's novel *Pendennis*, Robinson gained a wide reputation and little pay. By the outbreak of the Civil War, the family, back in Boston, was in desperate straits, with William forced to borrow money to pay the bills and Harriet obliged to make mittens for the army, at seventy-five cents a dozen.[52]

It was in the wake of this long, bitter journey through the journalistic wilderness that Robinson learned of the death of his old friend Henry Thoreau in May 1862. "Warrington" sat down immediately to pen a tribute. The piece was short, fulsome in its praise of *Walden* as "the best book ever written in Concord," and appreciative of the author who preferred the solitude of nature to the crowds in Boston. Ironically, the columnist observed, Thoreau's once-secluded retreat at Walden had become a popular destination for day-trippers from the city, thanks to promotional fares offered by the Fitchburg Railroad. Only in the now-deserted center of town, where his body lay at Sleepy Hollow Cemetery, would the poet-naturalist get any rest. Though the urban journalist loved the metropolis his old classmate "hated, or affected to hate," the two were kindred spirits, as Thoreau's biographer Franklin Sanborn discerned in an introduction to '*Warrington' Pen-Portraits*, Harriet Robinson's literary memorial to her husband. Though the "jesting" editor and the reserved writer differed in demeanor, they were "alike in their courageous support of unpopular opinions, their neglect of the cheap prizes of life, and in the steadiness of their friendship for those to whom they were allied." That connection may not have pleased Mrs. Robinson. She pointedly opened her text with an epigraph from Emerson.[53]

Few people would have heard of Horace Hosmer but for his connection to Thoreau. He was born into a family of long lineage and little property; his father, descended from original Puritan settlers of Concord, was a landless laborer all his life. The "titman" of the brood, a dozen years younger than his nearest sibling, the boy grew up in the countryside "alone among old folks." Books were his companions. By age five he had learned his letters from the family Bible and begun attending the district schools, where his brother Ben, years before, had become a great friend of John and David Henry Thoreau. Thanks to that connection, Horace was sent to their academy in 1840 and boarded in the Thoreau home for the year. The experience opened a new era of existence; to "a very green, bashful boy" who had seldom been off the farm, John Thoreau, Jr., made "all things [seem] possible in school life at least." But that schooling was cut short when Hosmer's sister got married the next year and money was needed for her dowry. The boy went home, despite an offer from the Thoreau brothers to teach him for free, and was left to pursue learning on his own. "Starved for something to read," he scrounged old newspapers and comforted himself with *Pilgrim's Progress*. He would remain "a great guzzler" of books all his life.[54]

Hosmer escaped the countryside for the commercial village. After coming of age, he clerked in a grocery store and then engaged in pencil-making for two decades. The business offered a step up in the world, but every time he started to make gains disaster hit. The Civil War stuck him with huge bills owed by southern customers, wiping him out. He rebuilt the business, based in Acton, in partnership with a stationery company in the capital only to watch his entire investment go up in smoke during the "Great Boston Fire" of 1873. In the aftermath, the middle-aged Hosmer was reduced to the laborer's life from which he had sprung, doing all sorts of manual work—painting carriages, mending harnesses, filing saws—and selling occasional articles to the local press in order to pay off his debts and sustain his family. His troubles mounted still more in 1875 after his wife, at age thirty-nine, fell victim to epilepsy, leaving Hosmer to care for her, with his daughter's help, for the next twenty years. By 1890, as he turned sixty, his own health began to fail. But the resourceful Yankee clung to independence, supplying basic necessities by his own efforts and stinting on store-bought goods. It was the familiar formula for self-sufficiency detailed in *Walden*. Hosmer took pride in that achievement: "we are not bloated capitalists, neither have we begged, but sometimes it seems as though God has forgotten us, but we get over that feeling, for he never does, and we have always had a living so far."[55]

Under these trying circumstances, an inquisitive visitor from

Ann Arbor, Michigan, walked into Hosmer's life and stoked his memories of those happy days, four decades before, when he had come to know the Thoreaus. A homeopathic physician with a keen interest in Transcendentalism, Samuel A. Jones had come east to Concord, in search of information about the author of *Walden.* Jones was an iconoclast with little truck for received wisdom in medicine or literature, and he was determined to get to the truth about Thoreau. When he met Franklin Sanborn, the self-appointed custodian of Thoreau's reputation, he was disgusted. The old abolitionist was no longer the radical Jones had admired from afar, and, though courteous, he did not welcome rivals in the business of writing about Thoreau. Turning elsewhere for sources, Jones found Hosmer, and their meeting spawned a correspondence lasting almost three years, from February 1891 to the day before Hosmer's death in January 1894. For the ailing laborer, the homeopath was just what his spirits needed. From his post in Acton, off the beaten path, he had waited in vain for the educated elite of Concord to pay Thoreau his due. Instead, while Emerson was being canonized, Thoreau's reputation remained in the untrustworthy hands of Sanborn. Hosmer was anxious to see the Ttranscendentalists rescued from the dubious care of the respectable, who had dominated Concord far too long. "Concord is a sheepfold," he told Jones, without any obstreperous goats. "These were found on the wild, rocky hills of Acton."[56]

The feisty old man was raring to enter the lists with Sanborn and correct his numerous errors. More than that, he wanted to explain just what the Thoreaus had meant in his life and in the cultural history of New England. As for Henry himself, there was not that much to say. At the academy, young Horace had come under the care of the older Thoreau brother, whom he worshiped, and hardly knew the younger. The preceptor of the advanced classes had a fearsome reputation—he was "merciless," "rigidly exacting," and when he called class into session "the bell tolled instead of rang"—that did not invite close inspection. Even so, the atmosphere in the Thoreau home, combined with the inspirational teaching of John, Jr., introduced the boy to a new world of culture. The father was "healthy, fine boned, fine trained, well bred, a gentleman by instinct," the mother a "large positive woman" with a forceful will, who "recognized his superiority to the coarse, unclean, unrefined crowd of human animals around her." Husband and wife shared a mutual love of nature and beauty and passed it along to their children. Dinners at their table were beautifully prepared and served, with "an abundance of fruit and vegetables, puddings and pies, and best of all to me, was the delicious brown and white bread and butter. There was an absence of heat, noise, fat greasy meat, of everything unpleasant." In this setting, it was natural for the Thoreau children to imbibe a higher, purer vision of life. The outgoing John was "the heart" of the family, the reserved Henry "the head." The writer developed into "the realization of the hopes and aspirations of the Thoreau family: he voiced their feelings, he made their flowers into immortal wreaths, and he formed the bricks made by the humble toilers into an Arch of strength and beauty." Concord had never seen his like. Spurned for the superior "intelligence, civilization," and faith that set the Thoreaus apart, Henry was twenty years ahead of his time. He had to wait for an audience.

What the wide-eyed boy saw in the progressive, village home of the Thoreaus was the new domestic culture of the middle class, with its premium on family affection, tasteful surroundings, and educational achievement. He had stepped off the farm into the bourgeois future. The vernacular world he had known was coarse, cruel, and benighted. "The Concord people were ignorant, low lived, unambitious save in the money making line, and many large estates were squandered by farmers who neglected their farms, and lounged in the Tavern bar rooms week in and week out." On the Sabbath "boozy congregations" heard warnings of "infant damnation and literal hell" from the "drunken lips" of preachers. Intemperate parents blighted the lives of the young. Their retarded children were tied to chairs and confined in backyard cages. Amidst "all this filth," the Thoreaus aspired to higher things and produced "Poets, Artists, Teachers, instead of fools," while Emerson labored through the lyceum to expand his neighbors' minds. As Hosmer looked back across the great divide separating "the age of homespun" from modern, middle-class America, the rural community of his youth resembled, in its meanness and bigotry, the "pathetic" enclaves of poverty and "stagnation" Thoreau had been shocked to discover in his travels through the backcountry.[57]

Yet, the moral improvement foretold by the Thoreau family had not occurred. No apologist of the middle-class order, Hosmer looked down from his Acton hilltop and spied in Concord center a smug, respectable, status-conscious society, as conformist as Thoreau had found it. This was the world made by Jarvis and Keyes, and Hosmer wanted nothing of it. Gilded Age Concord, like the nation as a whole, presented a dispiriting picture to the inveterate idealist. In 1851, on coming of age, he had cast his first ballot "for freedom" and done so "every time" until "Hayes made me tired." Like Robinson, he was disgusted by "the political market" ruled by the conventional parties. Nor was the literary scene more auspicious. To the man who had been among the first in Concord to read and admire *Leaves of Grass*, the town remained provincial, resistant to new currents of thought, as if "all knowledge outside of Concord was Apocryphal." So, in a move reminiscent of Thoreau, the old man withdrew into himself, put on a stoic face, and sought solace in Marcus Aurelius. But when Dr. Jones came along, he rose to the occasion:

> I love Liberty, not the 4th of July sort alone, but all that the word implies. It has cost me more than all else beside, and I value it accordingly. You may go to Concord for civilization, comfort, and refinement, and do well; when you want wood chucks, grass, rocks, rough ways and liberty, come to Acton.

No more than chanticleer on his roost, awakening the neighbors, could the Acton goat pass up the opportunity to butt the Concord sheep.[58]

On the small stage of individual life, then, large social forces played out, shaping fundamental choices about career and family, education and migration, politics and ideology and entering into the construction of personal identity and the perception of self and others. The four contemporaries of Thoreau we have considered here—Jarvis, Keyes, Robinson, and Hosmer—pursued paths

common to their generation. They broke with the rural community inherited from the past and claimed freedom from traditional
constraints. They seized upon the wider world to fashion a liberal,
capitalist order with its own set of opportunities and limits. As
they wrestled with decisions that were intensely personal, these
New Englanders called upon a heritage of thought about self and
society derived from the Puritans and modified in the Revolution.
Such ideas came into collision with changing social needs and
with fresh intellectual currents at home and abroad. The energy
generated by that encounter charged the political debates, cultural conversations, and literary achievements of the era. Central
to this process was the redefinition of boundaries between individual and community. On the personal level, it affected relations
among particular families, friends, and neighbors; on the collective, it generated connections—alliances and rivalries—of lasting
significance for reputations and legacies. And so it was that Henry
David Thoreau the writer came to represent larger meanings to
the people who had once known David Henry Thoreau the
schoolmate and neighbor. And through their lens, American readers at large gained distinctive notions of the man within and behind the texts. The making of Thoreau's reputation is a study in
the interplay between social history and cultural memory.

As a participant in an "age of Revolution," the Concord writer
experienced the same historical movements as his neighbors: the
advance of the market, the waning of traditional authority, the
quickening of migration and mobility, the democratization of
politics, the flourishing of voluntary associations, the superses-
sion of old hierarchies of status by new ones of class. "There was
a new consciousness," Emerson wrote in retrospect. "The former generations acted under the belief that a shining social prosperity was the beatitude of man, and sacrificed uniformly the
citizen to the state. The modern mind believed that the nation
existed for the individual, for the guardianship and education of
every man." In the spirit of the age, Thoreau pulled back from
inherited institutions and involuntary associations. With Jarvis,
he rebuffed older forms of sociability and resisted traditional
claims for allegiance. "I am not responsible for the successful
working of the machinery of society," he declared. "I am not the

son of the engineer." Whatever his roles as citizen, neighbor, and son, he would be, first and foremost, a separate, sovereign self. It was as an individual that he demanded to be judged, upon character and merit alone. To discover his unique gifts, what only he could say and do in this world, constituted his highest obligation. That was not selfishness, he affirmed with William S. Robinson, but true social service. Why was it, he complained, that "he who gives himself entirely to his fellow-men appears to them useless and selfish, but he who gives himself partially to them is pronounced a benefactor and philanthropist"? [59]

To fulfill this duty to self and society, Thoreau took the ideal of independence he shared with contemporaries and elevated it to new heights. Spurred by the rhetoric of the American Revolution, his generation sought self-determination in personal as well as national affairs. For Jarvis and Keyes, independence was a clarion call to cast off patriarchal authority and decide their own callings. For Hosmer, it meant liberation from rural ignorance and vice. But the pursuit of independence was entangled with capitalism and class. Where Jarvis, the successful professional, found a new freedom in the impersonal mechanisms of the market, Hosmer and Robinson suffered relentless insecurity. Dependent on others for a living, they took serious risks every time they asserted their own voice. In like manner, the independence Jarvis and Keyes claimed from intrusive neighbors served, intentionally or not, as a splendid instrument for consolidating a privileged class, free to enjoy separate associations behind closed doors, even as it presumed to public power over common citizens like Hosmer. In this setting, Henry Thoreau stands out for the rigor of his social analysis. In the nineteenth-century dialectic of change, as he saw it, an *ancien régime* of traditional hierarchy and communal constraint was giving way to a new order of market domination and middle-class conformity. In the name of independence, he repudiated both.

To that end, Thoreau employed the familiar strategy of Yankee economy—self-sufficiency and thrift—to secure freedom from arbitrary limits. Once a tool for sustaining independent households in an interdependent community, the formula enabled Thoreau to carry the logic of social withdrawal to its limits. At Walden, he maintained an independent household, consisting of a single member, with open hospitality for chipmunks and titmice and a mixed welcome for visitors from town. Subsidized by Emerson, the experiment in deliberate living was economically a losing venture, based on a curious commodity in everyday use—the Yankee bean—that nobody raised as a cash crop. But imaginatively, the enterprise was a vast success. It dramatized the power of the individual to declare independence from constraints and to speak his own mind free from all "slavemasters," including his well-socialized self. The symbolic figure Thoreau projected in *Walden* spoke powerfully to men like Robinson and Hosmer, engaged in their own struggles for self-expression against the tyrannies of censorship, conformity, and cash. That resonance illuminates the appeal of *Walden* to working-class as well as elite readers in his time down to our own.[60]

While Thoreau embraced independence in the service of freedom, he spurned the inequality and class consciousness that were its concomitants for Jarvis and Keyes. Educated to be a gentleman and scholar, he astonished the neighbors with his preference for the company of disreputable woodsmen, common farmers, and Irish laborers. Keyes observed that it was the "quaint people of the town, those who were racy in speech and personal in character," whom Thoreau favored. "The more of oddity he found in them the greater liking he had for their society, and the greater enjoyment he found in their expressions and ideas. . . . He seldom came into contact with the educated people of the village, with the exception of Emerson, Hawthorne, Channing, and the few others who were his special admirers and friends." With an inclusiveness rare for a Harvard graduate of his time, Thoreau transgressed the boundaries of class as naturally as he ignored the property lines he surveyed.[61]

For all his rhetorical proclamations of independence from family, Thoreau remained a faithful son. If he did not marry, neither did his siblings, his uncle, or aunts. Bachelorhood was in his blood. Apart from his stays with the Emersons and his sojourn in the woods, he lived always amidst kin. If he treasured his privacy in a room of his own, he gave much of his time to the family, working in the pencil business, caring for his ailing father, assuming the responsibilities of a head of household after John Thoreau's death. It may be, as Horace Hosmer speculated, that Cynthia Thoreau was "disappointed" that "Henry did not become a Lawyer, Doctor or Minister," but he persisted on his own course in the face of that disapproval. Precisely because he was so attached to the family, he denied its claims so fiercely in his texts. It took courage to cultivate independence among people who had known him all his life, and, as contemporary writers suggested, that struggle exacted a toll.[62]

Concord thus remained home to Thoreau, a constant source of inspiration and irritation. He ranged over the landscape as freely as he sought out its inhabitants. "Henry talks about Nature," observed one neighbor, "just as if she'd been born and brought up in Concord." The American Revolution was equally a local affair, an object of civic pride on which Thoreau rang numerous changes to spur the townspeople to new battles for liberty. The truth was that the hermit of Walden had absorbed Ezra Ripley's message. Locked in a quarrel with neighbors whose false values he decried, he could not leave them alone. With the passion of a Puritan preacher and the zeal of a temperance crusader, he spoke out from his independent pulpit and tried to wake them up. Far from being antisocial, he was a true son of the town. "If I forget thee, O Concord," he once pledged, "let my right hand forget her cunning." He never did.[63]

NOTES

1. Walter Harding, ed., *Thoreau as Seen by His Contemporaries* (New York: Dover, 1989), 32, 49, 50, 206; Edward W. Emerson, "Remains of Thoreau," undated lecture in his manuscript notes on Thoreau, Concord Free Public Library; George Hendrick, ed., *Remembrances of Concord and the Thoreaus: Letters of Horace Hosmer to Dr. S.A. Jones* (Urbana: University of Illinois Press, 1977), 14; F.B. Sanborn, *The Life of Henry David Thoreau Including Many Essays Hitherto Unpublished and Some Account of His Family and Friends* (Boston: Houghton Mifflin, 1917), 297.

2. Walter Harding, *The Days of Henry Thoreau: A Biography* (rev.

and corrected ed.; New York: Dover, 1982), 321–22; Henry D. Thoreau, *Walden and Resistance to Civil Government*, ed. William Rossi (2nd ed.; New York: W.W. Norton, 1992), 2, 5, 6.

3. Harding, *Days*, 52–54, 159–62; Journal of William S. Robinson and Harriet Hanson Robinson, entries for May 31, 1855 and August 26, 1856, Robinson-Shattuck Papers, M-110, Reel 3, Schlesinger Library, Harvard University, Cambridge, Mass.

4. Harding, ed., *Thoreau*, 202; Hendrick, ed., *Remembrances*, 32, 136.

5. Sanborn, *Life*, 462–63; *Reports of the School Committee, and Superintendent of the Schools, of the Town of Concord, Mass.* [for 1861] (Concord: Benjamin Tolman, 1861), 26; Bradford Torrey and Francis H. Allen, eds., *The Journal of Henry D. Thoreau* (14 vols.; Boston: Houghton Mifflin, 1906), IX:160; Lawrence Buell, *The Environmental Imagination: Thoreau, Nature Writing, and the Formation of American Culture* (Cambridge: Harvard University Press, 1995), 320–21.

6. Emerson, "Nature" and "Thoreau," both in *Selected Essays of Ralph Waldo Emerson*, ed. Larzer Ziff (New York: Penguin Books, 1982), 67, 393–415; Fritz Oehlschlaeger and George Hendrick, eds., *Toward the Making of Thoreau's Modern Reputation: Selected Correspondence of S.A. Jones, A.W. Hosmer, H.S. Salt, H.G.O. Blake, and D. Ricketson* (Urbana: University of Illinois Press, 1979), 14.

7. Robert Sattelmeyer, "Emerson and Thoreau," in *Cambridge Companion to Thoreau*, ed, Joel Myerson (New York: Cambridge University Press, 1995), 38; Oehlschlaeger and Hendrick, eds., *Toward the Making*, 15–17.

8. Sanborn, *Life*, 283–86; Mary Hosmer Brown, *Memories of Concord* (Boston: Four Seas Company, 1926), 92; Mary Elkins Moller, *Thoreau in the Human Community* (Amherst: University of Massachusetts Press, 1980), 6, 181-86, Oehlschlaeger and Hendrick, eds., *Toward the Making*.

9. Gamaliel Bailey, review of *Walden*, and Charles Frederick Briggs, "A Yankee Diogenes," both in Norton edition of *Walden*, 312, 314–17; Hosmer, *Remembrances*, 3–4; Robert A. Gross, "Lonesome in Eden: Dickinson, Thoreau and the Problem of Community in Nineteenth-Century New England," *Canadian Review of American Studies* 14 (Spring 1983): 3.

10. Thoreau, *Walden*, 1, 163; Robert A. Gross, "The Machine-Readable Transcendentalists: Cultural History on the Computer,"

American Quarterly 41 (September 1989): 501–21; Ezra Ripley, "On Gratitude to God and Man," ninth sermon on the social virtues, adapted to Thanksgiving, November 29, 1798, bMS AM 1835 (11), Box 2, Houghton Library, Harvard University; Emerson, "Thoreau," 410.

11. Emerson, "Thoreau," 395; Harding, *Days*, 72–73, 142–43, 200. A register of voters was prepared by the Concord selectmen in preparation for the November 1841 town meeting. It lists 377 enrolled voters, including John Thoreau, John Thoreau, Jr., and Henry D. Thoreau. Next to most names is an "x." That is the case for John Thoreau, and for 337 others. But no symbol adjoins the name of Henry D. Thoreau. Evidently, he was among the thirty-eight men who did not turn out to vote in the November election. See checklist of voters, November 8, 1841, in Concord Archives, Box 14, folder for October–December 1841, Concord Free Public Library.

12. John Wood Sweet, "The Liberal Dilemma and the Demise of the Town Church: Ezra Ripley's Pastorate in Concord, 1778–1841," *Proceedings of the Massachusetts Historical Society* 104 (1992): 102–3; Susan Kurland, "Democratization in Concord: A Political History, 1750–1850," in *Concord: The Social History of a New England Town 1750–1850*, ed. David Hackett Fischer (Waltham: Brandeis University, 1983), 270–71; Glenn C. Altschuler and Stuart M. Blumin, "'Where Is the Real America?': Politics and Popular Consciousness in the Antebellum Era," *American Quarterly* 49 (June 1997): 225–67.

13. Petition of Ezra Ripley and 127 others of Concord, Massachusetts against the annexation of Texas into the Union; petition of Josiah Bartlett and sixty-one others of Concord, praying for a ban on the admission of any new slaveholding states into the Union; and petition of Josiah Bartlett and sixty-nine others of Concord, praying for the abolition of slavery and the slave trade in the District of Columbia. All three petitions were submitted to the Twenty-Fifth Congress and are now held at the National Archives in Washington, D.C. The petition against Texas annexation, presented to the first session of the Congress on October 3, 1837, can be found in Petitions and Memorials of the House of Representatives: Annexation of Texas (25A-H1.1), Twenty-Fifth Congress, First Session, Record Group 233. The other two petitions, submitted to the second session on January 15 and 16, 1838, are contained in the Library of Congress Collection of Records of the House of Representatives: Massachusetts Antislavery Petitions (25A-H1.1), Twenty-Fifth Congress, Second Session,

National Archives Box 31 of Library of Congress Box 117, Record Group 233.

14. Thoreau, *Walden*, 74, 234; Harding, *Days*, 314–16, 416–17; Henry D. Thoreau, "A Plea for Captain John Brown," in *Reform Papers*, ed. Wendell Glick (Princeton: Princeton University Press, 1973), 111–38 (quotation, 115).

15. Ralph Waldo Emerson, "The American Scholar," in *Selected Essays*, ed. Ziff, 101; Robert A. Gross, "Culture and Cultivation: Agriculture and Society in Thoreau's Concord," *Journal of American History*, 69 (June, 1982): 42–61, and "Transcendentalism and Urbanism: Concord, Boston and the Wider World," *Journal of American Studies* 18 (December 1984): 361–81; Richard D. Brown, *Modernization: The Transformation of American Life, 1600–1865* (New York: Hill & Wang, 1976).

16. Emerson, "Fate," in *Selected Essays*, ed. Ziff, 361; Emerson, "American Scholar," 101; Thoreau, *Walden*, 5.

17. Robert A. Gross, *The Minutemen and Their World* (New York: Hill & Wang, 1976), 171–76, Gross, "Lonesome in Eden," 14–15; *English goods cheaper in Concord than at Boston! Concord variety store, kept by Richardson & Wheeler* (Boston, 1804), broadside in collection of American Antiquarian Society, Worcester, Mass.; Philip Zea and Robert C. Cheney, *Clock Making in New England, 1725–1825: An Interpretation of the Old Sturbridge Village Collection* (Sturbridge: Old Sturbridge Village, 1992), 69–70; Harding, *Days*, 5, 8.

18. Gross, "Transcendentalism and Urbanism," 369–71; Thoreau, *Walden*, 113; advertisement for How and Hidden's Dry Goods Store, *Yeoman's Gazette*, Septenber 2, 1837; entry for October 15, 1843, Directors Discount Sheet, Concord Bank Records, Old Sturbridge Village, Sturbridge, Mass.

19. Gross, "Culture and Cultivation"; Thoreau, *Walden*, 43, 106.

20. Gross, "Culture and Cultivation"; Ralph Waldo Emerson, "Historical Discourse at Concord . . . ," in Ralph Waldo Emerson, *Miscellanies* (Boston: Houghton Mifflin, 1883), 85; Jack Larkin, "'Labor Is the Great Thing in Farming': The Farm Laborers of the Ward Family of Shrewsbury, Massachusetts, 1787-1860," *Proceedings of the American Antiquarian Society* 99, pt. 1 (1989):189–226.

21. Gross, "Culture and Cultivation," 56, and "Transcendentalism and Urbanism," 374, n. 22; Edward Zimmer, "The Workers at the Damon Textile Factory, West Concord, Massachusetts: 1835–1837"

(paper written for Community Studies Seminar, Boston University, 1973), Concord Free Public Library; "Old School Fellows," *Concord Republican*, July 19, 1841; Harriet H. Robinson, *'Warrington' Pen-Portraits: A Collection of Personal and Political Reminiscences from 1848 to 1876, from the Writings of William S. Robinson, With Memoirs, and Extracts from Diary and Letters Never Before Published* (Boston: Mrs. W. S. Robinson, 1877), 22.

22. Gross, "Transcendentalism and Urbanism," 374–75; Ezra Ripley, lecture at Concord Lyceum, written March 1837, delivered April 19, 1837, in Samuel Ripley Sermons, Box 1 of 13, bMS AM 1835 (5), Houghton Library, Harvard University; Robert A. Gross, "The Celestial Village: Transcendentalism and Tourism in Concord," in *Transient and Permanent: The Transcendentalist Movement and Its Contexts*, ed. Conrad E. Wright and Charles Capper (Boston: Massachusetts Historical Society, 1999), 251–81.

23. Harding, *Days*, 4–12; Sanborn, *Life*, 441–47, 522–31; Gross, *Minutemen*, 59, 63.

24. Henry Petroski, *The Pencil: A History of Design and Circumstance* (New York: Knopf, 1990), 91–125; petition of Josiah Davis and fifty-four others of the town of Concord, Massachusetts, praying that Warren Bridge be made free, submitted to January 1835 session of the General Court, Massachusetts State Archives, Boston; Stanley I. Kutler, *Privilege and Creative Destruction: The Charles River Bridge Case* (Baltimore and London: Johns Hopkins University Press, 1971).

25. Lemuel Shattuck, *A History of the Town of Concord; Middlesex County, Massachusetts, From Its Earliest Settlement to 1832 . . .* (Boston: Russell, Odiorne, and Company, and Concord: John Stacy, 1835), 218; Harding, *Days*, 261–63; Ronald J. Zboray, *A Fictive People: Antebellum Economic Development and the American Reading Public* (New York: Oxford University Press, 1993), 9–11; Thoreau, *Walden*, 71, 83; Robert A. Gross, *Books and Libraries in Thoreau's Concord: Two Essays* (Worcester, Mass.: American Antiquarian Society, 1988).

26. Harding, *Days*, 11, 16, 23, 32, 44, 73, 177–78, 263–64; Hendrick, ed., *Remembrances*, 21; Timothy Prescott, Diary, entry for May 18, 1837, Houghton Library, Harvard University. On the 1850 assessment list, John Thoreau ranked in the second quintile of property-holders, with a taxable worth of $1,909.

27. Harding, Days, 32; Edward Jarvis, *Traditions and Reminiscences of Concord, Massachusetts, 1779–1878,* ed. Sarah Chapin (Amherst: Uni-

versity of Massachusetts Press, 1993), 235-38; Ronald Story, *The Forging of an Aristocracy: Harvard & the Boston Upper Class, 1800–1870* (Middletown, Conn.: Wesleyan University Press, 1980), 94–97, 108–34.

28. Harding, *Days,* 94–112, 145–56; Richard Lebeaux, *Young Man Thoreau* (Amherst: University of Massachusetts Press, 1977), 44–45; Sereno Edwards Todd, *Country Homes and How to Save Money . . .* (Hartford, Conn.: Hartford Publishing Company, 1870), 42–43. Thoreau seems to have given up on wedlock even before reaching age twenty-five, which had been the typical age for men to marry in Concord since the middle of the eighteenth century. Gross, *Minutemen,* 77; Marc Harris, "The People of Concord: A Demographic History, 1750–1850," in *Concord,* ed. Fischer, 89.

29. Sattelmeyer, "Emerson and Thoreau;" Emerson, "American Scholar," 104; R. Jackson Wilson, *Figures of Speech: American Writers and the Literary Marketplace, From Benjamin Franklin to Emily Dickinson* (New York: Knopf, 1989); entry for February 6, 1850, Directors Discount Sheet, Concord Bank Records; A. Forbes and J.W. Greene, *The Rich Men of Massachusetts . . .* (Boston: Fetridge, 1851), 101. The punctilious Thoreau paid off the bank loan on time.

30. Harding, *Days,* 66; Sattelmeyer, "Emerson and Thoreau," 28, 35; Thoreau, *A Week on the Concord and Merrimack Rivers,* ed. Carl F. Hovde (Princeton: Princeton University Press, 1980), 287.

31. Steven Fink, "Thoreau and his audience," in *The Cambridge Companion to Henry David Thoreau,* ed. Myerson, 83–88.

32. Thoreau, *Walden,* 12; Thoreau, "Life without Principle," in *Reform Papers,* ed. Glick, 156, 158.

33. Thoreau, *Walden,* 5, 8; Robert A. Gross, "Young Men and Women of Fairest Promise: Transcendentalism in Concord," *Concord Saunterer,* n.s. 2 (Fall 1994): 5–18.

34. This account of Thoreau's contemporaries is based on the following sources: for Edward Jarvis (1803–1884), see his "Autobiography," Houghton Library, Harvard University; Diaries, 1827–1842, Concord Free Public Library; and *Traditions and Reminiscences.* See also Robert A. Gross, "Preserving Culture: Edward Jarvis and the Memory of Concord," introduction to *Traditions and Reminiscences,* xv–xliv; and Gerald N. Grob, *Edward Jarvis and the Medical World of Nineteenth-Century America* (Knoxville: University of Tennessee Press, 1978); for John Shepard Keyes (1821–1910), see his Autobiography, Diaries 1837–1908, vols. 1–5, 7–13, and Reminiscences of Con-

cord, 1824–1867, Concord Free Public Library; Gross, "Young Men and Women of Fairest Promise;" for Robinson (1818–1876), see Robinson; *'Warrington Pen-Portraits.* For Hosmer (1830–1894), see Oehlschlaeger and Hendrick, eds., *Remembrances* (quotation, 9). For John Thoreau's management of the Jarvis store, see Harding, *Days,* 8, 11.

35. This account of Jarvis is based on my essay "Preserving Culture." In this and subsequent notes, I cite only quotations not referred to in that piece. See Jarvis, "Autobiography," 28–29.

36. Jarvis, Diary 1: 99–102, and "Autobiography," 28–29.

37. Jarvis, Diary 1: 210, 212-15.

38. Grob, *Edward Jarvis*, 232, n. 7.

39. Jarvis, Diary 2: 1–5, 94–96, 115–20, 142–47: "Autobiography," 79–82.

40. Grob, *Edward Jarvis*, 43–48; Jarvis, *Traditions and Reminiscences*; Robert A. Gross, "'The Most Estimable Place in All the World': A Debate on Progress in Nineteenth-Century Concord," *Studies in the American Renaissance* 2 (1978): 1–16.

41. Jarvis, "Houses and People in Concord, Massachusetts, 1810 to 1820," typescript of original manuscript, 1882, in Concord Free Public Library, 251–54.

42. Harding, ed., *Thoreau*, 81–83, 205; Keyes, Autobiography; Gross, "Young Men and Women of Fairest Promise." In subsequent notes, I cite only quotations from Keyes's manuscripts not referred to in my essay.

43. Keyes, Diary, vol. 2, entries for January 1, 1840, February 9, 1840, and September 19, 1841; Autobiography, 117–18; Thoreau, *Walden*, 33.

44. Keyes, Autobiography, 45$^{1/2}$.

45. Keyes, Diary, vol. 3: entries for July 28, 1840 and July 4 and 11 and August 24, 1841; vol. 4: entry for September 11 and 28, 1841;

46. Keyes, Autobiography, 100–104, 110, 115–17, 167–68; Thoreau, *Walden*, 107–8.

47. Keyes's letter to Underwood and interview with Cooke are available in Harding, ed., *Thoreau*, 81–87, 205–208. For Underwood's collection of biographical sketches, see *Builders of American Literature: Sketches of American Authors Born Previous to 1826* (Boston: Lee and Shepard, 1893). (The account of Thoreau appears on pp. 213–16.) The admirer in Cooke's piece may well have been Franklin B. San-

born, the biographer and sometime associate of Thoreau. There is a striking similarity between Cooke's report that "in his relations to his friends [Thoreau] was fidelity itself" and Sanborn's praise of Thoreau's "fidelity in friendship." (Sanborn, *Life*, 284.) However, Cooke refers directly and not altogether favorably to Sanborn in his piece. One of the "Secret Six" accused of aiding John Brown's raid at Harpers Ferry, Sanborn was identified as the person who cautioned Thoreau against speaking out in Brown's defense. If Cooke's informant was not Sanborn, it was, in all likelihood, the poet Ellery Channing, who had been an intimate of Thoreau in Concord.

48. Robinson, ed., '*Warrington*' *Pen-Portraits*, 49 50; Hendrick, ed, *Remembrances*, 21; Thoreau, *Walden*, 10.

49. Robinson, '*Warrington*' *Pen-Portraits*, 7–13; Jarvis, "Houses and People," 150–52.

50. Robinson, '*Warrington*' *Pen-Portraits*, 15–21; Emerson, "Address Delivered Before the Senior Class in Divinity College, Cambridge," in *Selected Essays*, ed. Ziff, 126.

51. Robinson, ed., '*Warrington*' *Pen-Portraits*, 90.

52. Robinson, ed., '*Warrington Pen-Portraits*, 22, 35–99: Harriet Hanson Robinson, Diary, entries for June 9, 1856 and June 23, 1858. Harriet Robinson explicitly tied her family's economizing measures to those of Thoreau. Quoting *Walden*, she reported that her husband "lived, as Thoreau said, 'close to the bone'" ('*Warrington*' *Pen-Portraits*, 49).

53. Robinson, '*Warrington*' *Pen-Portraits*, ix–x, 22. John S. Keyes, comp., Social Circle Records, List of nominations for membership, entry for November 1854, Concord Free Public Library. Interestingly, Harriet Robinson likened her late husband to the Stoic philosopher Diogenes (77), with whom Thoreau was disparagingly equated in reviews of *Walden*. See, for example, Briggs, "A Yankee Diogenes."

54. Hendrick, ed., *Remembrances*, 9, 27, 44, 76.

55. Hendrick, ed., *Remembrances*, 28–30.

56. Hendrick, ed., *Remembrances*, xv–xxvi, 4, 44: Oehlschlaeger and Hendrick, eds., *Toward the Making*, 1–54.

57. Hendrick, ed., *Remembrances*, 17, 20–22; Thoreau, "Life Misspent," typescript of lecture reconstructed from Thoreau manuscripts by Tom Blanding, Concord, Mass.

58. Hendrick, ed., *Remembrances*, 4, 47, 78, 133–34.

59. Emerson, "Historic Notes on Life and Letters in New En-

gland," in Ralph Waldo Emerson, *Lectures and Biographical Sketches* (Boston: Houghton Mifflin, 1883), 326; Thoreau, "Resistance to Civil Government," in *Walden*, 228, 238–39.

60. Robert A. Gross, "The Great Bean Field Hoax: Thoreau and the Agricultural Reformers," *Virginia Quarterly Review* 61 (Summer 1985): 483–97, and "Lonesome in Eden."

61. Harding, ed., *Thoreau*, 82–83.

62. Harding, *Days*, 112; Hosmer, *Remembrances*, 35.

63. Harding, ed., *Thoreau*, 59; Gross, "'The Most Estimable Place,'" 11.

ILLUSTRATED
CHRONOLOGY

Thoreau's Life

1817: July 12, born in Concord, Massachusetts; October 12, baptized as David Henry Thoreau.

1818: Family moves to Chelmsford, Massachusetts, ten miles north of Concord.

1821: Family moves to Boston, where father teaches school.

1822: First visit to Walden Pond.

1823: Family moves back to Concord; father runs pencil-making business.

1827: Earliest known work, "The Seasons."

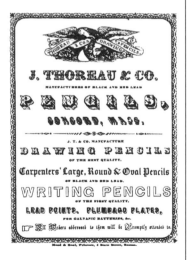

An advertisement, c. 1845, for the Thoreau family's pencil business.

Historical Events

1817: White settlers attack Seminole Indians, in Georgia and Florida, leading to First Seminole War (1817–1818).

1818: Benjamin Silliman (1779–1864), Connecticut chemist, establishes *American Journal of Sciences and Arts.*

1819: Supreme Court, under Chief Justice John Marshall (1755–1835), in *McCulloch v. Maryland,* asserts power of the federal government over the states. Spain cedes Florida to United States. American Geological Society formed, at Yale College, New Haven, Connecticut. Washington Irving (1783–1859), *The Sketch Book of Geoffrey Crayon, Gent.*

1820: March, Missouri Compromise: Missouri admitted to the Union as a slave state, Maine as a free state; slavery prohibited in Louisiana territory north of 36°30' latitude. United States population: 9.6 million.

1821: American Colonization Society establishes colony of Liberia in western Africa for freed black slaves; settlement begins in 1822. James Fenimore Cooper (1789–1851), *The Spy.* William Cullen Bryant (1794–1878), *Poems.*

1828: Thoreau and brother John (b. 1815) attend Concord Academy.

1833: Enters Harvard College.

1835: Between terms at Harvard, teaches school in Canton, Massachusetts.

1836: January/February, boards for six weeks with Orestes Brownson, minister and author. Summer, visits New York City with father.

1837: Graduates from Harvard; begins journal; teaches briefly in Concord public school; becomes friends with Ralph Waldo Emerson, Margaret Fuller, Jones Very, and Amos Bronson Alcott. Changes name from David Henry to Henry David.

1822: Denmark Vesey (b. 1767) and thirty-four followers hanged for plotting slave rebellion in Charleston, South Carolina.

1823: December, President James Monroe (1758–1831) declares Monroe Doctrine warning European powers against interfering in internal affairs of the Western Hemisphere and stating that the United States will keep distant from European conflicts.

1824: December, no candidate receives an electoral majority in presidential election; John Quincy Adams chosen as president by vote in U.S. House of Representatives in February 1825. First school of science and engineering opens in Troy, New York; later called Rensselaer Polytechnic Institute.

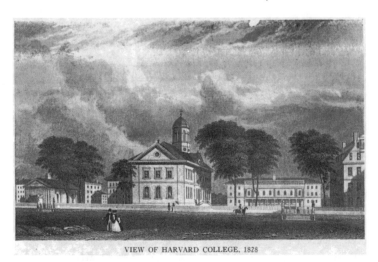

VIEW OF HARVARD COLLEGE, 1828

View of Harvard College, 1828. Thoreau graduated from Harvard in 1837.

This nineteenth-century drawing shows a passenger coach drown by horses, and the locomotive that would soon replace it.

1839: May, travels to Maine. With brother John, teaches school in Concord.

1839: July, meets and falls in love with Ellen Sewall. August/September, travels along Concord and Merrimack Rivers with John.

1840: July, publishes essay "Aulus Persius Flaccus" and poem "Sympathy" in Transcendentalist journal *The Dial.*

1841: April, stops teaching school; moves in with Emerson family, stays two years as gardener and handyman.

1842: January 11, brother John dies. Summer, meets Nathaniel Hawthorne.

1825: October, opening of the Erie Canal, 350 miles in length, connects Great Lakes and Hudson River and establishes route via the Hudson to the Atlantic Ocean at New York City.

1826: Josiah Holbrook (1788–1854), educational reformer, organizes first lyceum for community meetings and for lectures on literature, the arts, and public affairs. American Temperance Society formed. Cooper, *The Last of the Mohicans.*

1827: November, Creek Indians cede their remaining lands in the Southeast, including vast territory in Georgia, to United States. *Freedom's Journal*, first African-American newspaper, begins publication in New York. William Ladd (1778–1841) founds American Peace Society. John James Audubon (1785–1851), *The Birds of America* (1827–1838).

LAND SURVEYING

Of all kinds, according to the best
methods known; the necessary data supplied, in order that the boundaries of
Farms may be accurately described in
Deeds; *Woods* lotted off distinctly and
according to a regular plan; *Roads* laid
out, &c., &c. Distinct and accurate Plans
of Farms furnished, with the buildings
thereon, of any size, and with a scale of feet
attached, to accompany the Farm Book, so
that the land may be laid out in a winter
evening.

Areas warranted accurate within almost
any degree of exactness, and the Variation of the Compass given,
so that the lines can be run again.   Apply to

HENRY D. THOREAU,
near the depot
Concord Mass

Thoreau worked intermittently as a surveyor in Concord and the surrounding area.

1828: December, Andrew Jackson (1767–1845), candidate of newly formed Democratic Party, elected president. Noah Webster (1758-1843), *An American Dictionary of the English Language.*

1829: Workingmen's Party begins in Philadelphia and New York City, calls for non-imprisonment for debt and free public education.

1830: April, Joseph Smith (1805–1844), in Fayette, New York, founds the Church of Jesus Christ of Latter-Day Saints, known as the Mormon Church. New York inventor Peter Cooper (1791–1883) builds the first locomotive in the United States.

Peter Cooper's "Tom Thumb." Peter Cooper (1791–1883), a New York manufacturer and inventor, built the first steam locomotive, "Tom Thumb," in 1829–1830, at the Canton Iron Works in Baltimore, Maryland.

1843: Assists Emerson in editing *The Dial*. May-December, moves to Staten Island, New York, to tutor the children of Emerson's brother William. December, returns to Concord.

1844: April, by accident sets fire to Concord woods, 300 acres burned. July/August, Hudson River boat trip to Catskill Mountains, southeast New York state.

1845: March, begins work on cabin near Walden Pond. July 4, moves into cabin. Works on book about 1839 river trip and on essay about Scottish historian and essayist Thomas Carlyle.

1846: Begins writing *Walden*. July, arrested for failure to pay taxes. August/September, trip to Maine woods.

1847: September, leaves Walden cabin. October, moves into Emerson house, stays ten months. Begins note-taking on American Indians (3,000 pages of quotations and notes, 1847–1861).

1848: January, lecture, "The Rights and Duties of the Individual in Relation to Government," Concord Lyceum; returns to Thoreau family home.

1831: January, William Lloyd Garrison (1805–1879) begins *The Liberator*, abolitionist newspaper. August, slave insurrection in Southampton County, Virginia, led by Nat Turner (b. 1800); more than fifty whites killed; Turner tried and executed six weeks later.

1832: January, New England Anti-Slavery Society formed in Boston; April, Sauk Indians, led by Black Hawk (1767–1838), fight against settlers and Illinois militia (who massacre many Sauk women, children, and old men at Bad Axe River, Wisconsin); December, Nullification crisis—President Jackson issues proclamation asserting supremacy of federal law in reply to South Carolina's declaration of federal tariff null and void and threat to secede from the Union.

1833: December, American Anti-Slavery Society organized in Philadelphia. Oberlin College first to admit both men and women; admits black students in 1835.

1834: Whig Party formed, favors protective tariffs, internal improvements (roads, canals), and development of industry.

1835: November, warfare begins between U.S. forces and Seminole Indians in Florida. Alexis de Tocqueville (1805–1859), *De la Démocratie en Amérique* (English edition, *Democracy in America*, 1838).

1849: May, *A Week on the Concord and Merrimack Rivers*; June 14, sister Helen (b. 1812) dies. "Resistance to Civil Government" (later titled "Civil Disobedience") published in *Aesthetic Papers*. Works as surveyor. October, first trip to Cape Cod.

1850: June, second trip to Cape Cod. July, journeys to Fire Island, New York, to search for manuscripts of Margaret Fuller, drowned in shipwreck. September, travels by railway to Canada.

1851: Active in Underground Railroad, helping fugitive slaves flee to Canada.

1853: September, second trip to Maine.

The political opponents of Andrew Jackson (1767–1845), Democrat, seventh president of the United States (elected in 1828, reelected 1832), claimed that his frequent use of the veto showed that he sought to wield the absolute power of a king.

Frederic Edwin Church (1826–1900), Mt. Ktaadn (1853). Yale University Art Library. Thoreau explored Mount Ktaadn on a trip to Maine in August/September 1846 (while he was living at Walden). He published an essay about his experience in the Union Magazine, *July through November 1848, and a version of it was later included in his posthumous book* The Maine Woods *(1864).*

WALDEN;

OR,

LIFE IN THE WOODS.

By HENRY D. THOREAU,

AUTHOR OF "A WEEK ON THE CONCORD AND MERRIMACK RIVERS."

I do not propose to write an ode to dejection, but to brag as lustily as chanticleer in the morning, standing on his roost, if only to wake my neighbors up. — Page 92.

BOSTON:
TICKNOR AND FIELDS.
M DCCC LIV.

Henry David Thoreau, 1856. From a daguerreotype by B. W. Maxham. Photo used courtesy of Concord Free Public Library.

Henry David Thoreau. Title page of the first edition of Walden, *published in 1854. Thoreau's sister Sophia provided the drawing of the cabin, and he used it, but he complained that it was somewhat inaccurate (for instance, the roof was placed too high above the door).*

Items of furniture used by Thoreau at Walden. Concord Free Public Library.

1854: July 4, lecture, "Slavery in Massachusetts," in Framingham, Massachusetts. August 9, *Walden*. Lectures in northeast, "Getting a Living" (later published as "Life without Principle"). November, lectures in Philadelphia.

1855: July, third trip to Cape Cod.

1856: September, travels in Vermont and New Hampshire. October/November, travels to New Jersey and New York; in Brooklyn, meets Walt Whitman.

1857: March, meets abolitionist John Brown. June, final trip to Cape Cod. July/August, final trip to Maine woods.

1858: May, travels to New York City. July, explores White Mountains, in New Hampshire.

1859: February 3, father dies. October-November, lectures on John Brown, abolitionist leader of failed attack on federal arsenal in Harpers Ferry, Virginia.

1836: March–April, Texas wins independence from Mexico after battles at the Alamo, in San Antonio, and San Jacinto. Emerson and other intellectuals in Concord, Cambridge, and Boston form Transcendental Club. Ralph Waldo Emerson (1803–1882), *Nature*. Asa Gray (1810–1888), *Elements of Botany*.

1837: May, financial panic, economic collapse, beginnings of mass unemployment, effects linger for next seven years; November, mob kills anti-slavery editor Elijah P. Lovejoy (1802–1837) in Alton, Illinois. Emerson, "The American Scholar." Nathaniel Hawthorne (1804–1864), *Twice-Told Tales* (collection of eighteen previously published stories, including "The Minister's Black Veil," "The May-Pole of Merry Mount," "The Gentle Boy," and "Wakefield").

Concord Center, c. 1860. Concord Free Public Library.

BHĂGVĂT-GĒĒTĂ,

OR

DIALOGUES

OF

KRĔĔSHNĂ AND *ĂRĴŎŎN*;

IN EIGHTEEN LECTURES;

WITH

N   O   T   E   S.

TRANSLATED FROM THE ORIGINAL, IN THE *Sănskrĕĕt*, OR ANCIENT
LANGUAGE OF THE *Brahmins*,

BY

CHARLES WILKINS,

SENIOR MERCHANT IN THE SERVICE OF THE HONOURABLE THE EAST INDIA
COMPANY, ON THEIR BENGAL ESTABLISHMENT.

LONDON:
PRINTED FOR C. NOURSE,
OPPOSITE CATHARINE-STREET, IN THE STRAND.

M.DCC.LXXXV.

*The first Englishman to acquire a
thorough knowledge of Sanskrit, the
Orientalist Charles Wilkins (1749–1836)
published his translation of the
Bhagavad Gita in 1785, a book that
Emerson, Thoreau, and other
Transcendentalists highly esteemed.*

*Ralph Waldo Emerson, c. 1854–1855.
Concord Free Public Library.*

1838: Trail of Tears: beginning in
October, U.S. government forces
Cherokee nation to march from
native home in Georgia to Indian
Territory (Oklahoma). Edgar Allan
Poe (1809–1849), *Narrative of A.
Gordon Pym.* Emerson, "Divinity
School Address." Asa Gray and John
Torrey (1796–1873), *Flora of North
America* (seven parts, 1838–1843).

1839: November, Liberty Party,
antislavery political party, holds its
first convention in Warsaw, New
York.

1840: June, World's Anti-Slavery
Convention, meeting in London,
refuses to admit women delegates
from the United States; July, first
issue of Transcendentalist journal,
The Dial. United States population:
17 million. Richard Henry Dana, Jr.
(1815–1882), *Two Years before the
Mast.* Poe, *Tales of the Grotesque and
Arabesque.*

1841: April, Brook Farm community
in West Roxbury, Massachusetts,
residents include Hawthorne, who
later describes his experiences in the
novel *The Blithedale Romance* (1852).
Dorothea Dix (1802–1887) campaigns in Massachusetts to reform
prisons and insane asylums. Emerson, *Essays* (first series). Cooper, *The
Deerslayer.* Henry Wadsworth
Longfellow (1807–1882), *Ballads and
Other Poems.*

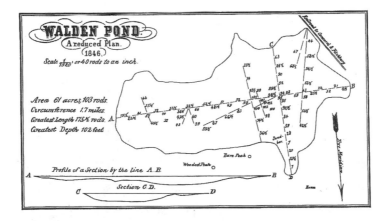

The lithograph of Thoreau's "reduced Plan" of Walden Pond, probably redrawn in 1854 from his fair copy map of 1846, and printed in the 1854 edition of Walden.

Walden Pond. Toward Fitchburg Rail-road, across Walden Pond (April 24, 1918). Photograph by Herbert W. Gleason. Concord Free Public Library.

1842: Massachusetts's child labor law limits workday of children under twelve to ten hours. Master showman P. T. Barnum (1810–1891) opens Barnum's American Museum in New York City.

1843: Utopian community based on principles of French social theorist Charles Fourier (1772–1837) established at Red Bank, New Jersey. Catharine Beecher (1800–1878), *Treatise on Domestic Economy for the Use of Young Ladies at Home and at School.* William Hickling Prescott (1796–1859), *The History of the Conquest of Mexico.*

Tompkins H. Mattheson. The Last of the Race *(1847). During the 1830s and 1840s the Native American tribes of the South were forced to relocate to the Oklahoma territory. This painting depicts the destiny that would befall Native Americans if such policies continued, showing them pushed to the very edge of the West Coast. Used with permission from the collection of the New-York Historical Society.*

1860: December, catches severe cold that turns into bronchitis.

1861: May, hoping to improve health, travels to Minnesota; studies Native American life and history. July, returns to Concord, still in poor health. September, final visit to Walden Pond. November 3, final entry in journal.

1862: May 6, dies of tuberculosis. May 9, buried in Concord.

1863: *Excursions*, edited by sister Sophia (b. 1819) and Emerson.

1844: June, Mormon leader Joseph Smith murdered by mob in Carthage, Illinois; Brigham Young (1801–1877) later leads Mormons on westward migration, 1846–1847, to Utah territory; December, Democrat James K. Polk (1795–1849) wins presidential election, defeating Whig candidate Henry Clay and abolitionist Liberty Party candidate James Birney (1792–1857). Emerson, *Essays* (second series).

DEATH OF JOSEPH SMITH.

The Mormon leader Joseph Smith (1805–1844) was killed by a mob in Carthage, Illinois, on June 27, 1844.

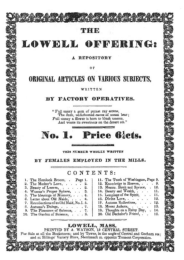

THE
LOWELL OFFERING:

A REPOSITORY

OF

ORIGINAL ARTICLES ON VARIOUS SUBJECTS,

WRITTEN

BY FACTORY OPERATIVES.

"Full many a gem of purest ray serene,
The dark, unfathomed caves of ocean bear;
Full many a flower is born to blush unseen,
And waste its sweetness on the desert air."

No. 1.   Price 6¼cts.

THIS NUMBER WHOLLY WRITTEN

BY FEMALES EMPLOYED IN THE MILLS.

CONTENTS:

1. The Hemlock Broom, . . Page 1.	11. The Tomb of Washington, Page 9.
2. The Mother's Love, . . . 2.	12. Knowledge is Heaven, . . 9.
3. Beauty of Leaves, . . . 3.	13. Mourn, Birch and Spruce, . 10.
4. Woman's Prayer Sphere, . . 3.	14. Beauty and Wealth, . . 11.
5. The blessings of Memory, . . 4.	15. Longings of the Spirit, . . 11.
6. Lines about Old Maids, . . 4.	16. Divine Love, ... 12.
7. Recollections of an Old Maid, No. 1. 5.	17. Autumn Reflections, . . 12.
8. Autumn's Doings, . . . 7.	18. Mount Auburn, ... 13.
9. The Pleasures of Science, . . 7.	19. Thoughts on a Rainy Day, . . 14.
10. The Garden of Science, . . 8.	20. Old Bachelor's Friend, . . 15.

LOWELL, MASS.
PRINTED BY A. WATSON, 12 CENTRAL STREET.
For Sale at all the Booksellers; and by Tower, in the angle of Central and Gorham sts; and at Billings' Variety Store, Merrimack st. opposite Tremont Corporation.

Title page of the first issue of The Lowell Offering, a literary magazine, published 1840–1845, which included poems, essays, and stories written by the "mill girls" who lived and worked at the Lowell Textile Mill in Massachusetts.

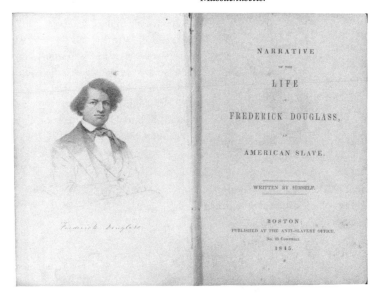

NARRATIVE

OF THE

LIFE

OF

FREDERICK DOUGLASS,

AN

AMERICAN SLAVE.

WRITTEN BY HIMSELF.

BOSTON:
PUBLISHED AT THE ANTI-SLAVERY OFFICE,
No. 25 CORNHILL
1845.

Frederick Douglass. Title page of his autobiographical Narrative, published in 1845. Special Collections, Wellesley College.

Boston abolitionists viewed the annexation of Texas as a southern plot to extend slavery and gain more congressional and Senate seats for the proslavery position. Congress annexed Texas in early 1845, and it became a state in June of the same year.

1864: *The Maine Woods*, edited by Sophia Thoreau and William Ellery Channing.

1865: *Cape Cod*, edited by Sophia Thoreau and Channing; *Letters to Various Persons*, edited by Emerson.

1866: *A Yankee in Canada, with Anti-Slavery and Reform Papers*, edited by Sophia Thoreau and Channing.

1894: Riverside edition of Thoreau's writings, eleven volumes.

1906: Walden edition of writings, twenty volumes, including fourteen volumes of the journals.

1845: July, *United States Magazine and Democratic Review* describes United States's "manifest destiny to overspread the continent"; December, Texas admitted to the Union, the twenty-eighth state. Frederick Douglass (1817–1895), *Narrative of the Life of Frederick Douglass, an American Slave, Written by Himself.* Margaret Fuller (1810–1850), *Woman in the Nineteenth Century.* Poe, *Tales; The Raven and Other Poems.*

1846: May, United States declares war on Mexico; August, Wilmot Proviso, proposed by Democratic congressmen from Pennsylvania, David Wilmot (1814–1868), states that slavery should be prohibited in any territory acquired during war with Mexico. Abraham Lincoln (1809–1865) elected to Congress from Illinois, serves 1847–1849. Herman Melville (1819–1891), *Typee.* Hawthorne, *Mosses from an Old Manse* (collection of stories, including "Young Goodman Brown," "Roger Malvin's Burial," "The Artist of the Beautiful").

1847: Emerson, *Poems.* Longfellow, *Evangeline.*

1848: January, gold discovered near sawmill in California owned by John Sutter (1803–1880), start of Gold Rush. February, Treaty of Guadalupe Hidalgo ends Mexican War; Mexico cedes 500,000 square miles of territory to the United States. July, American women led by Lucretia Mott (1793–1880) and Elizabeth Cady Stanton (1815–1902) meet in convention in Seneca Falls, New York, to call for women's rights. November, Zachary Taylor (1784–1850), Mexican War hero and Whig Party candidate, elected president. James Russell Lowell (1819–1891), *The Biglow Papers*; *A Fable for Critics.*

1849: Emerson, *Nature, Addresses, and Lectures.* Melville, *Mardi*; *Redburn.*

1850: September, Congress passes a series of compromise measures designed to end crisis over slavery; includes abolition of slave trade in Washington, D.C., and a more restrictive law for recapture of fugitive slaves. United States population: 23.1 million. 370,000 immigrants enter United States; 2.3 million arrive in United States during 1850s. Emerson, *Representative Men.* Hawthorne, *The Scarlet Letter.* Melville, *White-Jacket.*

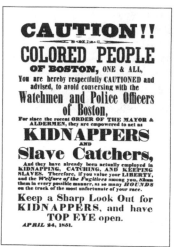

CAUTION!!

COLORED PEOPLE

OF BOSTON, ONE & ALL,

You are hereby respectfully CAUTIONED and
advised, to avoid conversing with the

Watchmen and Police Officers
of Boston,

For since the recent ORDER OF THE MAYOR &
ALDERMEN, they are empowered to act as

KIDNAPPERS

AND

Slave Catchers,

And they have already been actually employed in
KIDNAPPING, CATCHING, AND KEEPING
SLAVES. Therefore, if you value your LIBERTY,
and the *Welfare of the Fugitives* among you, *Shun*
them in every possible manner, as so many *HOUNDS*
on the track of the most unfortunate of your race.

Keep a Sharp Look Out for
KIDNAPPERS, and have
TOP EYE open.

APRIL 24, 1851.

Warning posted in Boston, April 24, 1851, cautioning African Americans to watch out for slave catchers. Earlier in the month, Thomas H. Sims, a seventeen-year-old escaped slave from Savannah, Georgia, had been arrested under the provisions of the Fugitive Slave Law of 1850, leading to massive protests by abolitionists. Simms was returned to his master in Savannah and punished with thirty-nine lashes in the public square.

1851: New York *Daily Times* (name changed in 1857 to the *Times*) begins publication. "Maine Law" prohibits manufacture and sale of intoxicating liquors; by 1855 thirteen states have such laws. Hawthorne, *The House of the Seven Gables*. Melville, *Moby-Dick*.

1852: November, Franklin Pierce (1804–1869), Democrat, elected president; supports southern rights and is opposed to abolition. Hawthorne, *The Blithedale Romance*. Melville, *Pierre*. Harriet Beecher Stowe (1811–1896), *Uncle Tom's Cabin*.

1853: July, Commodore Matthew Perry (1794–1858) arrives in Tokyo Bay and opens U.S. diplomatic relations with Japan. Formation of the American, or Know-Nothing, Party; contends that only the native-born should hold public office and calls for repeal of naturalization laws. The Crystal Palace Exhibition of the Industry of All Nations held in New York City, to demonstrate U.S. industrial and technological progress. William Wells Brown (1814–1884), *Clotel* (first novel by an African-American; published in London).

1854: May, Kansas-Nebraska Act, sponsored by Senator Stephen A. Douglas (1813–1861) of Illinois, repeals the Missouri Compromise of 1820 and calls for "popular sovereignty" (letting the people

An engraving of a mother, her child, and the child's African-American nurse, illustrating "southern fashions" for the fall season, from Godey's Magazine and Lady's Book *45 (1852).*

KIDNAPPING AGAIN!!

A MAN WAS STOLEN LAST NIGHT BY THE
Fugitive Slave Bill COMMISSIONER
HE WILL HAVE HIS
MOCK TRIAL
ON SATURDAY, MAY 27, AT 9 O'CLOCK
In the Kidnapper's 'Court,' before the Hon. Slave Bill Commissioner,
AT THE COURT HOUSE, IN COURT SQUARE.
SHALL BOSTON STEAL ANOTHER MAN?
Thursday, May 26, 1854.

Anthony Burns, a fugitive slave from Virginia, was seized by a U.S. marshal in Boston on May 24, 1854. This effort to enforce the Fugitive Slave Law of 1850 led to massive demonstrations by antislavery forces. Burns was returned to his master in June.

themselves decide) on the slavery question in the territories; May–June, abolitionists in Boston fail in violent attempt to rescue fugitive slave Anthony Burns; July, Republican Party formed, in Jackson, Michigan.

1855: May, feminist and abolitionist Lucy Stone (1818–1893) becomes first woman officially to keep maiden name in marriage. Violence in Kansas territory over the slavery question. John Bartlett (1820–1905), *Bartlett's Familiar Quotations.* Thomas Bullfinch (1796–1867), *The Age of Fable* (known as *Bullfinch's Mythology*). Douglass, *My Bondage and My Freedom.* Fanny Fern [Sara Payson Willis] (1811–1872), *Ruth Hall.* Longfellow, *Song of Hiawatha.* Walt Whitman (1819–1892), *Leaves of Grass.*

1856: May, congressman Preston Brooks (1819–1857) of South Carolina assaults Charles Sumner (1811–1874) of Massachusetts in the U.S. Senate for his antislavery "Crime against Kansas" speech; November, James Buchanan (1791–1868), Democrat, elected president. Emerson, *English Traits.* Melville, *The Piazza Tales.*

De Witt Clinton Boutelle (1820–1884). Indian Surveying a Landscape *(1855). This painting shows the majesty of a Native American warrior as he surveys a landscape that no longer belongs to him. Note the cabin in the foreground, and the sailing ships on the river in the background. Gift of Mrs. Maxim Karolik for the M. and M. Karolik Collection of American Paintings, 1815–1865. Museum of Fine Arts, Boston.*

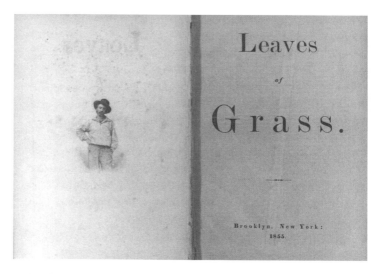

Walt Whitman. Title page of the first edition of Leaves of Grass, *published in 1855. Special Collections, Wellesley College.*

SOUTHERN CHIVALRY — ARGUMENTversus**CLUB'S.**

The Attack on Senator Sumner. This 1856 lithograph shows the brutal attack by Preston S. Brooks (1819–1857), member of Congress from South Carolina, on Senator Charles Sumner (1811–1874) of Massachusetts, who had denounced the South in a powerful antislavery speech, May 20, 1856. Brooks's assault took place two days later, in the Senate chamber.

George Inness (1825–1894), The Lackawanna Valley (c. 1856). The National Gallery of Art, Washington D.C. This painting displays both the progress of technology and its costs to the landscape.

"HERE! TAKE THIS AND FOLLOW ME!"
"Please God, Mr. Brown, dat is onpossible. We aint done seedin' yit at our house."

Racist cartoon that presents the response of a slave to the radical abolitionist John Brown, who led a doomed attempt to free and arm slaves with pikes and other weapons on October 16, 1859. Brown was captured, tried for treason, and executed on December 2d.

NEGROES
FOR SALE.

I will sell by Public Auction, on Tuesday of next Court, being the 29th of November, *Eight Valuable Family Servants,* consisting of one Negro Man, a first-rate field hand, one No. 1 Boy, 17 years o' age, a trusty house servant, one excellent Cook, one House-Maid, and one Seamstress. The balance are under 12 years of age. They are sold for no fault, but in consequence of my going to reside North. Also a quantity of Household and Kitchen Furniture, Stable Lot, &c. Terms accommodating, and made known on day of sale.

Jacob August.
P. J. TURNBULL, *Auctioneer.*
Warrenton, October 28, 1859.
Printed at the *News* office, Warrenton, North Carolina.

Poster advertising a slave auction, Warrenton, North Carolina.

1857: March, in *Dred Scott* case, Supreme Court declares that slaves are not citizens and that Congress cannot prohibit slavery in the territories; August, widespread banking failures and financial panic. *Atlantic Monthly*, edited by James Russell Lowell, and *Harper's Weekly*, edited by George William Curtis (1824–1892), begin publication. Louis Agassiz (1807–1873), *Contributions to the Natural History of the United States* (4 vols., 1855–1862).

1858: August–October, debates between Stephen Douglas and Abraham Lincoln, candidates for U.S. Senate seat from Illinois; Douglas wins reelection.

1859: October, antislavery forces led by John Brown (1800–1859) attempt to seize federal arsenal in Harpers Ferry, Virginia; Brown executed in December. Massachusetts Institute of Technology founded in Cambridge, Massachusetts. Harriet Wilson (1808?–1870), *Our Nig* (first novel by an African-American published in the United States).

1860: February, widespread strikes and labor unrest, beginning with shoemakers' strike in Lynn, Massachusetts; November, Lincoln elected president; December, South Carolina secedes from the Union. Emerson, *The Conduct of Life.* Hawthorne, *The Marble Faun.*

1861: April, Civil War begins with Confederate attack on Fort Sumter, in Charleston harbor, South Carolina. Rebecca Harding Davis (1831–1910), *Life in the Iron Mills.* Harriet Jacobs (1813–1897), *Incidents in the Life of a Slave Girl.*

1862: May, Homestead Act opens public lands in the West for settlement; July, Morrill Act, for support of higher education, signed by President Lincoln, provides for endowment of colleges of agriculture and industry.

1863: January, Lincoln issues Emancipation Proclamation, freeing slaves in territory under control by Confederacy.

AN HEIR TO THE THRONE,
OR THE NEXT REPUBLICAN CANDIDATE

A racist campaign poster that mocks the Republican Party and its candidate Abraham Lincoln (1809–1865) for their sympathy for the African-American race.

THE FIRST GOLD-HUNTERS.

"The First Gold-Hunters," from Harper's New Monthly Magazine *20 (April 1860). Reports of the discovery of gold in California began to appear in newspapers in the East in September 1848, and these led to a major migration westward, a frenzied quest for riches that Thoreau derided.*

Bibliographical Essay

William E. Cain

For the study of Thoreau's writings, Raymond R. Borst's *Henry David Thoreau: A Descriptive Bibliography* (1982) is an excellent resource. It presents a comprehensive list of Thoreau's publications as well as the title pages of first editions and other illustrations. For a list and description of Thoreau's papers and manuscripts in private and public collections, see William L. Howarth's *The Literary Manuscripts of Henry David Thoreau* (1974).

The standard edition is *The Writings of Henry D. Thoreau*, ed. Walter Harding, et al. (12 vols. to date, 1971–). Published volumes include: *Walden* (1971); *The Maine Woods* (1972); *Reform Papers* (1973); *Early Essays and Miscellanies* (1975); *A Week on the Concord and Merrimack Rivers* (1980); *Translations* (1986); *Cape Cod* (1993); and the *Journal* (5 vols. to date, extending thus far to 1852–1853; 1981–). For works not yet included in the Princeton edition, readers should consult *The Writings of Henry David Thoreau* (1893–1894) and *The Writings of Henry David Thoreau* (1906).

The Library of America volume of Thoreau's writings (1985) includes *A Week*, *Walden*, *The Maine Woods*, and *Cape Cod*, but it does not include the social and political essays or anything from the journals. For Thoreau's essays, collections include *The Natural History Essays*, ed. Robert Sattelmeyer (1980); and *Political Writings*, ed. Nancy L. Rosenblum (1996). For Thoreau's letters, see the *Correspondence*, ed. Harding and Carl Bode (1958). Other primary sources are *Collected Poems of Henry Thoreau*, ed. Bode (1943); *Faith in a Seed: "The Dispersion of Seeds" and Other Late Natural History Writings*, ed. Bradley P. Dean (1993); and *Wild Fruits: Thoreau's Rediscovered Last Manuscript*, ed. Dean (2000).

Thoreau's development as a writer, and the complex processes by which his books came into being, are traced in Stephen Adams and Donald Ross, Jr., *Revising Mythologies: The Composition of Thoreau's Major Works* (1988). See also Linck C. Johnson, *Thoreau's Complex Weave: The Writing of "A Week on the Concord and Merrimack Rivers," with a Text of the First Draft* (1986). For *Walden*, J. Lyndon Shanley, *The Making of "Walden," with the Text of the First Version* (1957), is illuminating.

There are a number of books and essays devoted to *Walden* that readers will find rewarding. Starting points include *The Annotated "Walden,"* ed. Philip Van Doren Stern (1970); and *"Walden": An Annotated Edition*, ed. Harding (1995). Critical insights as well as textual information can be found in Ross and Adams, "The Endings of *Walden* and Stages of Its Composition" (1981); and Sattelmeyer, "The Remaking of *Walden*" (1990).

The best biography is Harding's *The Days of Henry Thoreau* (1965; repr. 1992). Briefer biographies have been written by Edward Wagenknecht (1981), Howarth (1982), and Richard J. Schneider (1987). For an intellectual biography that is enlightening throughout on Thoreau's responses to an array of literary and philosophical sources, see Robert D. Richardson, Jr., *Henry Thoreau: A Life of the Mind* (1986). Borst, *A Thoreau Log: A Documentary Life of Henry David Thoreau, 1817–1862* (1992), chronicles Thoreau's activities day-by-day. A stimulating collection is *Thoreau as Seen by His Contemporaries*, ed. Harding (1989), which includes more than 200 documents and reports by friends, Concord neighbors, and others who knew Thoreau.

Also relevant for the biography is Borst, *Henry David Thoreau: A Reference Guide, 1835–1899* (1987), and Gary Scharnhorst, *Henry David Thoreau: A Case Study in Canonization* (1993). Readers will benefit too from the detailed biography and cogent critical analysis in two bibliographical surveys of Thoreau as a lecturer: Bradley P. Dean and Ronald Wesley Hoag, "Thoreau's Lectures before *Walden*: An Annotated Calendar" (1995); and Dean and Hoag, "Thoreau's Lectures after *Walden*: An Annotated Calendar" (1996). Joel Myerson's *The Cambridge Companion to Henry David Thoreau* (1995) includes a range of essays on various aspects of Thoreau's life and writings.

For nineteenth-century reviews of, and responses to, Thoreau's writings, consult John C. Broderick, "American Reviews of Thoreau's Posthumous Books, 1863–1866: Checklist and Analysis" (1955); Dean and Scharnhorst, "The Contemporary Reception of *Walden*" (1990); and Myerson, ed., *Emerson and Thoreau: The Contemporary Reviews* (1992). Also useful is Scharnhorst, *Henry David Thoreau: An Annotated Bibliography of Comment and Criticism before 1900* (1992).

For critical analysis, F. O. Matthiessen's *American Renaissance: Art and Expression in the Age of Emerson and Whitman* (1941) remains stimulating for its treatment of Thoreau's understanding of literary form and his relationship with Emerson. Still pertinent, too, are the chapters on Thoreau in Leo Marx's *The Machine in the Garden: Technology and the Pastoral Ideal in America* (1964), and in Richard Poirier's *A World Elsewhere: The Place of Style in American Literature* (1966).

Of the many books on Thoreau, two merit special notice: Sherman Paul's *The Shores of America: Thoreau's Inward Exploration* (1958), and Stanley Cavell's *The Senses of "Walden": An Expanded Edition* (1981). Paul examines Thoreau's writings from the Harvard undergraduate essays through the major works, while Cavell concentrates on the style and the moral and philosophical themes of Thoreau's greatest text. Neither of these studies, however, delves into the antislavery and political essays. On this topic, one should turn to Michael Meyer, *Several More Lives to Live: Thoreau's Political Reputation in America* (1977).

Frederick Garber has written two books that give rigorous attention to Thoreau's texts: *Thoreau's Redemptive Imagination* (1977) and *Thoreau's Fable of Inscribing* (1991). Lawrence Buell also has written two books that include incisive commentary on Thoreau's literary style and ideas: *Literary Transcendentalism: Style and Vision in the American Renaissance* (1973) and *The Environmental*

Imagination: Thoreau, Nature Writing, and the Formation of American Culture (1995).

For broad surveys of twentieth-century criticism, the best books to begin with are the collections of essays edited by Philip F. Gura and Myerson (1982) and Harold Bloom (1987). For *Walden*, the collections edited by Myerson (1988) and Robert F. Sayre (1992) are excellent.

Many monographs and specialized studies have focused on Thoreau. Richard Lebeaux (1977, 1984) and Richard Bridgman (1982) have explored the writer's psychology as revealed in the writings. This issue also receives attention in Joel Porte's *Emerson and Thoreau: Transcendentalists in Conflict* (1966). Charles Anderson (1968) and Martin Bickman (1992) have written cogently about *Walden*. Richard Francis, in *Transcendental Utopias* (1997), relates Thoreau's experiment at Walden Pond to the communities at Brook Farm and Fruitlands. Sharon Cameron (1985) has examined his journal in detail.

Sattelmeyer's treatment of Thoreau's reading (1988) is informative. Also insightful are the books by Steven Fink (1992), Leonard N. Neufeldt (1989), and Richard F. Teichgraeber (1995) on Thoreau's economic ideas and interests, including his efforts to establish himself in the literary marketplace. There is rewarding analysis of Thoreau's work as a scientist and naturalist in the studies by David R. Foster (1999), John Hildebidle (1983), and Laura Walls (1995). See also the books by Robert Kuhn McGregor (1997) and James McIntosh (1974), which similarly trace Thoreau's inquiry into nature. Sayre (1977) discusses Thoreau's research on Native Americans. For further consideration of important themes in Thoreau's writings, the books by Joan Burbick (1987), Henry Golemba (1990), Robert Milder (1995), Mary Elkins Moller (1980), and H. Daniel Peck (1990) are recommended.

Students seeking further bibliographical guidance on editions of Thoreau's writings, scholarly books and articles, and key topics in Thoreau criticism should refer to the useful, if dated, essay by Lewis Leary in *Eight American Authors* (1971), and then proceed to Meyer, "Henry David Thoreau" (1984). Bibliography and commentary can also be found in Harding and Meyer, *The New Thoreau Handbook* (1980), which includes chapters on Thoreau's life, works, sources, ideas, literary art, and reputation. For Thoreau's reception in other parts of the world, consult Eugene F. Timpe, ed., *Thoreau Abroad: Twelve Bibliographical Essays* (1971). For up-to-date coverage, see the annual *American Literary Scholarship* (1963–); *The Thoreau Society Bulletin* (1941–); and *The Thoreau Quarterly* (1982–).

Internet resources are also helpful:

The Writings of Henry D. Thoreau
<http://www.library.ucsb.edu/depts/thoreau/thoreau.html>
Designed by Elizabeth Witherell, Louisa Dennis, Russ Coon, and Betty Koed, this site complements the Princeton University Press edition of Thoreau's writings. It includes a list of Thoreau sites on the Internet, a biography, and a bibliography.

Cybersaunter: Henry David Thoreau
<http://usmh12.usmd.edu/thoreau/>
Still in development, this site includes biography and images.

The Thoreau Institute
<http://www.walden.org/institute/>
The Thoreau Institute, located a mile from Walden Pond, in Concord, Massachusetts, features a collection of material by and about Thoreau, a media center, and a reading room. It hosts educational programs and provides accommodations for visiting scholars.

The Thoreau Society
<http://www.walden.org/society/>
This site supports the Thoreau Society and its activities and events. It includes a helpful list of links to other Internet sites.

For further information, contact the Thoreau Society, 44 Baker Farm, Lincoln, Mass. 01773-3004. Phone: 781-259-4750. Fax: (781) 259-4760. E-mail: ThoreauSociety@walden.org

WORKS CITED

Adams, Stephen, and Donald Ross, Jr. *Revising Mythologies: The Composition of Thoreau's Major Works*. Charlottesville: University Press of Virginia, 1988.

American Literary Scholarship. Durham: Duke University Press, 1963–.

Anderson, Charles. *The Magic Circle of "Walden."* New York: Holt, 1968.

Bickman, Martin. *"Walden": Volatile Truths*. New York: Twayne, 1992.

Bloom, Harold, ed. *Henry David Thoreau*. New York: Chelsea, 1987.

Borst, Raymond R. *Henry David Thoreau: A Descriptive Bibliography*. Pittsburgh: University of Pittsburgh Press, 1982.

———. *Henry David Thoreau: A Reference Guide, 1835–1899*. Boston: Hall, 1987.

———. *A Thoreau Log: A Documentary Life of Henry David Thoreau, 1817–1862*. New York: Hall, 1992.

Bridgman, Richard. *Dark Thoreau*. Lincoln: University of Nebraska Press, 1982.

Broderick, John C. "American Reviews of Thoreau's Posthumous Books, 1863–1866: Checklist and Analysis." *University of Texas Studies in English* 34 (1955): 125–39.

Buell, Lawrence. *The Environmental Imagination: Thoreau, Nature Writing, and the Formation of American Culture*. Cambridge: Harvard University Press, 1995.

———. *Literary Transcendentalism: Style and Vision in the American Renaissance*. Ithaca, N.Y.: Cornell University Press, 1973.

Burbick, Joan. *Thoreau's Alternative History: Changing Perspectives on Nature, Culture, and Language*. Philadelphia: University of Pennsylvania Press, 1987.

Cameron, Sharon. *Writing Nature: Henry Thoreau's "Journal."* New York: Oxford University Press, 1985.

Cavell, Stanley. *The Senses of "Walden": An Expanded Edition*. San Francisco: North Point, 1981.

Dean, Bradley P., and Ronald Wesley Hoag. "Thoreau's Lectures after *Walden*: An Annotated Calendar." In *Studies in the American Renaissance 1996*, edited by Joel Myerson, 241–362. Charlottesville: University of Virginia Press, 1996.

———. "Thoreau's Lectures before *Walden*: An Annotated Calendar." In *Studies in the American Renaissance 1995*, edited by Joel Myerson, 127–228. Charlottesville: University of Virginia Press, 1995.

Dean, Bradley P., and Gary Scharnhorst. "The Contemporary Reception of *Walden*." In *Studies in the American Renaissance 1990*, edited by Joel Myerson, 293–328. Charlottesville: University of Virginia Press, 1990.

Fink, Steven. *Prophet in the Marketplace: Thoreau's Development as a Professional Writer*. Princeton: Princeton University Press, 1992.

Foster, David R. *Thoreau's Country: Journey through a Transformed Landscape*. Cambridge: Harvard University Press, 1999.

Francis, Richard. *Transcendental Utopias: Individual and Community at Brook Farm, Fruitlands, and Walden*. Ithaca, N.Y.: Cornell University Press, 1997.

Garber, Frederick. *Thoreau's Fable of Inscribing*. Princeton: Princeton University Press, 1991.

———. *Thoreau's Redemptive Imagination*. New York: New York University Press, 1977.

Golemba, Henry. *Thoreau's Wild Rhetoric*. New York: New York University Press, 1990.

Gura, Philip F., and Joel Myerson, eds. *Critical Essays on American Transcendentalism*. Boston: G. K. Hall, 1982.

Harding, Walter. *The Days of Henry Thoreau*. 1965, rev. 1982. Reprint, with a new afterword, Princeton: Princeton University Press, 1992.

———, ed. *Thoreau as Seen by His Contemporaries*. New York: Dover, 1989.

Harding, Walter, and Michael Meyer. *The New Thoreau Handbook*. New York: New York University Press, 1980.

Hildebidle, John. *Thoreau: A Naturalist's Liberty*. Cambridge: Harvard University Press, 1983.

Howarth, William L. *The Book of Concord: Thoreau's Life as a Writer*. New York: Viking, 1982.

———. *The Literary Manuscripts of Henry David Thoreau*. Columbus: Ohio State University Press, 1974.

Johnson, Linck C. *Thoreau's Complex Weave: The Writing of "A Week on the Concord and Merrimack Rivers," with a Text of the First Draft*. Charlottesville: University of Virginia Press, 1986.

Leary, Lewis. "Henry David Thoreau." In *Eight American Authors*, edited by James Woodress, 129–71. New York: Norton, 1971.

Lebeaux, Richard. *Thoreau's Seasons*. Amherst: University of Massachusetts Press, 1984.

———. *Young Man Thoreau*. Amherst: University of Massachusetts Press, 1977.

McGregor, Robert Kuhn. *A Wider View of the Universe: Henry Thoreau's Study of Nature*. Urbana: University of Illinois Press, 1997.

McIntosh, James. *Thoreau as Romantic Naturalist: His Shifting Stance toward Nature.* Ithaca, N.Y.: Cornell University Press, 1974.

Marx, Leo. *The Machine in the Garden: Technology and the Pastoral Ideal in America.* New York: Oxford University Press, 1964.

Matthiessen, F. O. *American Renaissance: Art and Expression in the Age of Emerson and Whitman.* New York: Oxford University Press, 1941.

Meyer, Michael. "Henry David Thoreau." In *The Transcendentalists: A Review of Research and Criticism,* edited by Joel Myerson, 260-85. New York: Modern Language Association, 1984.

Meyer, Michael. *Several More Lives to Live: Thoreau's Political Reputation in America.* Westport, Conn.: Greenwood, 1977.

Milder, Robert. *Reimagining Thoreau.* New York: Cambridge University Press, 1995.

Moller, Mary Elkins. *Thoreau in the Human Community.* Amherst: University of Massachusetts Press, 1980.

Myerson, Joel, ed. *The Cambridge Companion to Henry David Thoreau.* New York: Cambridge University Press, 1995.

———. *Critical Essays on Henry David Thoreau's "Walden."* Boston: G. K. Hall, 1988.

———, ed. *Emerson and Thoreau: The Contemporary Reviews.* New York: Cambridge University Press, 1992.

Neufeldt, Leonard N. *The Economist: Henry Thoreau and Enterprise.* New York: Oxford University Press, 1989.

Paul, Sherman. *The Shores of America: Thoreau's Inward Exploration.* Urbana: University of Illinois Press, 1958.

Peck, H. Daniel. *Thoreau's Morning Work: Memory and Perception in "A Week on the Concord and Merrimack Rivers," the "Journal," and "Walden."* New Haven: Yale University Press, 1990.

Poirier, Richard. *A World Elsewhere: The Place of Style in American Literature.* New York: Oxford University Press, 1966.

Porte, Joel. *Emerson and Thoreau: Transcendentalists in Conflict.* Middletown, Conn.: Wesleyan University Press, 1966.

Richardson, Robert D., Jr. *Henry Thoreau: A Life of the Mind.* Berkeley: University of California Press, 1986.

Ross, Donald, Jr., and Stephen Adams. "The Endings of *Walden* and Stages of Its Composition." *Bulletin of Research in the Humanities* 84 (Winter 1981): 451–69.

Sattelmeyer, Robert. "The Remaking of *Walden.*" In *Writing the*

American Classics, edited by James Barbour and Tom Quirk, 53–78. Chapel Hill: University of North Carolina Press, 1990.

———. *Thoreau's Reading: A Study in Intellectual History, with Bibliographical Catalogue.* Princeton: Princeton University Press, 1988.

Sayre, Robert F., ed. *New Essays on "Walden."* New York: Cambridge University Press, 1992.

———. *Thoreau and the American Indians.* Princeton: Princeton University Press, 1977.

Scharnhorst, Gary. *Henry David Thoreau: An Annotated Bibliography of Comment and Criticism before 1900.* New York: Garland, 1992.

———. *Henry David Thoreau: A Case Study in Canonization.* Columbia, S.C.: Camden House, 1993.

Schneider, Richard J. *Henry David Thoreau.* Boston: G. K. Hall, 1987.

Shanley, J. Lyndon. *The Making of "Walden," with the Text of the First Version.* Chicago: University of Chicago Press, 1957.

Teichgraeber, Richard F. *Sublime Thoughts/Penny Wisdom: Situating Emerson and Thoreau in the American Market.* Baltimore: Johns Hopkins University Press, 1995.

Thoreau, Henry David. *The Annotated "Walden."* Edited by Philip Van Doren Stern. New York: Potter, 1970.

———. *Collected Poems of Henry Thoreau.* Edited by Carl Bode. Chicago: Packard, 1943.

———. *Correspondence.* Edited by Walter Harding and Carl Bode. New York: New York University Press, 1958.

———. *Faith in a Seed: "The Dispersion of Seeds" and Other Late Natural History Writings.* Edited by Bradley P. Dean. Washington, D.C.: Island Press, 1993.

———. *The Natural History Essays.* Edited by. Robert Sattelmeyer. Salt Lake City: Peregrine Smith, 1980.

———. *Political Writings.* Edited by Nancy L. Rosenblum. New York: Cambridge University Press, 1996.

———. *"Walden": An Annotated Edition.* Edited by Walter Harding. Boston: Houghton Mifflin, 1995.

———. *Wild Fruits: Thoreau's Rediscovered Last Manuscript.* Edited by Bradley P. Dean. New York: Norton, 2000.

———. *Writings.* Edited by Robert F. Sayre. New York: Library of America, 1985.

———. *The Writings of Henry D. Thoreau.* Edited by Walter Harding et al., 12 vols. to date. Princeton: Princeton University Press, 1971–.

————. *The Writings of Henry David Thoreau*. With bibliographical introductions and full indexes. 11 vols. Boston: Houghton Mifflin, 1893–1894.

————. *The Writings of Henry David Thoreau*. 20 vols. Boston: Houghton Mifflin, 1906.

The Thoreau Quarterly. 1982–.

The Thoreau Society Bulletin. 1941–.

Timpe, Eugene F., ed. *Thoreau Abroad: Twelve Bibliographical Essays*. Hamden, Conn.: Shoe String Press, 1971.

Wagenknecht, Edward. *Henry David Thoreau: What Manner of Man?* Amherst: University of Massachusetts Press, 1981.

Walls, Laura Dassow. *Seeing New Worlds: Henry David Thoreau and Nineteenth-Century Natural Science*. Madison: University of Wisconsin Press, 1995.

Contributors

WILLIAM E. CAIN is Mary Jewett Gaiser Professor of English at Wellesley College. He is the editor of *William Lloyd Garrison and the Fight Against Slavery: Selections from "The Liberator"* (1995) and *Nathaniel Hawthorne's "The Blithedale Romance": A Critical and Cultural Edition* (1996), and he has coauthored, with Sylvan Barnet, a number of textbooks for literature and composition courses.

ROBERT A. GROSS is the Forrest D. Murden, Jr., Professor of History and American Studies at the College of William and Mary. Author of *The Minutemen and Their World* (1976) and *Books and Libraries in Thoreau's Concord* (1988), he has written numerous essays on the social and cultural history of Concord in the era of Emerson and Thoreau. His book, *The Making of Emerson's Concord, 1790–1840*, will be published by Hill & Wang in 2002.

DANA D. NELSON is professor of English and social theory at the University of Kentucky. She is the author of *National Manhood: Capitalist Citizenship and the Imagined Fraternity of White Men* (1998), and is currently co-editing two essay collections, *Materializing Democracy*, with Russ Castronovo, and a special issue of *American Literature* on Violence, the Body and "The South," with Houston Baker.

LAWRENCE A. ROSENWALD is Anne Pierce Rogers Professor of American Literature at Wellesley College. He is the author of *Emerson and the Art of the Diary* (1988) and the translator, with Everett Fox, of *Scripture and Translation* (1994), a collection of essays by Martin Buber and Franz Rosenzweig. He also has written on translation theory, on the relations between words and music, and on war tax resistance. Currently he is at work on a study of how American literature, both in English and in other languages, has represented language contact and language difference.

CECELIA TICHI is William R. Kenan, Jr., Professor of English at Vanderbilt University. Her publications include *New World, New Earth: Environmental Reform in American Literature from the Puritans through Whitman* (1979); *Shifting Gears: Technology, Literature, Culture in Modernist America* (1987); *Electronic Hearth: Creating an American Television Culture* (1991); and *High Lonesome: The American Culture of Country Music* (1994). Recently, under the pseudonym *"Tishy,"* she has published three mystery novels, *Jealous Heart, Cryin' Time,* and *Fall to Pieces* (1997–2000). In addition, her *Bodies of Nature's Nation: Environment, Nation, and Bodily Identity in Nineteenth- and Twentieth-Century America* will appear in 2001.

LAURA DASSOW WALLS is associate professor of English at Lafayette College, where she is also coordinator of the Values and Science/Technology Program. She is the author of *Seeing New Worlds: Henry David Thoreau and Nineteenth-Century Natural Science* (1995), which traces the intersection of literature and science in the writings of Thoreau, and the editor of *Material Faith: Thoreau on Science* (1999). She has published articles in *American Quarterly, Configurations, Nineteenth-Century Contexts*, and *ISLE (Interdisciplinary Studies in Literature and the Environment)*, and elsewhere on Thoreau, Emerson, Humboldt, Louis Agassiz, S. Weir Mitchell, and Michel Serres. Her current book project is on Emerson and science.

INDEX